DO TRUST ME:
I'm Not A *veterinarian*!

...No Dog Before His Time!

By Jim Schwartz, Man of Dog (in training)

Next-to-Kin Foundation
www.trustmeimnotaveterinarian.com
www.next2kin.org

Copyright © 2008 James D. Schwartz
All rights reserved.

ISBN: 1-4196-9619-X
ISBN-13: 9781419696190

Visit www.booksurge.com to order additional copies.

Disclaimer

This book details the author's personal experiences with, and opinions about, the state of small-animal veterinarian care, pet health insurance, and companion animal emergency care, as well as current governmental disaster preparedness for dogs and cats. I am also concerned about other issues related to the well being of our companion animals.

The author and publisher are providing this book and its contents on an "as is" basis and make no representations or warranties of any kind with respect to this book or its contents. The author and publisher disclaim all such representations and warranties. In addition, the author and publisher do not represent or warrant that the information accessible via this book, or referenced therein, is accurate, complete or current.

The statements made about products and services may not have been evaluated by the U.S. Department of Agriculture or the U.S. Food and Drug Administration. They are not intended to diagnose, treat, cure, or prevent any condition or disease. Please consult with your veterinarian or healthcare specialist regarding the suggestions and recommendations made in this book.

Except as specifically stated in this book, neither the author or publisher, nor any authors, contributors, or other representatives will be liable for damages arising out of or in connection with the use of the book. This is a comprehensive limitation of liability that applies to all damages of any kind, including (without limitation) compensatory; direct, indirect or consequential damages; loss of data, income or profit; loss of or damage to property and claims of third parties.

The reader should understand that this book is not intended as a substitute for consultation with a licensed companion-animal healthcare professional, such as your veterinarian. Before you begin any pet healthcare program, or change your companion animal's lifestyle in any way, you should consult your veterinarian or other licensed healthcare practitioner to ensure that your companion animal's health will not be compromised by employing any of the ideas in this book and that doing so will not harm your dog(s) or cat(s).

The reader will have to deal with any situation arising out of any veterinarian's disagreement with this material, which I believe to be factual and responsible.

This book provides content related to topics concerning health and safety issues for your companion animal(s). Any use of this book implies your acceptance of this disclaimer.

James D. Schwartz

DEDICATION

'For Being There Al*ways*'

To my 'K9 Stars of David,'
Past, Present, Future & Thereafter (Again!)

Nature Boy 'Buddy'

The Fabulous 'Moolah'

Tricki 'Nicki'

'Slick' Ricki

Elle 'The Excellence of Elle-cution'

Max 'Mossad'

'Holy' Moses

&

Godwin* to come…

---

* About 1/3 of the way through radiation, I had a dream I was in a veterinarian's office. A breeder comes into the waiting room with 5 or 6 black standard poodle puppies. All the puppies roam, visiting each in the room – except one. This poodle puppy came right to me and stayed with me – leaning against me tail a waggin'. I asked the breeder the puppy's name. She replied, "Godwin – God wins." Of all the hundreds – thousands of names – Godwin – my *next* poodle.

> I am I because a little dog knows me
> – *Gertrude Stein*

Acknowledgments

Our animals shepherd us through certain eras of our lives. When we are ready to turn the corner and make it on our own…they let us go

Anonymous

Dingo (dog) makes us human

Australian Aboriginal saying

Through creatures and creation one can realize divinity

St. Francis of Assisi

Listen to the animals…for they shall teach thee

The Book of Job

Thank you, my friends, teachers, and colleagues through the years: Senator Hugh Fowler, Rabbis Raphael Sonnenfeld and Howard Hoffman, Bamboo-Bill Hensel, Skip Netzorg, Rich Saul, Cassie Pazour, Margot Nacey, Louis Dominick, Dr. Mark Linkow, Brad Rhodes, Pam Nicols, DVM, Karon Van Winkle and The King of Men – The Rock Doc – Buzz Reifman.

Table of Contents

Prologue 1

Chapter One:
Buddy Call 3

Chapter Two:
Nicki – Call Waiting 25

Chapter Three:
Moolah – The Call, Connecting the Doc$ 57

Chapter Four:
Moolah II – The Economic$ 105

Chapter Five:
Moolah III – The Ethics 113

Chapter Six:
Elle and Max – Emergency Call – K911 169

Chapter Seven:
Ricki – Re-calling 235

Chapter Eight:
Moses – Caller ID 249

Chapter Seven:
Epilogue 255

Exhibits 263

Coda 321

Prologue

The call came.

I knew.

The vet tech from the animal hospital said, "Mr. Schwartz, you should come down now to see Moolah."

It was Moolah's time.

I learned later, too late, it should not have been Moolah's time.

Chapter I
'Buddy' Call

Nature Boy 'Buddy'
TNT – Tongues & Tails & Co, Inc.
Parts Unknown, Colorado

The original watchdog of personal finance never lets sleeping dogs (or people) lie. Bud Light- The Mooch Pooch – protects Fort Schwartz from going to the dogs. In this person-eat-person world of high finance, the Nature Boy's finishing hold is: 'dogleg to the right.'

I didn't have dogs as a kid.

My brother had a dog – 'Terry' – until one day I came home to find out Terry had been given to my cousin in Indiana, PA, "where he would be happier and have more room to roam" – unlike the front yard of our row house in Overbrook Park in Philadelphia.

At best, dogs were incidental to my childhood.

It wasn't until I was married that dogs came to my life – eventually changing my life (dogs, not marriage) – giving my soul a way to go – *'no dog before his time.'*

Despite the commandment not to covet, I was envious of the love and attention that my former spouse's dog, Barkley, gave to her.

I wanted this friendship, acceptance, and multiple 15 minutes of daily fame without the responsibility that owning a dog entails.

So, due to my self-indulgent attitude – compounded by my wife's not wanting another dog – Sushi, a Bichon, was adopted out to an elderly couple who loved her dearly.

I still wanted the companionship and love of a dog – and this time, I swore, I would do whatever it took – even sneaking my friend into the office every day.

Pooping, peeing, feeding, walks be damned.

And so, Buddy, a silver miniature poodle, arrived.

> Dogs are not my whole life but they make my life whole
> *Roger Caras*

(I have always been interested in professional wrestling.) Each of my first generation of dogs was named after a professional wrestler. Moolah was named for the "Fabulous Moolah," considered the greatest female wrestling champion of all time. Slick Ricki, my female Maltese, was named for Rick Flair – the 16-time World Wrestling Champion still going strong in his 50's. Tricki Nicki, my female black lab Shepherd mix was named for AWA Champion Nick Bockwinkle and my first puppy love at the age of 13.

The first was Buddy.

Buddy was named for "Nature Boy" Buddy Rogers, the first wrestling champion to hold simultaneously both the NWA and WWF championships. Rogers' finishing submission hold was 'the figure-four grapevine' (today called the figure-four leg-lock by succeeding pretenders).

Submitting to my Buddy was easy.

No tap out required.

As the divorce approached, Buddy and I moved out to my present house. Devoid of furniture, cable not yet installed, still awaiting a telephone connection, that first night, it was Buddy by my side as I ate a TV dinner and fiddled with the rabbit ears. That night and for 14 more years, Buddy was cuddled against my right thigh like Velcro.

For 14 years, every morning as I lifted an eyebrow, there

was Buddy within an eighth-inch of my face.

And then, when I would cover my face and ask, "where's Jim?" he would burrow under my hands as we played this game repeatedly for 14 years.

And for 14 years, at my request, he would jump into my arms, immediately putting his right front paw around my shoulder.

For 14 years, daily, he would give me that loving stare of "you are the one, you are my person" ignoring others (though I feigned apologies for him).

For 14 years.

Then, in the wee hours of one morning in the 15th year, I awoke to a restless Buddy.

He wasn't against my side.

He kept wanting to go out.

And then each time he came back through the dog door, he would move to a different position on the bed. He wouldn't put his head down.

Every guardian knows.

Every guardian knows their dog and when something is not right.

I knew.

And he was very sick.

Dr. Kris Abbey brought Buddy back from his illness – not through the conventional vet medicine she had practiced for years – but as her first patient for acupuncture. Dr. Jan

Fascinelli helped her to apply it to Buddy.

But he was never the same.

His mind was never the same.

He never again slept by my side.

He never again was at my cheek, within 1/8", awaiting my raised eyebrow and question, "where's Jim," so he could burrow his snout under my hands.

He would sit with me and even put his arm around my shoulder when lifted, but he was never the same.

Little did it occur to me that the change in Buddy's behavior and sudden deterioration of his health could have been connected to getting his annual shots all at once (the rabies, parvo, distemper – now called the wombo combo) just a few weeks (or possibly days) before. Only later would I learn how dangerous those shots were for Buddy, especially in light of his advanced age (14), allergies, and other maladies which should have exempted him from ANY shots.

Little did I realize then the harmful physical impact of fiscally-driven overvaccination which would revisit me with Moolah's passing.

The next two years were filled with medications, rotational conditions, and new maladies from collapsing trachea, to heart murmur, to ear problems and on and on. The weeks were filled with vet visits, homeopathic approaches, more acupuncture, and even laser therapy for Buddy.

Then one Wednesday afternoon after returning from Talmud study, I first went downstairs to my home office to get my messages.

I heard an intermittent thumping.

I went back upstairs.

Buddy would walk a step and then his right hind leg would go out and thump.

I knew it was time.

I lifted him up.

He put his arm around my shoulder.

I then sat with him in the chair where we had meditated for 15 years – one last time

I took off his harness.

He shook his head as if to say, "Thanks, I'm free."

It was time to release Buddy.

My late friend and first self-protection teacher, Fred Burke, once said to me about his dogs, "Jim, if I bring them into this world, then I owe it to them to be the one that takes them out."

I wasn't going to help Buddy graduate on some barren floor in a cold vet's office.

He would pass on in the home we shared together for 14+ years.

My veterinarian from VCA made the house call.

After she administered the valium to calm Buddy, she engaged the barbiturate needle into the site for euthanasia.

I then pushed in the syringe administering the injection.

Buddy passed easily on August 2, 1999, in my arms.

I bring my dogs into my life and it is my duty to ease their transition to the World That Comes – The Hidden That Awaits.

> "Do dogs go to heaven (the world to come)," someone asked author Elizabeth Thomas.
>
> "Of course," she replied, "what would heaven be without dogs?"

Sidebar: Memo To God

Every day for his 14+ years, Buddy and I meditated together. And almost every day, after meditation, I would write my daily journal as he slept on the carpet nearby.

Just a few days before that Wednesday afternoon after Talmud, I knew the day was approaching for Buddy.

I wrote the following "Memo To God", subsequently published in the *Intermountain Jewish News*, in all of 10 minutes.

It was if something was moving through my fingers – irrespective of me.

Memo to G-d

To: G-d
From: Jim Schwartz, Buddy's Human Companion
Subject: Buddy's Promotion
Date: July 25, 1999

Background & Assumptions:

Earth is a correction (Tikkun) facility. The purpose of this correction/repair is for the return (Teshuvah) to You. To earn this ascension and re-fusion, You have created an obstacle course but provided several tools: lures, temptations, and guides - teachers - ambassadors.

Through deeds (applied giving, service, and teaching) and with the gentle and not so gentle assistance of guides, teachers, ambassadors, man manifests his worthiness - "to earn his wings" and return.

You have given this "man," several of your "canine ambassadors" for his training. It appears that a 15-year-old-male miniature poodle ambassador's, Buddy's tour of duty is coming to an end.

Steps Taken To Date:

Awards abound for the large, bigger than life, life-saving-man-from-the-fire, heroic acts of canines. (Rin-Tin-Tin and Lassie probably have their own Wheaties Box.) While not minimizing these singular acts of courage, it is the smaller but sustained acts of the everyday canine hero that have the greater impact.

Buddy has been *there*.

- *"there"* - comforting through the first nights of an empty house during a divorce
- *"there"* upon opening an eyelid with a smiling face though you dread the close up: approaching day
- *"there"* routing his nose under my hands covering my face to the daily ritual question of "where's Jim?"
- *"there"* with his arm around my shoulder - every time I'd pick him up - even now

- *"there"* no matter how high the temperature or how low the mood
- *"there"* - closer than Velcro against my body as we sleep or in my lap mediating

There.

Everyday.

These are the acts of the everyday hero demonstrating endurance and courage, while keeping "Your word" with grace.

When I'd be in the line of life's fire, he'd scrunch up even closer. Without a doubt, he'd take a bullet for me as would I for him.

Buddy routed, guided and directed this so-called "professional" planner, such that he has given my soul a way to go.

Conclusions:

In the Talmud, it is said, *"save a life and you save the world."*

Buddy has saved this life even as his life force grows weaker. Old age and numerous afflictions have taken their toll - not the least of which is absorbing his human companion's negativity. The time is rapidly - too rapidly approaching - for your ambassador to come home again - canine grata.

Recommendation:

Buddy deserves "caninization."
He has earned his return - Teshuvah with unlimited cookies.
Buddy merits promotion - 5 stars on his wings - a canine flight

instructor teaching other ambassadors to assist in man's return to you.

He is, has been, and always will be my hero....

Signed: Jim

Buddy's Epitaph: *You don't have to be a* Rabbi *to be a* Rebbe [1] [2]

1. Rebbe – When a Rabbi is late for a meeting with the President of the Synagogue, he's fired. When a Rebbe is late, they tell stories about him.

2. Another story: A Rebbe and his students (Yeshiva Bokers – not a baseball team) were invited to a poor widow's for Shabbas. The widow brought out the chicken for the Rebbe to inspect prior to adjourning to the kitchen to make further preparations. The Rebbe looked under the wings and the popik and returned the bird for her saying, "yes, this chicken is kosher." Now one of the Yeshiva Bokers turned to the Rebbe out of the widow's earshot and said, "But Rebbe, this bird is not Kosher." To which the Rebbe gave the student an immediate Dr. Evil "Shhhh!!!." After the Shabbas dinner and goodbyes, the Rebbe and the students proceeded to walk back to the Yeshiva. Immediately, the student began about the chicken not being Kosher. The Rebbe stopped in his tracks, and turning around was within 2 inches of the Yeshiva Bokers face and said, "You are right. The chicken was not Kosher. But I, as a Rebbe, have additional authority. Out of ethics and intent, I declare this chicken Kosher." Two inches from the student's face.

Are These Buddy's Ashes?

> "Cremation (private or otherwise) is typically performed within 1 to 2 days (of receipt of the body after death). The private cremation process requires a resetting or 'cleaning' which takes 1-2 hours and assures identification of cremains."
>
> *(Peter Down of The International Association of Pet Cemeteries in conversation with author subsequently related via email to Dr. Earl Wenngren, Director of local VCA Animal Hospital, August, 1999.)*

Buddy was the first of my four 'chaverim (friends) of the soul' to graduate over the next two years.

For the first few days, as most guardians will tell you who have experienced the loss of a companion animal, and sometimes a few weeks, they will swear they saw their deceased dog around a corner, in that certain place, for a glimpse. And so it was with each of my dogs that have passed as well as Buddy.

Buddy, oh, maybe once a month, regardless of training, bitter orange, barricades etc., had a place he would mark. (I could never catch him!) And yes, I became quite adept with different spot removers.

It's interesting how those irritating markings become 'landmarks' once 'the friends of our soul' have passed.

(The only other times Buddy marked were submission pees on the shoes of two professionals. They were both trial lawyers.)

> **Contracts break; covenants stretch**
> *Rabbi Gershon Winkler*

I remembered how Tim Russert counseled Mike Gartner about the loss of his teenage son – and applied the same logic to Buddy's graduation.

If the Almighty offered me a deal: I could be with Buddy for 15 years but then he would return to the Almighty, or not be with Buddy at all in my life, of course, I would take the first deal. And, I believe, if Buddy were offered the same deal, he would take being 15 years with me.

It was a good contract – better yet wonderful covenant – that expanded over 15 years physically – that stretched *fur*ever my being. The body may be gone, but the relationship – the connection – continues – to this day, and especially on Shabbat.

Before every Shabbat, I stand in front of the portrait of my Buddy, Ricki, Nicki, and Moolah re-membering – glancing, ever so often at their urns.

Though cremation is frowned upon in most Judaic circles, I do accept the Judaic concept of "the watchman." The watchman's role is to "watch" over the body until it is buried (or cremated in Buddy's situation).

Some would argue that the first watchman, in biblical history, was Abel's dog.

So, on that afternoon of **August 2, 1999**, the vet took

Buddy's body back to the VCA Animal Hospital for holding (for watching?) until the crematorium people would take him for final settlement of his remains.

I wanted and paid for the more expensive private cremation. I was told by the vet that the crematorium people would pick up Buddy and in a few days I would have Buddy's ashes.

August 9th came, and no ashes. Seven days, not 1 or 2, and no word of Buddy's ashes; I was seeing glimpses of Buddy more frequently it seemed.

August 9th - 7 days.

After finding out from VCA that Denver Pet Cemetery was to have cremated Buddy, I called three times on **August 9th** – leaving an urgent message. The last call I made at approximately 4:15 PM, receiving a recorded message stating that Denver Pet Cemetery closes at 4:30 PM.

It turns out the Managing Veterinarian/Director of VCA's local animal hospital, Dr. Wenngren, by his own admission, "may have mis-tagged" Buddy for identification and "he remained frozen for 7 days," as I recall his words.

VCA Animal Hospital not only failed the precept of "substitute reliance" but also the role of "the watchman."

So in light of 7 days to cremate when the standard is 1 to 2 days (especially for the more costly private cremation), freezing for the same period, mis-tagging, and no response from Denver Pet Cemetery, I was concerned: "are these Buddy's ashes?"

(Later, Denver Pet Cemetery would claim a storm knocked out their phone line on the 9th. Qwest/US West indicated that was not the case on **August 9th**. Furthermore, how could Denver Pet Cemetery get my messages if the phone line was out?)

I finally got what were (are) supposed to be Buddy's ashes on **August 11th**.

Just coincidentally, the certificate of cremation was dated August 9th, the date that Denver Pet Cemetery supposedly did not get my phone calls due to the storm.

As Gomer Pyle would say, "Surprise! Surprise!"

I contacted Mike Booth of *The Denver Post*. He had done a feature on pet deaths: " 'Body' Of Evidence in Doubt." He had so much response that he did a follow-on story, "Grief Over Cremations Stays With Pet Owners," where other guardians related their cremation horror stories.

What was VCA Veterinarian Director Wenngren's response to Booth? Not facts. Not admission, as he had to me, that Buddy was improperly tagged. Not admission that the Vet Hospital had a duty to supervise as they were subcontracting to Denver Pet Cemetery (which at the time had 70% of the market share for cremation and burial of pets). Not an admission that vets get a commission, kick-back, whatever you wish to call it, of 50% of cost of cremation (private cremation $90-$250 versus $45-$125 for "communal") and urns.

Nope.

VCA's Dr. Wenngren's responses were:

- he (Wenngren) understands why his "intense" client was distraught
- "Jim's a sensitive guy, that's the best word I can think of ... What he got from the scenario was more perception than fact"
- "the pet cemetery handles animals with dignity...Bass' (owner of Denver Pet Cemetery) explanation of delaying Buddy's cremation because of a backlog of business is a credit to the cemetery because it shows he takes the time to do things right…"

There was no mention of VCA's duty to supervise subcontractors nor the remuneration received by VCA from Pet Cemetery let alone VCA's mis-tagging.

See sidebar "Difficult" (which should be supplemented with the accusing deflection "he/she is distraught.")

Sidebar: You're Difficult, etc.

There's an old legal saying: "When you have the facts, argue the facts; when you have the law, argue the law; and when you have neither, attack your opponent." But this cliché was before "sensitive" political correctness and hostile environmental argument fallbacks were added to the arsenal of responsibility avoidance language. Now when caught (and "I'm sorry" and "biting one's lip" doesn't work to avoid responsibility and restitution) you might use, "it's how you said it" to deflect responsibility. And if that doesn't work, divert with "you're difficult!" Finally, there is always, "we're all responsible" (so no one is responsible and has to pay!).

But scratching beneath the "it's how you said it" retort is exoneration, dare I say justification, for their wrong-doing – a priori – by manner – culpability be damned. Scratching beneath, the "you're difficult" assertion to avoid blame let alone having to make the situation "right" is "I'm not getting my way."

"You're difficult" is often just a projection of the accuser being "difficult" because he or she, ironically, is "not getting his way."

So, really, who is being difficult?

And what were Denver Pet Cemetery owner Bob Bass' responses:

- "the ashes are definitely Buddy's" (though he can't prove it)
- that "the cemetery has earned the trust of thousands of pet lovers"
- "there was a rush for private cremations"
- "maybe he's grieving the loss of his pet and is taking it out on everybody around him. About one in 300 people do that."
- "I would encourage them to bury the pet...That costs about four times as much as cremation. *But they want to do the cheap thing,* and they want the assurance, too, *and I don't know how you do that.*"
- "I (Bass) deal with veterinarians not owners."
- "His (Schwartz's) messages were 'so profane' (I) didn't care to talk with him."

As to Bass' last assertion, how could he know my messages were profane (which I deny) if his machine was out of order due to a storm? Furthermore, how could he state he would have talked with me when "(I) only deal with the vet, not the owner?"

"When you have the facts, argue the facts. When you have the law, argue the law. When you have neither: yell baloney, impeach the other's character deflecting responsibility calling the opponent 'intense, difficult, distraught' adding 'and it's how they said it.' Of course, there was no mention of VCA's primary responsibility for Buddy's remains, nor their duty to supervise subcontractors, nor the remuneration received by VCA from Pet Cemetery, let alone VCA's mis-tagging according to Dr. Wenngren for purposes of the article.

The response to the first feature caused Booth to follow up the article with another entitled, "Grief Over Cremations Stays With Pet Owners."

Seems my experience was not isolated.

To add insult to injury, it was discovered that certain pet cemeteries (including Bass' Denver Pet Cemetery) charge extra if the owner wishes to observe the cremation!

Booth reported boxes of ashes coming back to the vet weighing more than the small dog that left the vet.

Pet advocacy groups indicated they wanted a tracking system for privately cremated pets that would survive the burning process.

A Pamela Dunn related how a week and half later after contracting through her vet for the cremation of her cat – no remains. She contacted the crematorium directly, and "a man said he had the cat in front of him and just about to conduct the cremation. She asked him to describe it, and it turned out to be the wrong cat. Her vet finally admitted she had mis-tagged

Dunn's cat in the first place."

And my phone was ringing off the hook with callers indicating similar and worse experiences.

> "Denver Pet Cemetery has earned the respect of thousand of other pet lovers"
> *Bob Bass*

And approximately 70% of the commission-paying burial/cremation business of veterinarians in Denver (without disclosure to the guardians) at one time belonged to Denver Pet Cemetery.

> "I would encourage them to bury the pet. That costs about four times as much as cremation. ***But they want to do the cheap thing,*** and they want the assurance, too, *and I don't know how you do that.*"
> *Bob Bass, Denver Pet Cemetery*

We tend to do what is *in*spected, not what is *ex*pected.

There was and still is no effective interdictive deterrent, no checks and balances on the crematoriums other than 'good intentions.'

Of little consequence (and with little effective recourse) after the fact is the weight of the ashes. An average 50-65 pound dog will produce 1 to 2 pounds of ashes according to Allen Rutherford, then of Pet Cremation Services. But then, the crematorium might argue the dog was sick – so there are fewer ashes (I've heard this one.)

Even the vets know they have a problem (though they won't admit it) as shown by their actions.

Then Denver Vet Medical Society president Dr. Paul Oberbroeckling said that cremation profit doesn't motivate the vet, but when the Society considered starting its own crematorium "the costs were too high." He further stated, "you hope the crematory service is doing the same good job every day as they were on the day you went out to see them."

Without any admission of culpability or responsibility, the Denver area veterinarians, obviously fearing liability for failure to supervise in these situations, almost one-year to the day of Buddy's passing, offered a new 'member benefit." In particular, in the summer issue of the Denver Area Veterinary Medical Society's Pulse Summer Newsletter 2000 (one-year after "Are These Buddy's Ashes") there is an ad for this New Member Benefit – Cremation Tags.

"To address the concern over cremains being returned to the proper owner, the DAVMS is offering members a way to better track individual cremations. Veterinarians may be unaware that hiring a crematory to contract business makes them legally responsible for the proper return of the animal's remains. Human crematoriums place a numbered metal tag on the deceased person's body. The number is then checked with the numbered tag in the ashes after cremation. The DAVMS Board, after much discussion, decided that using a similar system would offer another way to assure clients they are getting back the proper ashes. ***It would ease the possible liability concerns on the veterinarian's end***.

The tag would be placed on the outside of the pet's body using a plastic tie. The SAVMS will write a letter to all crematoriums letting them know this system is being put into place and to place the tag on the outside of the box of cremains so it can be checked. Is this a foolproof system? No. Problems can still probably occur but the idea is that the veterinarian has made a conscious effort on his/her part to reduce the possibility of errors."

    Difficult?

    Distraught?

    Intense?

    'Disgruntled?'

    Sensitive?

    Profane?

    Talk to the paw.

> Better done than said.
> *Ben Franklin*

In passing, Buddy made his loss matter for thousands of companion animals, despite the protestations of Mr. Bass, despite the deflecting characterizations of VCA Vet Dr. Wenngren, and despite the denials of economic motivation by the vet association.

The Denver Area Veterinary Medical Society has the cremation tags in place – now going on 6 years.

Still, additional safeguards are necessary.

Since companion animals are by law property, and depreciated property at that (unless they are show, breeding or stud animals), prevailing in law against negligent mis-tagging and or deceptive practices would cost the guardian more in legal fees than what would be recovered.

Recommendation: a state mandated <u>rider</u> on the crematorium's general liability policy – allowing for a stated value of, for instance, a minimum of $50,000 in liquidated damages plus legal costs per incident for wrongful acts (p.e., wrong ashes).

Insurance companies don't like to pay claims (believe me, I know, as a former fee- only financial planner for 20 years dealing with insurers). Thus, unlike the commission-receiving veterinarian, the insurance carrier would have a self-interest in random inspections to minimize incompetent and or deceptive practices by their insured.

Enactment of this <u>rider</u> – **as a mandate** - would go a long way to answering the question of "are these Buddy's ashes!" of our **fur**-ever companions.

What You Can Do If You Wish Your Companion Animal To Be Privately Cremated:

Yes	No	
		Ask the vet if they tag your dog upon your request for cremation. If not, you may wish to consider another veterinary hospital for cremation. Ask for at least two crematorium referrals Ask, even if you feel uncomfortable, what the crematorium pays the veterinarian for his/her referral Ask the crematorium if you can view the private cremation. If they say no, or wish to charge you for your viewing, I would not use them and quite frankly would wonder about the referring veterinarian's due care and due diligence in his referral.

Buddy's 'adventures' turned me in the direction of making loss matter. With Nicki, my female black Lab-Shepherd mix, I started down the path of 'no dog before his time.'

Chapter II
Nicki: Call Waiting

Tricki Nicki
(The Red Light District)

Often accused of dogging it, this 'Slut Puppy'
the hot-diggity-dog – can be B-B-B-Bad to the bone.
The original junk food dog, the tender lick,
Nicki doggedly protects and preserves the
dogma of the Monetary Mongoose.
Finishing Hold: The Dog *Pound!*

Slut puppy.

Indiscriminate.

Nicki, my female Black Lab-Shepherd mix, never met a hand she wouldn't rollover for a tummy rub.

I thought.

The late Fred 'One Man Gang' Burke was giving me a 'hand to hand' self-defense combat lesson on my front lawn. When I reentered the house, my then financial planning partner, Karon Van Winkle, told me that Nicki had to be restrained from jumping out the living room window, to get Fred and defend me.

Nicki, the slut puppy!

Nicki defended me, and it would be time for me to defend her - and hopefully other canine Ambassadors from God.

Pet 'Peeved' Health Insurance – A Bone To Pick

"And, Mr. Schwartz," then Colorado State Insurance 'O'-missioner Richard Barnes stated with the added finger-pointing emphasis of a principal admonishing a wayward student, "if you don't like it (commission fixing – no rebating allowed in life insurance), start your own insurance company," as he slammed shut his briefcase embossed with The Traveler's Umbrella.

At the time, as a fee-only financial planner on behalf of a client in collaboration with his estate attorney, we determined the design and the amount of insurance this client would need. Thus, an insurance agent would get a full commission for merely taking an order. The idea was to negotiate a lower fee as the agent did not have to: find the client, create the product design, nor select the carrier. So, why can't one unbundle the services and negotiate the commission down? Here's why: It's illegal – it's called rebating. So insurance agents can negotiate the price of a car they buy, for example, but by law, their clients cannot negotiate a 'rebate,' in part or in full, of the commission, irrespective of the level of service!

Now this wouldn't be the first time, nor the last time, I would go toe-to-toe, bark-to-yap, with these State Insurance Omissioners. Supposedly bastions protecting the public, these irregulators, in my opinion, are, too often, in reality, captives (some say lapdogs) of the Insurance industry. It is not unusual after a decent or not-so-decent interval, for the former commissioner to wind up representing or lobbying for those he or she 'regulated.' This game of musical chairs – or revolving doors between the insurance industry is anathema to the interests of consumers and the basic tenets of capitalism. The National Association of Insurance Commissioners is nothing more than a self-dealing trade organization/employment agency. (As for protecting the consumer, the NAIC as of June, 2007, continues to hold closed meetings excluding consumers – so much for transparency by this taxpayer-subsidized Trade Organization). The audacity of the NAIC's sanctimonious proclamation of consumer protection – is like the ship captain's lecture on navigation as his ship sinks.

Barnes' pompous snit in the early '80's energized me to create a low-load (no agent commission) no-load insurance product – I believe the first ever. It was issued by Bradford National Life. Now, despite revolving self-dealing regulator hurdles, Ameritas, Southland Life (ING), and others have a thriving small market in the United States. Interestingly, no-load low-load now has a substantial market share in Britain.

I made 14 cents an hour for my trouble (return/time invested).

I was 30 – still idealistic – confusing should be's and can be's.

But I learned – hopefully. (Remember, hope is deferred disappointment [per Ambrose Bierce] and yet a feather residing in the heart according to Emily Dickinson.)

(Colorado State Insurer Omissioners Barnes, Ehnes, 'Dealin' Doug Dean, etc.: wherever you are – talk to the paw.)

Nicki was loving but stoic when it came to her maladies. She would just stretch, while her dad, on the other hand, would kvetch.

But for her and my other canine companions, I secured pet health insurance – when available.

You would think I would know better–with my experience.

Pet insurers, in the US, have come and gone, as I had experienced with Medipet (issued by Fireman's Fund, then owned by American Express). So I sought to secure coverage from VPI, which had been in the pet insurance business the longest time.

VPI is the largest provider of pet health insurance in the country. The Wall Street Journal and others indicate VPI has 80%+ of the market share at this writing.

80% of what? Of the 2% or less of all guardians securing pet health insurance! Now that's spin on steroids. Two-thirds of American households have companion animals; only one third have children (per the American Pet Manufacturers Association). Yet after 20+ years, pet insurance has sold only 2%-3% of the market. In Britain approximately 25% have pet insurance and the Brits spend less per capita on companion animals than we do as Americans!

Why?

Draw your own conclusions but here's a hint: Kiplinger's has questioned the value of pet insurance in general (VPI in particular at one point), and Consumer Reports in 2003 preferred self-insurance (self-funding) to pet insurance in general in its (July, 2007) article: 'Why Pet Insurance Is Usually *A Dog.*' (Sorry.)

I believed the VPI policy I purchased was a $50 deductible, 80/20 cost sharing split (the company 80%, the owner 20%) thereafter with an out-of-pocket maximum *per incident* of $2500 but $10,000 lifetime coverage. I understood that charges must be reasonable and customary, and furthermore, hereditary illnesses would not be covered. I would have preferred (and paid for) a $100 or even $250 deductible, 80/20 split – *per year* – not per incident – but that was not available.

Thus, when Nicki required a $1300 anterior cruciate ligament surgery, I expected the following payment:

$1300	cost of surgery (reasonable and customary in the Denver area)
−50	deductible
$1250	basis for 80/20 sharing ratio
−250	my 20% of the cost
$1000	to be received from the insurance company.

That's how you would figure your normal (human) health plan benefit. I received approximately $400 (and not $400 initially but only after review after review.)

It's really embarrassing for an insurance guy to find out stuff too late. I wasn't provided with this information at point of sale, nor upon receipt of paid contract, but it turns out reimbursements were not only restricted by the per-incident limit, the deductible, the 80/20 split, and reasonable and customary charges (the surveys of which are not provided by the insurer and lag a good year or two thus creating an inflation discount on how much is paid) but also subject to *"inner limits"* (a schedule of maximum payments per procedure).

Inner limits state that for xyz operation – regardless of reasonable and customary – we will only pay up to abc amount.

And not only did VPI have an inner limit per procedure – but it further limited the inner limits by whether the procedure was primary, secondary or tertiary – meaning the primary cause or incidental to some other procedure, factor, etc.

In effect, this VPI policy, at that time, wasn't in my opinion, insurance, but rather in effect a discount policy – like these health cards which give you a discount but are not insurance.

To add insult to the injury, if you did not bunch your claims together within a certain period of time, then a whole new deductible started – even if it was the same incident.

But the *coup de grâce* for this VPI policy – which effectively recaptured a significant part of the $400 claim payment – was the hidden authority for the insurer to surcharge the premium upon renewal – due to usage!!! Whoa!

That was 1996.

In 1996, I had almost completely phased out of my fee-only personal financial practice. I still did a good bit of business consulting, but "when love and skill come together, expect a masterpiece" and the love wasn't so much gone as superceded.

This commitment was leapfrogged by a greater and ever growing call for my dogs, and canines in general. I became involved as National Chair of The Delta Society's Beyond Limits Program and the Chairman of the Assistance Dog United Campaign as my ardor increased.

Though these other activities broadened my outlook and background relative to companion animals, Nicki's experience with VPI, in light of my financial service industry and consulting background, kept gnawing at me. Finally, these so-called pet insurance experiences ignited the impetus for creation of no-games, easily affordable and acquirable major pet health insurance. And the following experience with Pethealth's (un)coverage for my female black standard poodle, Elle (the Excellence of Elle-cution), raised the inspiration to lightning proportions. I knew I had to create an insurance product that would be 'There' – through better, and through worse – NO DOG BEFORE ITS TIME.

Sidebar: Nicki Semper Fido

Nicki & The Juniata Express

Better one good week – one good month for Nicki rather than six more months of suffering.

As such, I have chosen comfort over "getting better" as Nicki isn't doing very well.

Her eating - even the good stuff - is about a quarter of normal - regardless of ground beef, premium hard, soft - out of the dish, on the floor or from the hand. She isn't stealing at all. She is falling more and whimpering either in pain or frustration from the mylopathy or herniated discs. She favors one side of her mouth eating. She is restless at night. While she still wants affection – only standing up – and then not as much. Her tail wagging is infrequent. She sleeps a lot.

Acupuncture has run its course as well as the Myristan experiment.

So, she had a shot of steroids which absorbs faster and better than the steroidal pills – now ineffective. The steroids will bring the end closer – but up till the end – in comfort.

Most believe I named Nicki for Nick Bockwinkle – the three time AWA Heavyweight Wrestling Champion. After all, her name fit the genre with Nature Boy Buddy, The Fabulous Moolah and Slick Ric.

But she was also named for my first "puppy" love, Nicki R.

I was 14.

Every summer, for 2 weeks, we visited relatives in Indiana, Pa – the Xmas Tree Capital of the World or as my father sarcastically would say, "the garden spot of the world."

Mom and I would take the Pennsylvania RR's Juniata Express out of 30th St. Station in Philadelphia making stops in Coatsville, Lancaster, Harrisburg, Lewistown (rounding the horse shoe curve), finally into Altoona and Johnstown where Aunt Sissy would pick us up.

It was that summer I fell for Nicki R.

And then the two weeks were up and back on the Juniata Express: Johnstown, Altoona, Lewistown, Harrisburg, Lancaster, Coatsville, Philadelphia.

It was the longest 5-hour trip with an emptiness in the pit of my stomach – 36 years later – I still remember that feeling.

True, memory does believe before knowing remembers. And true, those were the eyes of a 14-year-old. But those two weeks were both wonderful and terrible.

Whereas Buddy was "there" for me allowing belonging and trust again in my life – filling the hole in my soul – giving it a way to go, over the past 14+ years Nicki has been guardian, surrogate mom to Ricki (my Maltese lion), and inspiration.

Nicki, who never met a hand she couldn't lick, and yet, had to be restrained from jumping through the window to get at Fred Burke who was teaching me self-protection holds on the lawn.

It was Nicki who mothered my Maltese Ricki as a puppy. It may have been false motherhood – but it was motherhood.

And it is Nicki through her illnesses who has inspired my work and dedication reducing unnecessary companion animal death and suffering due to cost – my companion animal insurance project. Had it not been for VPI's Pet "Insurance" paying but maybe $400 on a $1300 ACL operation for Nicki, I wouldn't be attempting to get 20 million dogs and cats covered under their guardians' home owner/ or health insurance policies.

I believe we are given each of our companion animals as G-d's ambassadors sent to us for a reason. Nicki's was inspiration – a muse. Nicki's tour of duty is coming up.

And so, I have chosen for her comfort.

But the emptiness is the same as returning home – Johnstown, Altoona, Lewistown, Harrisburg, Lancaster, Coatsville, Philadelphia.

It's just a very short time till Nicki returns to the way station.

And I know Buddy will be there to greet her.

Nicki graduated January 3, 2000.

Nicki – Semper Fido

Petshealth Insurance offered a $100 per-year deductible (per-year – not per- incident), 80/20 sharing of subsequent costs up to $3500 per incident with a maximum of $10,000, supposedly.

Finally, real coverage, I thought.

I thought wrong.

No one in their right mind would buy a health insurance policy which states up front that an illness for which a claim is paid this year becomes a "pre-existing illness" and therefore not covered when the policy is renewed. Would you? I hope not.

Think of someone who unfortunately contracted cancer three-years after paying premiums month in and month out, year in and year out to the same health insurance carrier. Then upon annual renewal (and continued payment of premium), the insurance carrier held that the cancer is now considered a preexisting illness and therefore not covered.

Who would buy this 'coverage' knowing this – let alone someone who had spent 20 years as a fee-only financial planner, author of two editions of the book *ENOUGH: A Handbook for Your Personal Financial Planning*, and a pioneer in the creation of no-load, low-load life insurance – especially after Nicki's VPI incident?

In Petshealth's policy in 2003 it is stated, "there is a thirty (30) day waiting period after the effective date of this policy during which we will not cover any illness to your pet. This thirty (30) day waiting period will not apply to any renewal of this policy if continuous coverage is maintained."

(A waiting period is to avoid adverse selection – meaning someone knows their companion animal has a problem and buys the insurance knowing this – sticking it to the insurance company. The waiting period protects the insurer from attempted larceny.)

Thus, if one meets the initial waiting period upon original issue of the policy, and if one pays their premiums, a plain reading of the above clause would indicate that upon renewal, there is no waiting period – the illness coverage from the prior period continues. Yet, when denying a later claim for Nicki's successor Elle, Petshealth declared that the illness was now a preexisting illness which upon renewal became subject to exclusion.

The reality of this policy: the heck with $100 deductible per year, 80/20 sharing arrangement, $2500-$3000 per incident, we'll just make any claim from the previous year going into the renewal year "a pre-existing illness!"

Yet even later, in 2006, Petshealth's spokesperson said "the exclusion (rewriting the policy each year) has raised issues among customers, but it is 'clearly identified' in policy certificates" (which are issued after the policy has been paid for!) ('Pet Peeved,' Smart Money Magazine, February 2006)

Clearly identified?

Is that why now in 2007, when renewing a policy, Petshealth offers 'continuing coverage' for an illness in the prior premium year – *for an additional premium*? Who will understand this?

Full & timely disclosure or Fool disclosure!

The resources of the Colorado State Insurance Division are either "strained but effective" or "without jurisdiction and strained" depending on whether the Omissioner is seeking additional budget from the legislature or just arguing with citizens. The division chose to pass on pursuing a fraudulent practices suit against Petshealth in 2003 (after collecting a fine for the Department itself from Petshealth for violating the "prompt claims statute.") Then State Insurance O-missioner Dean failed to act upon the question of market and or management misconduct (let alone 'bad faith') even though Clarendon (Petshealth's underwriter at the time) had demonstrated a course of conduct adverse to consumers evidenced by a complaint ratio of over 168% on the National Association of Insurance Commissioners' Complaint Scale! Dean, subsequently appointed as a Public Utility Commissioner, punted – suggesting 'you may wish to pursue this through Small Claims Court' – for which he provided the telephone number.

911 is needed for reforming (or chloro-forming) this insurance division.

So much for protecting the consumer's interest.

It should be noted that State Insurance Departments have systemically conflicting missions. On one hand, these commissioners are to protect the consumer indirectly by insuring the solvency of the insurers. On the other hand, they are to directly protect the consumer against malpractice. However, agents are subject to fines and potentially jail, if they disclose the risk-based capital position (i.e. rating of solvency) to the insured!

Censorship to protect the consumer? Furthermore, the National Association of Insurance Commissioners (a trade organization masquerading as a professional organization – probably funded by your tax dollars) holds closed meetings excluding even its de-facto consumer representatives from deliberations about industry offenses. So much for transparency by these 'consumer' protectors.

No Dog Before His Time - Insurance Innovation An Oxymoron

The terms "insurance company" and "innovative new product development" are almost never used in the same sentence...Product development is reactionary... Lack of product ingenuity has contributed to poor financial results for property/casualty companies...

Something Different, Something New, Best's Review, **February, 2001.**

As I researched the market for pet insurance more thoroughly, I learned the following:

- Every year 6 to 8 million companion animals are euthanized.
- Approximately 25% of these euthanasias are for monetary reasons. Thus, 1,500,000 to 2,000,000 dogs and cats are put down due to cost. This is called **economic euthanasia.**
- An annual survey by the Animal Hospital Association showed that 70% of pet owners said they would spend $1000 in a life threatening illness or accident involving their companion animal – 40% said they would spend 'anything'.
- There are over 160,000,000 companion animals in US households
- 65%-70% of the US households have a companion animal (48% have multiple dogs and cats) (Compare: only one-third have children!)
- 76% of the companion animals sleep in their guardian's bed (Sealy Posturepedic Study 2005)
- There are **40 million singles** with companion animals
- 82% feed premium dog food (AAHA study), and raw feeding (more costly) according to several purveyors was increasing in excess of 100% a year.
- Alternative veterinary care (i.e. homeopathy, acupuncture, Chinese herbs, massage) utilization increased from 4% in 1995 to over 34% in 1998, an average annual increase of 187%.

- Pet expense was growing three times faster than GNP (Gross National Product).
- 80% + of owners would put themselves in harm's way to protect their companion animals.

Thus, we are having more companion animals than kids, we are spending more and faster on dogs and cats than the growth of GNP, we would put ourselves in harm's way for them, and yet the guerrilla-marketing US Insurance Industry has convinced only 2% of the potential market to buy pet health insurance, while 25% of pet owners in Britain, for instance, have such insurance.

Earth to overpaid insurance executives!

Exploiting the insurance principle of the "law of large numbers," where else in America is there an untapped market of 160 million insureds – where the risk can be limited to $15-$20,000 each? There isn't one that I'm aware of. The insurance geniuses are too busy doing finite insurance resulting in massive fines extracted by former New York Attorney General and former Governor Elliot Spitzer, rather than by the bobbing-head revolving-door State Insurance O-missioners.

Is it any wonder that although innovation spawns hundreds of thousands of patents in the health and pharmaceutical industries, only fewer than 330 patents have issued since 1977 in the business methods category relative to insurance?

The insurance geniuses will argue that they are encumbered in Pet Health Insurance by regulatory problems (i.e., not being able to pay veterinarians a commission to sell umbrellas when it isn't going to rain).

Furthermore, they will argue that insurance ideas are free ('open architecture') and good for the consumer – just like the McCarran-Ferguson law which exempts them from anti-trust regulation, just like their exclusion from the Federal Trade Commission further investigating the industry, and just like their censorship of agents who reveal the capital strength of individual companies (called Risk-Based Capital) by threatening those agents with fines and possible jail time.

Talk to the paw.

And what has this privileged status – exemption from market forces – spawned? Mutual Benefit Life, Executive Life, Confederation Life, going under; bailouts (using the name merger) of General American and New England Life due to risky assets and practices in the late '80's, early '90's; property and casualty bid rigging; not to mention the widespread disappointing (as proved by their landmark settlement) of disability claimants by UNUM in the '90's and early 2000's while the revolving door Insurance Omissioners sat on their tuchasses whining "we don't have the resources, we are strained, but effective – give us more money, legislators, so I can update my resume."

(And I reluctantly report this as a Goldwater Conservative Republican!)

The insurance industry's exemption from the meritocracy of the marketplace has also led to legalized theft. Rarely does a large insurance company invent anything other than good lunch in the executive dining hall amidst expensive paintings. If anything, this exemption from anti-trust has allowed the large companies to shift research and development costs to smaller companies. They encourage the smaller insurers to invent and educate – and then knock off the ideas without compensation.

Isn't it stupid to spend resources on innovation when one can steal it without cost or retribution?

The second bite of the apple wins in this privileged structure. Forget merit – forget the better mousetrap – since the cheese can be stolen without any penalties. As a result, innovation is rare. And the losers are society as a whole, and in this case, our companion animal owners and their guardians are harmed.

Lowering The Incidence of Economic Euthanasia & Extending The Quality of Healthy Longevity for our Companion Animals while Increasing Insurers' Profitability

Dogs and cats are home.

Companion animals have gone from the backyard to the bedroom.

They are members of the family (some, would argue, the preferred members of the family).

And, while considered by law 'sentient' beings in Britain, in the US they are property. Depreciated property at that.

Granted, they are implicitly beyond mere property in the more than 30 states which allow pets to be beneficiaries of trusts (52" HDTV's cannot be heirs). Furthermore, dogs and cats are protected by cruelty laws – while other property is not (though Richard Simmons exercise tapes should be considered cruel and unusual punishment.)

We insure not only our homes but the personal property within the residence. Since dogs and cats are 'living property,' why not attach major medical pet health insurance (which is therefore property insurance) to the homeowners' policy or for that matter to the family health insurance coverage?

Besides reducing the probability of economic euthanasia, here are the benefits:

To the guardian:
- Easily acquirable as the pet insurance is a convenient rider to the underlying homeowner's policy
- Less expensive. The underlying policy is already sold and has typically paid a 10%-15% commission to the agent. The added policy would not require 50%-100%+ upfront commissions and acquisition costs (typical of the industry) which could double the cost of the pet policy
- With a $500 to $1000 deductible (per year) and $15,000 lifetime coverage (including alternative veterinary care), the cost would be $10-$20 level per month (of course, adjusted for breed and area). The cost should be less than a lunch for two at Chili's once a month. (As it is, PetsMart is opening up 100 Pet Hotels a year which are charging $26 -$36 **per night!**)
- Being 'there' for their friend – through the better and worse (as he has been for you) – giving a 'new leash on life' – a second chance – not having to make an economic euthanasia decision because of finances.
- Potential longer healthier lifespan due to a 'minimum vaccination by law discount' (which is discussed later) and to the use of alternative approaches to health care.

For the insurance company (policy writer) (inside info you can skip):

- Increased persistency (retention – lowering lapse rates of policies in force) which results in additional profitability of the underlying homeowners or health insurance block of the insurer's business. One insurer estimated that for every 1% increase in retention on a block of 40000 policies, an additional $14 million went to the bottom line.
- Reduced switching of policies. In a 2005 J.D. Powers' study, 22% of those homeowner policyholders who have been with their present insurer 10 or more years, were shopping other policies. (The older the policy, the more profitable the homeowner's policy is to the insurer as the 'acquisition cost' (commissions, marketing etc.) has been spread over a longer period of time)
- New premium – at an average premium of $15 per month, 15% of market share would translate to $4.3 billion in premium, with a maximum exposure of $15,000 per companion animal spreading the risk.
- Increased market share – with 65%-70% of homeowners having companion animals, an affordable, no games, easily acquirable major medical pet health insurance policy would take market share away from competitors securing more homeowner policies for the insurer offering this rider. 'Heal!' Pet Health Insurance ™ would be what is called an ingredient brand – like 'Intel inside' or 'Ethyl' – acquiring new homeowners policies for the company.

- Reduced costs of acquisition – as the rider is an 'add-on' to an underlying policy, or bundled with the underlying policy.
- Reduced administration cost per claim. Claims are accumulated by the policyholder until the $500 or $1000 deductible is met; thereafter, all covered claims are paid.

More importantly, companion animals would be saved from economic euthanasia – as many as 150,000/yr assuming 15% market share. Furthermore, if the minimum vaccination by law discount extended the quality of healthy life by only 1 year per pet, this feature alone would save in effect 1,250,000 companion animal lives per year.

Through insurance connections, I initially made contact with the key Chubb Insurance VP in charge of new products.

One thing led to another; Chubb sent out a key executive with the understanding that this individual could make the deal.

We agreed to a deal, on the spot, on how Chubb might develop major-medical pet health insurance on its homeowners' policies

Subsequently, apparently distracted by the potential of the China market, Chubb changed its mind on our deal. The legal department changed the parameters of the deal beyond what I believe had been agreed to – with a handshake – "on the spot."

Talk to the paw.

I really thought that, since I had insisted on it, the executive they sent had all the authority he needed to do so. He subsequently championed this project, and then took a good deal of ribbing in the Chubb executive suite, derisively being called "Dog Boy."

Most of the old Chubb executive team is now gone (and coincidentally, Chubb's stock has subsequently climbed) but don't worry about Dog Boy – he has since moved on to a much higher level and (deserved) executive positions in the insurance industry.

Chubb 'changing its mind' was just as well. Their homeowner policy market is at the high end ($1,000,000+ homes). Whereas the average homeowner's premium is approximately $800, Chubb's is probably three times that amount. Their policyholder would more likely be able to self-insure (pay out of pocket) the pet health/economic euthanasia risk – unlike many an average homeowner.

I pursued the major carriers – State Farm, All State, Travelers, etc. I couldn't even get a response to calls, letters, or even introductions via other insurance execs in the business. And, I couldn't even get a response from the 'new ventures, new products' areas of these companies.

New products – new ventures – is an oxymoron at insurance companies.

But State Farm wins the prize for "moat" mentality, corporate insulation and arrogance.

I was a State Farm policyholder for all but 1 out of 39 years up until 2006 despite their recent problems with OEM's (Original Manufacturer's Equipment losses in the Supreme Court and now Katrina).

I couldn't get through to State Farm's executive offices, neither could my agent, nor a super agent of theirs (let alone other insurance executives) for even a phone call – let alone a response to correspondence.

Yet, during the most recent years under the third generation of Rust family leadership, State Farm has 'burned' surplus (depleted net worth) and lost market share as a "mutually owned" company (with third generation leadership.)

Rust-o-leum?

(And they still haven't dealt with coverage for ID theft (unlike its competition) though estimates are 40% of US homeowners are concerned about ID theft!)

What was I doing wrong that I couldn't even get an audience with these property and casualty insurers?

These property and casualty insurers were losing profit, market share, having their book of business churned, going into questionable markets of low profit and high risk when there was a virtually uncovered market of 160 million companion animals – loved, and lavished increasingly – with minimum exposure per liability – that hadn't even been 'scratched' (though many an owner had been bitten by scam pet insurance.)

There had to be another way.

I had to think outside the litter box of property and casualty insurers (since they weren't).

Ok, the landscape was littered with money-loser *<u>standalone</u>* pet insurance policies.

The key is 'standalone'!

The doors of property and casualty insurers were not just closed – shut, sealed, hardened with 'only authorized personnel' labels under a skull and cross bones symbol.

There was no listening outside the box.

My access had gone dark. The question becomes how to penetrate the property and casualty and or health insurer lack of imagination?

> **Coincidences are God's way of remaining anonymous**
>
> *Another Judaic saying*

By coincidence, as my quandary compounded during this process, an article in the Wall Street Journal featured 'the only certified pet actuary' in the English speaking world, Sally Schreiber. Schreiber, for 20 years, had been the actuary for Pet Plan in England owned by Allianz, one of the largest reinsurers in the world.

(Reinsurance is where an insurer – typically called a direct writer like State Farm – sells part of the risk ((the insurance)) to another insurer ((called a reinsurer)) to spread its risk. Think of the reinsurer as the insurer's insurer!)

My thinking was since pet insurance (as a standalone policy) had failed several times, direct insurance writers like Allstate and State Farm were afraid of the risk. Thus, if they could spread the risk – reinsure part of the risk – they might be more amenable to trying pet insurance attached as a rider to their underlying homeowner's policy and or health insurance policies.

Simultaneously the reinsurer is looking for new business – and business that will have a longer product life cycle for them.

Now, typically, insurers reinsure excess risk (over a certain amount per individual policy or cumulatively) and more often than not on new products with which the original insurers are not as familiar. As the direct writer becomes more comfortable with the product, he cedes (sells) less and less of the risk to the reinsurers.

Pet health insurance attached as a rider offers a unique opportunity for a <u>reinsurer</u> to have a longer life cycle (with more insurance ceded) – especially if the reinsurance is offered on what is called a 'facultative' reinsurance basis.

Facultative reinsurance has the reinsurer doing all the underwriting (original paperwork) of the pet health insurance policy rather than the direct write.

Thus, the reinsurer effectively becomes the underwriting department for the direct writer on the pet insurance element - accumulating underwriting experience and data. The reinsurer could accumulate proprietary data from several homeowner direct writers (as I envisioned the process). The direct writer would become more not less dependent on the reinsurer – constantly reducing costs – and thus premiums.

Finally, I conceived pet health insurance attached to the homeowners (or health insurance policy) as an "ingredient brand."

Think "Intel Inside."

Ingredient brand.

Now originally when I conceived this concept, Hulk Hogan (yes, the wrestler Hulk Hogan) was a bad guy (in wrestling parlance 'a heel') as the leader of the infamous "NWO" (New World Order). At of each of his interviews, he would hold 4 fingers up and then clinch in the middle three fingers (making an 'L") stating 'NWO, 4 Life.'

That was it – 4Life Pet Health Insurance – the brand.

The purpose of this pet health insurance was to reduce economic euthanasia – 4Life – 'no companion animal before their time' – 'through the better and worse' – 4Life.

4Life Pet Health Insurance – the ingredient branding.

(Subsequently, since the 4Life brand was in use elsewhere and not available, I changed the name to Heal! Pet Health Insurance™ at the suggestion of my friend and former Colorado State Senator Hugh Fowler.)

The concept was for the reinsurer to advertise directly to the ultimate consumer – as does Intel. While there is no 'Intel computer' the concept of the *ingredient brand* is to pull the consumer through to a brand – in this case to direct writers who offer Heal! Pet Health Insurance™ "inside" (bundled with their policies as an option)!

But before a discussion of marketing and "ingredient brands" could get underway, despite Allianz's interest and their actuary's seal of approval, I withdrew from any further discussion of a deal.

Allianz was to be sued by Holocaust survivors!

4Life Pet Health Insurance™ was dead before arrival.

> **Jews and Dogs Not Allowed**
>
> *Sign in store window in the movie, Life is Beautiful*

One or two weeks prior to the start of the survivors' suit against Allianz, during Shabbos dinner, Rabbi Howard (Henoch Dov) Hoffman told a story about his late mother Lillian, who at the time, was one of the leaders in the Soviet Jewry Movement. Rabbi Howard was then maybe 17. It seems Lillian called the Russian Gulag where Natan Sharansky was a prisoner. She gave Hell to its commander (who spoke English!) about Sharansky's imprisonment. (Lillian even reversed the charges).

After she hung up, Howard asked her, "Mom, why are you calling them. It's futile. It won't do any good."

Lillian got within an eighth inch of Howard's face and said, "every Jew is collateral for every other Jew."

'Coincidentally,' I had just seen *Life is Beautiful* and remembered the sign in the shop: "No Jews or Dogs Allowed."

Just a few days later, I was reading the story *The Precious Stone* in <u>Bedtime Stories of Jewish Values</u> by Shmeul Blitz.

Plot of *The Precious Stone*: there was a valuable sapphire stone in one of the eyes of an idol that a faraway king was now 'missing.' The king's trusted advisor, Salmen (not to be confused with Solomon) knew there was only one such sapphire in the entire kingdom – and Reb Yitzchak had it. Salmen sailed to purchase the jewel from Reb Yitzchak.

Now for a Jew, God the Almighty is one – oneness. Idolatry is a sin. So how could Reb Yitchak sell the stone – regardless of price – to the king's emissary for such a purpose? Yes, he and his wife could use the money, but he knew he could be an accomplice to this idolatry – regardless of price.

The king's emissary threatened death. Since life comes first in Judaism, the Rabbi consented to sell the jewel and boarded the boat, sapphire jewel in hand, to present it to the king.

On the boat, Salmen asked see the jewel. With shaking hand Reb Yitzchak acceded to his request. As he handed the jewel for inspection by Salmen, with his supposedly shaking hand, the jewel 'accidentally on purpose' was thrown overboard into the water.

So the king didn't get his Jewel and Reb Yitzchak was not an accomplice to idolatry. Nor did he bow to any idol.

A year after the sapphire was lost, Reb Yitzchak and his wife, who had been childless, conceived a baby boy named Shlomo. Shlomo grew up to become Rashi, one of the greatest teachers of the Jewish people.

Trifecta?

'Coincidences' – God's way of winking?

So, between Lillian Hoffman, *Life is Beautiful,* and Rashi, I had to throw 4Life overboard – walking away from Allianz.

If Allianz would not pay the rightful claims of Holocaust victims, how could I think they would make good on 'no companion animal before his time' 4Life claims?

To say I wasn't conflicted would be a lie. Many years, many hours had been put into this project, including even storyboards for 4Life commercials titled 'There' for my Nicki, Buddy, Moolah and Ricki. Many lives that could succumb to economic euthanasia were at stake. And yes, I did consider the economic consequences – which were not small – but then again, the proof of the puddin' is in the eatin', and yours truly had just written two editions of the personal financial planning book, *ENOUGH…*

A word for miracle in Hebrew – nes – also is defined as test.

When the Jews crossed the Reed Sea (not red, Bruce Almighty fans), it wasn't until Nashon led first in taking the test of going into the water up to his nostrils that the sea parted – without flashbacks to Charlton Heston.

The miracle is in the test.

I walked from the potential Allianz deal.

4Life was not only dead with Allianz but also 'coincidentally', the other major reinsurers, who once indicated an initial interest, were no longer returning phone calls.

4Life was grey-balled.

Talk to the paw.

I hadn't forgotten Nicki and 'no dog before her time' – it wasn't time. Another deadly factor would have to come into place to resurrect 4Life as Heal! Pet Health Insurance™: overvaccination and the unnecessary death of my Moolah.

> **Steps To Consider**
>
> **Let's face it, there is no such thing as a free dog or cat. Whether it's the original cost, or maintenance, or vet bills, etc., companion animals are costly (but, from a cost/benefit ratio, I contend, very inexpensive). Therefore, instead of wasting money on pet insurance premiums until real, affordable, no games, convenient major-medical pet health insurance comes to fruition, I suggest the following:**
>
> - Self-Insure: for each companion animal put aside initially $500 -$1000 and then $50-$75 a month in a separate account. (For example, I have set up my own self-insurance for each of my dogs – investing in Vanguard Health mutual fund.)

The positive of this approach is 100 cents on a dollar (other than gains or losses on your chosen investment) are available to pay healthcare costs versus maybe 60 cents from a dollar of insurance premium. After commissions, administration, marketing costs – typically 60 cents are available for claims.

The negative – God forbid a major illness(s) or accident(s) occurs of a magnitude of $5000 in the first couple years – the amount accumulated would not be sufficient to offset the total cost of the $5000 illness injury, but neither would any existing pet health insurance with a $2500 per-incident limit or, worse, inner limits (lowered maximums per illness or injury) when you've accumulated only $2300 to $3700 (giving no value to investment gains or loses).

Making the case - $5000 injury or illness at the end of three-years
Self-insurance vs Today's Pet Health Insurance:

Accumulation (Initial Deposit)	$500	$1000
Earnings at 6% after tax	95	191
Per month deposit		
$35	$1260	$1260
6% earn. After tax	116	116
Total available	$1971	$2567
$50	$1800	$1800
6% earn After tax	167	167
Total Available	$2562	$3158
$75	$2700	$2700
6% earn After tax	250	250
Total Available	$3545	$4141
For $5000 claim		

Of course, you could have paid $30 - $50+ per month depending on age etc, with the $2500 per incident limitation. You would have paid out the following:

	$35/mo	$45/mo	$50/mo
Premiums	$1260	$1620	$1800
Loss of earnings @ 6%	116	150	166
$2500 of the $5000 claim	$2500	$2500	$2500
Out of pocket on $5000	$3876	$4270	$4466
Net insurance coverage	$1124	$780	$534

Of course, if you have no claims, you are ahead by self-insuring $3545-$4141 versus having paid premium of $1260 to $1800 (not including lost earnings during the period.)

Self-insurance is even better versus today's insurance – the longer the time till a big claim (and remember, not even calculated in this contrast is the fact that today's pet insurance premiums typically rise annually – and at the 7th + year, coverage decreases.)

The only time today's questionable pet health insurance wins versus this self-insurance is in the first year or two – assuming there are no inner limits, no 'continuing coverage claims', etc.

So until real, affordable, no games major-medical pet insurance (like Heal!) is available as described previously, given the history with pet insurer claims, etc., my choice is to self-insure which, in effect, is the same recommendation of Consumer Reports which prefers paying 'out of pocket' to any Pet Health Insurance coverage available today.

SETTING FOR NEXT CHAPTER

> From 1980 to 2004, only 56 instances of human rabies (from all sources including bats-*jds*) were reported in the U.S.*
>
> Dr. Ranit Mishori, "How Worried Should You Be?" Parade, September, 2006

* If the average US population during these 25 years were only 200 million, this report of rabies would amount to an annual incidence rate of less than 11 *billionths* of 1%. Furthermore, since the vast majority of these incidents involved bats or miscellaneous critters, the incidence involving dogs is <u>even lower</u>.

> Custom will reconcile people to any atrocity
> *George Bernard Shaw*

Chapter III
Moolah I: The Call (Connecting The Doc$)

THE FABULOUS 'MOOLAH'

(a.k.c. THE POOCHINI OF BELCH)

The 'Standard of Excellence' aids the Monetary
Mongoose in hounding, pounding and mounting the
SINdication Distribution Complex & other 'MORE-ons.'
Win, Lose or Claw, the Wizard of Paws makes no bones
in protecting Ft. Schwartz and its clients.
Finishing Holds: Sniff & Tell or The Tax Bite.
(Moolah's Baseball Card)

> He (Charlie) feels that he is a first-rate dog, and has no wish to be a second-rate human
>
> *Travels With Charlie*, John Steinbeck

There are champions and there are champions.

There is being one of the best, and then there is that special champion of champions.

Professional wrestling, which is no different than life in its predetermined endings, has had some great champions – Buddy Rodgers (for whom Buddy was named in part), Nick Bockwinkle (for whom – in part – Nicki was named), and Ric Flair the namesake for Ricki.

All great – and no more than a hair's difference in their greatness.

And then there was The Fabulous Moolah (Lillian Ellison – passed late 2007).

Moolah was for 27 years the undisputed female wrestling champion. The others before and after most people don't remember and the knowledgeable must rack their brains to recall.

In female wrestling, there was Moolah – then all the rest.

Not just one of the greats. Not just first class. World class – in a category all by herself.

Each of the 10 black Standard Poodle puppies had a colored soft-cotton collar to identify it.

I chose the "purple lady" almost 20 years ago.

That was Moolah.

After but one night in a carrier, she was a permanent presence on my bed, nightly warming my side prior to my retiring. Ever conscious of the others, she dutifully waited her turn in succession for loving prior to starting the day's activities. However, she managed to double up her "loving" by first lying down face to face with me and then, sensing her time was up, plopping against me with her back for more, turning her face back toward me.

During Buddy's prolonged illness and then Nicki's imminent demise, Moolah increased her affection, filling Buddy's void as he battled; Nicki's kisses diminishing as her energy dissipated.

Moolah loved her walks – striding with confidence – perfectly – by my side, never pulling – always there.

Always there.

By my side.

With class.

As a puppy she had a very high respiration rate. CSU Vet School, several doctors, and thousands later – it turned out – the rapid breathing – not typical – was normal for her. As one vet said, she could have a normal life with it of 10 years.

As Buddy grew older, she became the leader – a benign leader.

However, outside of Nicki, Ricki, and Buddy – she avoided other dogs.

She didn't fight. She just avoided them.

Beneath tables – behind my legs – she avoided.

Not that she was a snob – just naturally regal.

Not often does one have *assigned* a bashert (to be) dog .

The Fabulous Moolah's *assignment* has been to polish and 'fix' the rough edges of her guardian's eccentric panache into a smoother flair – an unfinished futile dog trick.

Everyday she proved to me there is a G-d.

As only G-d could create "the purple lady," The Fabulous Moolah – The Standard of Excellence.

Always there.

By my side.

World(s) Class.

The Fabulous Moolah – The Best There Is; The Best There Was; The Best There Ever Will Be – The Standard of Excellence*

---

* As we all know, the best, a superlative, is plural in one instance – our companion animals, past, present & future

The Story: OVER-VACCINATION, *OVERKILL?*

On October 29, 1999, I brought Moolah in for her annual rabies shot at VCA's Wingate Hospital in Englewood (now Centennial), Colorado. At that time, I asked the vet, "Can we do the rabies shot every three-years - like we are doing with parvo and distemper?" (Exhibit 1; Rabies Certificate signed by Dr. Earl Wenngren, Director)

"No," I was told. "Arapahoe County [Colorado] still requires the annual rabies vaccination."

Now Moolah, at the time, was not in the best of health to begin with. Secondly, she was 11 years of age. I would later learn that both of these are critical concerns. Also, I would later learn that the rabies-vaccine label typically states "only administer to healthy dogs." I would also learn that the research is pretty overwhelming that older dogs *do not need the vaccination* - especially if they are kept in a confined area and out of the woods.

However, at that time, I was not aware of those points. Nor was I aware that Colorado had passed a bill allowing the three-year rabies vaccination - or that it had been enacted into law in July of 1999, four months prior to Moolah's unnecessary rabies shot. The Colorado veterinarians, however, had to have known (or should have known) of this option, as both the Denver vet newsletter as well as the cover story of the spring issue of the Colorado Veterinarian magazine in 1999 featured stories on the three-year rabies vaccination option.

Again, prior to vaccination, I had asked, "could we not go every three-years like we are on parvo and distemper?" I was told, "No. Arapahoe County (where I live outside of Denver) requires the annual rabies vaccination." (Exhibit 2; Health Record shows Moolah was given the 'Wombo Combo' – Parvo Distemper & Rabies all at once the year prior on 11/3/98)

Shortly after the unnecessary rabies vaccination, Moolah developed autoimmune hemolytic illness.

Every guardian knows his or her dog. I knew she was sick. Moolah wasn't herself. Normally upon my calling, she would be up instantly. Now she wasn't. Moolah always ate very well. (Once she got into my Werther's Original gold-wrapped butterscotch candies, devouring them. When I looked for them and accused her, she gave me a "who me?" look even as the wrappers dangled like tinsel from her ears). Now she wasn't eating well, at all.

Moolah had always been at my side. Now, she stayed in the cool hallway - panting and panting and panting. Her gums became pale. She was transferred to Alameda East Animal Hospital. Her blood platelet counts dropped like a rock; Oxyglobin was used, and I administered special medication which required my wearing gloves. Her platelets continued to drop. Her dosages of the steroid Prednisone were increased.

She still wasn't eating – not even hand-fed Good Times hamburgers with cheese.

I was advised to leave her at the vet's for a 24-hour watch. It went on for days; I visited her several times daily. The last day she looked at me as if to say, "Take me home to die." I didn't. I can still see her face as she went back into the cage.

Then came the call from Alameda East on December 28, 1999: "You ought to come down."

Five-six-seven thousand dollars later - all to no avail - she could hardly get up; she could hardly breathe. Hearing my voice when I entered, for the first and last time, she raised her head.

It was time. I had promised my late-friend Fred Burke to do what he had done: "I bring them into my life," he said, "I will be the one that takes them out."

I sang to Moolah Debbie Friedman's *"Let Us Light These Lights"* as I held her head on my lap. The vet sedated her.

I kept my promise to Fred Burke .

Her limp body now in my arms, I thanked the Alm-ghty for the 11 years He had given me on this earth with her.

G-d gave me 11 years with Moolah. The Alm-ghty, the TRUE guardian, reclaimed Moolah.

Moolah's case of over-vaccination is not isolated. It unfortunately happens every day – now 8 years after the enactment in 1999 in Colorado.

I left VCA when my previous veterinarian from Tendercare, Dr. Kris Abbey, went to affiliate with Hampden Family Pet Hospital. Kris and Dr. Jan Fascinelli had brought Buddy back from over-vaccination (now in hindsight) years before, utilizing homeopathy and acupuncture. It was early 2000 - February or maybe March. It was time to look into shots for Elle, my black female Standard Poodle (Moolah's successor). I asked Kris about giving Elle the annual rabies vaccination.

"No, we can do a three-year vaccination," she said.

I asked, "Did change just occur?"

Dr. Abbey replied, "No. I mean, we've had it (the three-year option) in Arapahoe County since 1999."

Well, that was interesting to me. So, I called VCA Wingate and talked with Beverly, the office manager, and asked, "Do you still do the annual rabies vaccination?"

She replied, "Yes."

I asked, "Is it still required by Arapahoe County?"

She said, "Yes, Arapahoe County requires it."

I was convinced that Arapahoe County was at fault. Why would I think otherwise? Why would VCA's vets mislead me? So I inquired at Arapahoe County Animal Control and eventually learned, after initial bureaucratic obfuscation, non-response and double talk, that Arapahoe County was not at fault. As a matter of fact, Arapahoe County Animal Control had notified vet hospitals in the county of the change in the rabies vaccination law. Additionally, I learned that the vaccination period was not set by county ordinance but by state law. (And this was reaffirmed in correspondence between Tri-County Health and Centennial's Mayor Randy Pye – Exhibit 3.)

Quoting Mayor Pye's letter to me of April 3, 2001, "The Colorado Department of Public Health and Environment was very helpful in pointing out that under Colorado law, 25-4-607 C.R.S. 1973 as amended, they clearly delegate the authority to enact mandatory rabies vaccination laws to local jurisdictions and the responsible Public Health officer for those jurisdictions. In Arapahoe County and Centennial (*my county and city respectively of residence*), it would be Tri-County Health Department.

"I (Mayor Pye) spoke with Mr. Bruce Wilson at Tri-County Health and he referred my attention to their Regulation II-99, Section 2 that states that animals shall be inoculated in accordance with the provisions of the Compendium of Animal Rabies Control. In reviewing that document, under Part I, titled **Recommendations for Parenteral Immunization Procedures,** Part B – Vaccine Selection, it states in part, 'only vaccines with a 3 year duration of immunity should be used.' I asked Mr. Wilson if under those guidelines it is required that only 3-year vaccines be used? He clearly stated that these were only **recommendations** and that it was up to each veterinarian to make a choice between 1 and 3 year vaccines or using both.

I then asked him how veterinarians were notified of the recommended change to 3-year inoculations since it is Tri-County Health's charge to oversee the program. I was told that it was done through several conduits (*seconded by Ms. Thompson at Arapahoe County Animal Control*). They are:

1. State-wide contact through the "Compendium of Animal Rabies Control" as published by the National Association of State Public Health Veterinarians, Inc. This is the compendium accepted and used by all veterinarians.
2. Through their office, Tri-County Health which notified:

    Colorado Veterinarian Medical Association

    Denver Area Veterinarian Medical Society

    Colorado Association of Animal Control Officers

    Colorado Federation of Animal Welfare Agencies"

(All the above from Mayor Pye – and thanks to him for the interest/effort.)

Prior notification was seconded to me by Ms. Thea Thompson of the Arapahoe County Animal Control Department listing VCA Wingate as having had contact relative to the three-year rabies option (Exhibit 4).

Apologies and a good ration of crow were in order. Having been initially red-taped by Arapahoe Animal Control, (compounding my anger at Moolah's unnecessarily premature death), I had spent $1400 taking out full-page ads in the *Centennial Citizen* to get city council and Mayor Pye off their tuchasses. After all, VCA Wingate told me of Arapahoe County's annual rabies shot requirement in late 1999 and maintained the same story in 2001. Why would this animal hospital, part of a national public chain of then 300 now over 435 veterinary hospitals, misinform me?

Subsequently, Brian Reagan took his dog, Lucy, to VCA Wingate in February, 2001, 18 months after the passage of the three-year rabies option, and was told by the Managing Director that the annual rabies shot was required by Douglas County. But a Mr. Lloyd Williams of Tri-County Health told Brian that Douglas County allowed the three-year option. Lucy died 3 months after her annual shot.

The question becomes was this particular VCA hospital misinformed? Was this just an isolated problem in one of VCA's several hundred veterinary hospitals?

Sabra Chandler, a resident of Denver County, suffered the same policy pronouncement ("the requirement is an annual rabies shot") from VCA Wingate in June of 2001. She requested Dr. Winton, at Wingate, to get the position of VCA-National on their rabies vaccination protocol. She received back a letter (see Exhibit 5) from Rocky McKelvey, D.V.M, Regional Medical Director Southwest Region of VCA. McKelvey, representing VCA National Headquarters, stated on June 25, 2001, "As a company we have chosen to 'err' on the side of conservative medicine (giving the annual rabies shot) until we can see some solid evidence to change our recommendation."

Yet, according to the American Veterinary Medical Association in 2001, "the practice of annual rabies vaccination is based *on historical precedent* and *government regulation, not* scientific data." Yet, in June of the same year, McKelvey asserted that the AVMA needed "more solid research 'under our belts' before making sweeping changes in vaccine protocol."

How could there be *more* solid research on the three-year option when there wasn't *any* research on the annual rabies shot to begin with?

Furthermore, *informed consent* is part of the canon of ethics of the AVMA. There was no *informed consent* given to myself in October of 1999, nor to Brian Regan in February of 2001, nor to Sabra Chandler in June of 2001. Nor to how many million others? To you?

It is interesting to note that a year later there was a front page feature *"Are Annual Shots Overkill?"* (Exhibit 6) in the Marketplace Section of the Wall Street Journal (July 31, 2002). According to the feature's writer, VCA Corporation would not let McKelvey talk to her for the purposes of her feature! Instead, Dr. Todd R. Tams, chief medical officer of VCA, the nation's largest owner of veterinary hospitals, three-and-a-half years after the passage of the three-year rabies option in Colorado stated, "the concern is that if we move too quickly to decrease vaccine frequency across the board, we may be opening the door for some animals to become infected when we could have prevented the problem." (Exhibit 5)

(Here, after Moolah's 'premature death,' Dr. Wenngren of Wingate VCA issued shot waivers for my also aging and not-in-the-best-of-health surviving dogs – Ricki and Nicki.)

Again per the AVMA Journal 9/01, "the practice of annual rabies vaccination is based (only) on historical precedent and government regulation, *not scientific data.*"

On 2/18/03, Dr. Jean Dodds, a pioneer on the question of over-vaccination of companion animals, stated, "in light of the new emphasis on doing titers rather than annual boosters – I've just given 5 area seminars on vaccine issues generally, all sold out in attendance to vets. They were very well received and sponsored by **VCA/Antech (the same VCA Corp**.). So, we hope that VCA policy will be changing to be more flexible, because that's what their vet staff want, i.e., the option to use their own professional judgment on this issue of boosters, etc."

So let's review:

1. 1/99, Colorado passes the three-year rabies option effective 7/99
2. pring 1999, the cover story of the Colorado Vet Magazine features the new Colorado rabies protocol option
3. Spring 1999, The Denver Vets newsletter features new Colorado rabies protocol option
4. October 29, 1999 – VCA requires the annual rabies shot for my dog Moolah (already older and not in the best of health) stating we could not go three-years

between shots because Arapahoe County requires the annual shot.

5. December 27, 1999, Moolah dies from auto-immune hemolytic disease

6. February or March 2000, in taking my dog Elle for her 'annual rabies vaccination' – I am told by Dr. Kris Abbey – that Elle can go three-years between rabies shots. When I said that Arapahoe county required annual rabies shots, she said that that was not the case.

7. February or March 2000, I call VCA Wingate and talk with their office manager, Beverly, and she reiterated that Arapahoe County requires the annual rabies shot and that has been the case since 1999.

8. February 2001, Brian Regan takes his dog into VCA Wingate. They require the annual rabies shot for his dog.

9. April 3, 2001, Centennial Mayor Pye confirms that Tri-County Health (which includes Arapahoe County and Centennial) has allowed the three-years rabies option since passage of the law in 1999.

10. June 25, 2001, Dr. Rocky McKelvey, Regional Medical Director of VCA states, "As a company (VCA) we have chosen to 'err' on the side of conservative medicine (giving the annual rabies vaccination) until we can see some solid evidence to change our recommendation."

11. Sept 1, 2001, The Journal of The American Veterinary Medical Association states, "The one-year (rabies) re-vaccination frequency recommendation found on many vaccine labels is based on historical

precedent and government regulation (United States Department of Agriculture regulation- USDA) NOT ON SCIENTIFIC DATA."

12. July 31, 2002, in a Wall Street Journal feature article *"Are Annual Shots Overkill,"* Dr. Todd R. Tams, chief medical officer of VCA, the nation's largest owner of veterinary hospitals, 3½ years after passage of the three-years rabies option in Colorado and 10 months after the AVMA Journal statement in #11, states: "The concern is that if we move too quickly to decrease vaccine frequency across the board, we may be opening the door for some animals to become infected when we could have prevented the problem." (Furthermore, it should be noted that the writer for the WSJ article, Ms. Rundles, indicated that VCA would not allow Dr. Rocky McKelvey to be interviewed for the article.)

13. February 18, 2003 (now 4 years since passage of the Colorado legislation, Dr. Jean Dodds relates that VCA/Antech (same company) sponsored 5 seminars on doing antibody titers (an alternative to annual rabies vaccinations which measures the companion animal's ability to fend off this disease!)

14. *VCA's Antech division now sells blood titering panels!*

As for VCA, let's do a little math. Let's assume during the period of October, 1999, through February, 2003, that VCA had 300+ hospitals – on average. And each hospital had 3 full-time vets each with approximately 2500 companion animals under his/her care. Assume just a 50% 'compliance rate' to an annual rabies vaccination requirement (not even considering annual parvo and distemper shots – which are now said to last 7+ years). And let's assume the period to consider is just 3 years – in two of which the rabies shot should not have been given.

- 300 hospitals * 3 vets * 1250 companion animals (2500 *.5 (50%) 'compliance') = 1,125,000 annual rabies shots/ year (as of January, 2008: 435 hospitals, 1100 vets)
- 2 years of unnecessary shots per the three-year option (for illustration purposes) or 2.25 million questionable shots.
- An office visit (average $45) is required by law for the administration of the rabies shot; add the price of the rabies shot (let's assume $25 on average) or a total of $70
- $70 * 2,250,000 questionably necessary rabies shots (not including parvo and distemper) = $157,500,000 gross revenues to VCA during that period under these assumptions. Cost of these shots (.60 *2.250,000) = $1,350,000.
- Gross profit margin from over-vaccinating pets unnecessarily over 3 years = $156,150,000!

And of course, the above does not factor in the cost to the companion animal owner of *adverse reactions* from over-vaccination. For example, a 1% *adverse reaction* with just one additional $100 (average transaction cost [ATC] per American Animal Hospital Association in their 2003 edition of <u>Financial</u>

& Productivity Pulsepoints small-animal practice was actually $108.90) cost to the owner/guardian multiplied by the 1,125,000 visits per year (2,250,000 visits over the two years) yields another $11 million per year of additional expense. Since it is doubtful that the average *adverse reaction* causes only one "transaction," at $200 would yield $22 million a year or at 5% *adverse reactions* over $110 million additional cost to guardians. Of course, at 5% *adverse reaction*, this is $55 million per year additional revenue. This writing is as of late 2007 – think the ATC has gone down in the past 5 years? (Consider the 2003 edition's data is probably 2002!). Check your vet bills; I doubt it.

Lastly, the above does not even consider the economic value of 'the up-sell': additional services/procedures and fees generated, i.e., pediatric needs, parasite and fecal screens, nutritional issues, skin surveillance, genetic predispositions, senior programs, chronic condition surveillance, etc. And all from the spit-it-out-from-the-computer-initiate-the-annual-vaccination-visit reminder!

Talk to the Paw$$$.

I couldn't, I didn't want to believe – and still to this day find it hard to believe even the possibility that this systemic, harmful over-vaccination could be economically motivated and covered up by our veterinarians whom we trust with our dogs and cats. Not by our friendly vets. And certainly, I couldn't fathom this from veterinarians in the largest vet chain (now, 435 sites) with a supervising manager on site, let alone national quality control and supervisory policy relative to shots which contribute 65%-

70% of all small-animal veterinarian visits happening without *informed consent* or other options by law. Veterinarians wouldn't, couldn't, daily, hourly, as a matter of policy, not tell guardians about alternatives to annual rabies vaccinations. After all, we give vets our trust – our substitute reliance, and, at a minimum and per the veterinarians' own canon of ethics, we deserve *informed consent*. But, lack of *informed consent* and over-vaccination was the case – and not – and I repeat, <u>not</u> an isolated case but rather a systemic norm – hardwired into the very essence of the small-animal veterinary practice business model.

Okay, Sammy Sosa had a corked bat; yes, Mark McGuire wouldn't talk about steroids; and as Simon & Garfunkle sang, Joe DiMaggio is dead. And of course, Rex Allen, frontier veterinarian, was a myth. But the reality was and is **A BETRAYAL OF TRUST** embedded in the small-animal veterinary practice management to the potential physical detriment of our companion animals.

Subsequently, I learned of a study in Europe indicating that 7% to 12%+ of all vaccinated companion animals experience *adverse reactions* to vaccination within the first 45 days (at the 99% confidence level in a study of 1000 dogs and 1000 cats), including death and auto-immune illness. The '1-in-10,000' and '1-in-100,000' *adverse reaction* statistics, thrown around by some veterinarians, have not been validated scientifically and are based on reactions reported by veterinarians themselves. That's sort of like Dracula guarding the blood bank. These mythological statistics are now even repudiated by the vet association itself (Journal of the American Veterinary Association) while trying to deflect the blame to the vaccine manufacturers! The problem with this finger pointing is that the vets are 'sophisticated users' especially when 63%-70% of small-animal vet practice visits are for 'vaccination.'

In addition, from the veterinarian's own economic literature, using conservative assumptions, the 10% to 15% of small-animal veterinarian practice revenues derived from vaccination, could constitute 70%-150% of the practice's gross profit! (And this estimate does not include derivative tests, procedures, up-sell etc. that result from the vaccination- elicited visit!!)

Let's review the economics. Without even including the parvo and distemper shot revenue (or other derivative revenue), the cost of the rabies shot is approximately 60 cents. Other than at a shot clinic, the typical rabies shot can cost $20-$35 with another $35-$48 for an office visit required by law as only a veterinarian can administer the rabies shot. The rabies shot and required office visit thus create a markup of 12,000%+. To put this in perspective, a $2.25 package of Oreo's would have to sell for approximately $270 sans the milk using these assumptions. At $25 for the shot and $45 for the office visit, the Oreo's would cost less – about $263 per package. Is it any wonder, in the words of Dr. Jim Irwin, who states: "Some practitioners may dread it (the American Animal Hospital Association's released canine vaccine guidelines) and consider the recommendations as a *'practice buster.'*...The concern of course is the loss of our *'vaccine hook'*...our image has become that of a *'vaccinator'* and not 'a physician for animals.' (*"What Do We Tell Our Clients"*, DVM News Magazine, July 1, 2003).

The economics, the science, the lack of legal accountability dots were connecting, and continue to connect and to be covered up.

The question wasn't 'revenge' on any one veterinarian as the problem is systemic. The mission was to 'make Moolah's loss matter" – no dog before his time.

What happened to Moolah, need not, should not, happen to another companion animal.

The Fabulous Moolah – The Best There Is; The Best There Was; The Best There Ever Will Be

---

Executive Guardian Summary: Connecting The Dot$$$$:

THE "SCIENCE":

> "The one-year vaccination frequency recommendation (for rabies) found on many vaccine labels is based only on historical precedent and United States Department of Agriculture (USDA) regulation, NOT on scientific data."
>
> *The Principles of Vaccination, American Veterinary Medicine Association (AVMA) Journal, No. 5, 9/1/01*

> Vaccine medicine is no longer a one-size-fits-all fantasy.
>
> Dr. Paul, past president American Animal Hospital Association, Lakewood, Colorado
>
> *December, 2003 Issue AAHA Trends Magazine*
>
> *Cover Story "Vaccine Legal Jitters"*

THE ETHICS:

> "Veterinarians should not allow their medical judgment to be influenced by agreements by which they stand to profit through referring clients to other providers of services or products."
>
> *Section V. Influence of Judgment:*
>
> *The Principles of Veterinary Medical Ethics of the American Veterinarian Medical Association*
>
> *(2003 Revision)*

THE ECONOMICS:

> "Many practices generate 15% to 25% of their gross incomes from vaccination visits. This income is supplemented by fees for additional services generated by the vaccination visit (e.g., dental procedures)...The immediate result of extended vaccination intervals will be the loss of this relatively easily-generated income. Some veterinary practices may not be able to survive financially. Those operating on close profit margins and depending heavily on vaccination income will be the first fatalities."
>
> *Gary D. Norsworthy, D.V.M., "Another Perspective on the Vaccination Controversy: Proposed Changes in the Standard Feline Vaccination Protocol," Veterinary Medicine (August, 1999): 731.*

THE VETERINARY CANON OF ETHICS AND LEGAL COMPLIANCE RECORD:

We have to change our focus from yearly vaccination to that of a yearly physical."

– Dr. Fred Scott, Professor of Virology and Director of the Cornell Feline Health Center in "Are We Vaccinating Too Much?" *Journal of American Veterinary Medical Association,* 1995.

"Clients Should Be Informed About Vaccine Use."

"There are legal and professional reasons to adequately inform clients about the vaccines practitioners use in their patients. Clients should be informed about the relative benefits and risks of vaccine use. They also should understand that vaccination does not guarantee protection and they should be informed about the potential adverse effects of vaccines. In general, clients should receive sufficient information to enable a reasonable person to reach an informed decision regarding an animal's medical care."

– "Vaccination Issues of Concern To Practitioners,"
Journal of American Veterinary Medical Association, April 1, 1999.

> "The final decision concerning individual vaccines to be administered should be based on risk and benefit assessment by the client and the vet."
>
> – *Small-animal Vaccination Protocol*, Colorado State University, College of Veterinary Science.

> Information about the benefits and risks of vaccination are important to owners' decisions about individual vaccine selection and vaccination program choices
>
> ***Principles of Vaccination***,
>
> *approved by the AVMA Executive Board, April, 2001*

> "Attending veterinarians are responsible for choosing the treatment regimens for patients.
>
> *It is the attending veterinarian's responsibility to inform the client of the expected results and costs, and the related risks of each treatment regimen."*
>
> *Section VI. Therapies:*
> *The Principles of Veterinary Medical Ethics of the American Veterinarian Medical Association*
> *(2003 Revision)*

> **"*Do not assume that vaccines cannot harm a patient.*"**
> "Vaccines are potent, medically active agents and have a real potential of producing adverse events."
> Report of the AAHA Canine Vaccine Task Force
> 2003 Canine Vaccine Guidelines and recommendations
> *Appendix 2. Important Vaccination 'Do's' and 'Don't s'*

> **What constitutes *informed consent*?**
> *The legal doctrine of informed consent arises out of the obligation to obtain consent prior to providing care to a patient. The essence of informed consent is that a practitioner informs the client of the material risks of a proposed treatment or procedure and potential alternatives, including the risk of no treatment; the client/patient, having been informed, either gives or withholds consent.*
> *2006 AAHA (American Animal Hospital Association) Vaccine Guidelines, p.17*

"I would like to make you aware that all 27 veterinary schools in North America are in the process of changing their protocols for vaccinating dogs and cats. Some of this information will present an ethical and economic challenge to vets and there will be skeptics. Some organizations have come up with **A POLITICAL COMPROMISE SUGGESTING VACCINATIONS EVERY 3 YEARS TO APPEASE THOSE WHO FEAR LOSS OF INCOME VS THOSE CONCERNED ABOUT POTENTIAL SIDE EFFECTS.**

Politics, traditions, or the doctor's economic well-being should not be a factor in a medical decision.

Email text attachment sent to author by Dr. Jean Dodds, August 25, 2005

YET...

Colorado pet owners were asked:

"Does your veterinarian recommend an annual rabies vaccination for your pet?"

79% said Yes!!

- <u>despite Colorado law allowing a three-year rabies option passed in **1999**</u>.

Next-to-Kin's First Annual Over-vaccination Survey Conducted Statewide in Colorado

September 27-28, 2005

by Hill Research Consultants

Betrayal of Trust: The Harmful & Unnecessary Over-vaccination of Companion Animals? Connecting The _Doc$_

> Things not worth doing are not worth doing well.
>
> *Anonymous but wise*

The question is not "vaccination or no vaccination" as some would like to frame the debate. The question is *over*-vaccination.

And in this regard, I shall delineate in greater detail the following material factors relative to the continued practice of non-*informed consent* for vaccination of dogs and cats:

- The Science
- The Economics
- The Ethics & Legal Implications

The "Science"

> "Although manufacturers label rabies vaccines as "good" for one to three-years, <u>*usually they are the same vaccine*</u>, only packaged with different labels. How would you determine how long a vaccine would be effective? Logic would suggest that for veterinary use an animal would be vaccinated and then "challenged" (injected with live virus). That *point in time when **susceptibility** returns (i.e. protection wanes) would delineate the endpoint of vaccine duration of effectiveness.* <u>In actuality, animals (dogs and cats) are only kept alive for one or three-years as needed, challenged, and **then killed once the challenge is proven "successful."**</u> Further testing is not done to determine the actual duration of immunity, as manufacturers only seek to show minimum rather than maximum duration." (edited for clarity)
>
> Don Hamilton, DVM, <u>Homeopathic Care for Cats and Dogs,</u> North Atlantic Books, <u>1999,</u> p.304

It was not my goal in life to delve even peripherally into the science of vaccination and over-vaccination. I, like you, want to trust our professionals. Unlike *caveat emptor* (buyer beware) there is an *implied* trust – a fiduciary responsibility of the professional to the client (as opposed to customer) and in this case to the guardian/owner and the companion animal. This trust rests on the concept of professional "substitute reliance." To argue 'science' relative to the question of standardized annual rabies vaccination (and other eminent immunologists would add "annual parvo and distemper shots") is like arguing fornicating for virginity. For example, The Federal Drug Administration (FDA), according to Consumer Reports (August, 2001 issue) said this: "Most vaccines (human) come to market with an incomplete safety record. A new vaccine is typically tested on 10,000 to 20,000 people before the FDA approves it. That's enough to study disease protection but *not enough* to reliably detect rare complications." Thus, typically 10,000 to 20,000 trials (challenges) of humans occur before the okay is given relative to safety and efficacy by the FDA.

Do you know what the United States Department of Agriculture (USDA) requires relative to the safety and efficacy of rabies shots for your pet? The USDA only requires a challenge of "a" (sic) duration at the 80% confidence level. Now what is critical is that little word "a." The USDA does not require a specific length of time or "**The**" duration – only "a" non-specified duration. Code of Federal Regulations: Title 9, Sec 113.209 (b) (1) & (3)(iv)

In light of the USDA code, the 'three-year' rabies vaccine was challenged for a duration arbitrarily chosen at three-years, not **The** (or some specified) duration. Furthermore, while there are over 160 million dogs and cats in the US alone, this challenge of "a" duration of 3 years, involved only 7 **dogs** (as reported by Veterinarian Advice Line, Dr. Chambreau, DVM)! Finally, when the arbitrary challenge period of 3 years was over, the dogs were euthanized – because the question/challenge is one of "a" duration not "**The**" duration: "was the vaccine effective for THREE-YEARS?" not "For how long was the vaccine effective?" (note how economics factored into the euthanasia decision, for if the dogs had lived beyond the challenge of "a" duration of 3 years – the shot then could be deemed to last longer than that, decreasing the frequency of vaccination even further.)

7 dogs to make the decision for 70+ million dogs and 80+ million cats!

7 dogs for an arbitrary challenge at the 80% - not 99% confidence level.

7 dogs euthanized.

And you are asked by your vet to make a life or death decision about your pet based on this so-called science.

The "$cience."

Paw$ and con$ider

Of course, we will never know how much longer the duration of effectiveness would be in a challenge of this kind. But if it *is* longer (which any decent serology method would suggest, one can only wonder if the economics of the shot-based small-animal veterinary practice influenced The "$cience."

For years, "The" $cience has been questioned – to no avail in journals, vet schools, and by a few (very, very, very few) courageous practitioners. Below are some excerpts from the experts:

> "The practice of annual (pet) vaccinations lacks scientific validity or verification. There is no immunological requirement for annual vaccinations. The practice of annual vaccinations should be considered of questionable efficacy."
>
> – *Kirk's Current Veterinary Therapy (The Textbook Bible for Veterinarians)*

"Our adoption of this routine vaccination program (three-year vaccination) is based on the lack of scientific evidence to support the current practice of annual vaccination and increasing documentation showing that over-vaccination has been associated with harmful effects. Of particular note in this regard has been the association of autoimmune hemolytic anemia with vaccination of dogs and vaccine-associated sarcomas in cats –

BOTH OF WHICH ARE OFTEN FATAL"

Colorado State University's Small-animal Vaccination Protocol

---

"There is strong and growing consensus among immunology and infectious disease experts that annual vaccination (of dogs and cats) is neither necessary nor advisable. The vast majority, if not all, of the North American veterinarian schools are currently recommending reduced frequency of vaccination."

– "Does My Pet Need Annual Vaccinations", **American Animal Hospital Association,** *1999*

"To insure efficacy, manufacturers (of vaccines) for years have made vaccines 10 times more potent than what is needed to challenge the immune system."

– "The Nature of Animal Healing", Martin Goldstein, DVM

> "Dr. Mark Wood, representing the Animal Health Institute, a trade organization for vaccine manufacturers, has indicated the arbitrary re-vaccination label on vaccines has no legal significance."
>
> –Cite 24, **Small-animal Vaccination Protocols**, Veterinary Teaching Hospital, College of Veterinary Medicine and Biomedical Sciences, Colorado State University

> "Almost without exception there is no immunologic requirement for annual re-vaccination. Successful vaccination to most bacterial pathogens produces an immunologic memory that remains for years. Furthermore, re-vaccination with most viral vaccines fails to stimulate an anamnestic (secondary response) as a result of interference by existing antibody."
>
> – Professors Tom Phillips and Ron Schultz, "Canine and Feline Vaccines," **Kirk's Current Veterinarian Therapy XI**

"The incidence of this often fatal cancer in cats (sarcoma development at the vaccine site) has been documented by several studies to be 1 to 3.2 per 10,000 cats receiving a rabies vaccine. If all the cats in Denver (estimated to be 400,000) were to be vaccinated yearly for rabies, the unneeded additional vaccinations would result in an additional 26 to 84 vaccine cancer sites per year! I estimate 22,000 vaccine-associated tumors per year. Since surgery is usually unsuccessful, radiation treatment is necessary. Treating all these cats would cost $66 million per year."

— *"Are We Vaccinating Too Much," Journal of the American Veterinary Medical Association, 1995 Professor Dennis Macy, Colorado State University*

"Vets and kennels are demanding that pets are vaccinated unnecessarily, and the owners are being fleeced. The veterinary profession and the vaccine manufacturers should be subject to adequate external monitoring."

— *Professor Richard Lacey, former member of the Ministry of Agriculture Veterinary Products Committee (VPC), United Kingdom*

"The Science" & The Three-Year (Triennial) Vaccination and Its Impact on Public Health

Dr. Kevin Reilly, DVM, is quoted as saying, "It is clear from both controlled laboratory challenged studies and more than 20 years of field experience with the triennial (every three-years vaccination) rabies programs, that the three-year rabies vaccines are extremely effective."

> "Reilly, a vet and public health officer in charge of rabies control for the state of California, where the risk of rabies is much higher having both bat and skunk rabies and ten million dogs and cats at risk, has used the triennial vaccination program in dogs and cats for the last 20 years. No currently vaccinated dogs or cats have developed rabies during the two decades. In addition, no animal receiving just two rabies vaccines *in its lifetime*, regardless of current rabies vaccine status, developed rabies in California during the last 20 years!"
>
> *(Source: "Denver's Rabies Laws - Take Another Look!", Professor Dennis Macy, DVM, MS, Professor, Internal Medicine/Oncology (Colorado State University, College of Veterinary Medicine and Bio- medical Sciences), Head, Treatment Sect. of AVMA Feline Vaccine-Associated Sarcoma Task Force.)*

> "Even Rabies vaccine is probably good for more than 3 years, since it is a viral vaccine. The tests done by the vaccine manufacturers on the required 7 dogs were carried out only at three-years post-vaccine. If they had tested dogs longer post-vaccine, rabies [vaccine] may have been good **for their lifetimes.**"
>
> —"Veterinarian Advice Line", Christina Chambreau, DVM

> The minimum DOI (Duration of Immunity) for killed rabies vaccine based on *challenge studies* is <u>3</u> years; based on *antibody titers*, it is considered to be up to <u>7</u> years
>
> (Report of the AAHA – American Animal Canine Vaccine Task Force 2003, p.13)

*This is "The $cience" of Annual Rabies **Vaccination?***?*?*?*

I have heard from countless guardians about "how long will a vaccine last?" Often they have been told the now-debunked ditty that <u>*adverse reaction*</u> to rabies vaccination was "rare," "1 in 10,000," "1 in 100,000."

Really?

(Definition: **adverse event** or **reaction**: when your pet gets very sick or dies from over-vaccination)

> "Little or no practical safety information exists on vaccine labels or the literature, and current **adverse event** reporting systems need great improvement…multiple parties are to blame for the current system's failure: veterinarians, manufacturers, and the government…Historically veterinarians have both demanded information from the USDA or manufacturers, and **veterinarians lack the commitment to reporting observations…They might also think an adverse event isn't related so they don't bother to report it."**
>
> *Dr. David Hustead, member at large of the AVMA Council on Biologic and Therapeutic Agents (COBTA), JAVMA (Journal of American Medical Association) News, September 15, 2003*

Furthermore, these "rare," "1/10,000," "1/100,000," *adverse reactions* are "**self- reported**" by small-animal veterinarians. Remember those friendly reminders "it's time for Cammy's vaccination!" The Talmud states, "There is no messenger in the case of sin." Thus, the defense 'the manufacturers made us do it" doesn't hold water for sophisticated users giving 5 shots a day, 5 days week, 52 weeks a years (and this is only rabies!), the hired hit man isn't exempted for his hit, or in this case, over-vaccination.

In March of 2001, an independent study (not self-reported study) conducted and reported by Canine Health Concern of 1000 cats and 1000 dogs showed (at the 99% confidence level, not the lower 80% required by the USDA) **7.54% minimum to 12.42%** *adverse reactions* **within 45 days of vaccination.**

Titering blood antibodies is an accepted method of measuring immunity – and whether or not your dog or cat needs the annual- or three-year rabies, parvo and/or distemper shot or not. In a 6/23/2003 email from Dr. Jean Dodds she stated…'(acceptable) **titer** levels are *already* established for purposes of export/import of animals to rabies-free countries all over the world, and for import to other countries just to ensure that pet dogs and cats entering these places are adequately immunized/protected. Furthermore, the CDC (The Center for Disease Control) and WHO (The World Health Organization) have determined what they consider to be protective rabies titer levels for people – namely, **1:5(CDC)** and **1:50(WHO)**, respectively, so – how can anyone say that rabies titers don't reflect immunity. Must be political issues here."

My 9-year-old black standard poodle, Max ('the knife') was due for a three-year rabies shot. I had him titered.

It was 1:1800. Not 1:5. Not 1:50.

1:1800. Max, at 70 lbs is 160 times more "protected" than a 200 lb. human! (Exhibit 7)

Would you think Max's immune system might have been compromised, as was Moolah's, with auto-immune hemolytic anemia by giving him a rabies shot at the time?

Max did <u>not</u> get another shot. The titer proved his antibodies were (are) vastly more than sufficient. He was current.

Had Max gotten the shot – he might have had the same fate as Moolah.

The "$cience?"

> "Vaccination should not be considered an innocuous procedure, since vaccines may have harmful consequences to patients as well as owners. The patient receives no benefit and may be placed at serious risk when an unnecessary vaccine is given. The owner also risks economic and emotional hardship in exchange for questionable benefit."
>
> *Current and Future Canine and Feline Vaccination Programs, Ronald D. Schultz, PhD, Department of Pathobiological Sciences, School of Veterinary Medicine, University of Wisconsin – Madison Veterinary Medicine, March, 1999.*

Another point you may wish to ponder: The Defensor 3 Pfizer Rabies Vaccine (three-year vaccine) is recommended (on a voluntary basis) for cattle and sheep – annually. Can you believe it's the same shot for Big Mac the Great Dane and Sherri Lewis' Lambchop?

Sidebar: The "Science" – The AVMA Under Attack, Responds (To Cut Off Potential Future Collateral Liability of the Association ???)

Below is the AVMA's Study of Vaccination Issues, 2001.

It should be noted that the AVMA per this study calls for *'customization'* of vaccination protocols. Does this mean that the 'standard of care' previously was <u>*standardized malpractice*</u> – little or no *informed consent* with one-size-fits-all for the shots – giving the same dosage to Scooby Doo or the Taco Bell Chihuahua? Que Sera, Over-vaccination???

The AVMA Has Studied Vaccination Issues (*aka CYA*)

(The following section is rather long, but it should be **REQUIRED READING** for anyone who really wants the best for animal companions. Get a coffee or coke, a red pencil, and dive into it. All italicization, underlining or bold-facing is mine. Jds)

Approved by the American Veterinary Medical Association Executive Board, April 2001, published in the Journal of the American Veterinary Medical Association, Volume 219, No. 5, September 1, 2001.

INTRODUCTION

Medical decisions about vaccine selection and protocols have become more complex. Selecting vaccine products and recommending vaccine programs are among the most complicated of medical decisions facing veterinarians. The reasons are numerous: continued evolution of our understanding of the immune system; increased value of animals to the owner/client; improved medical-record systems, and longer life-spans allowing the emergence of chronic sequellae. Improved understanding of infectious diseases, the strengths and limitations of the biologic regulatory-approval process, and adverse events associated with vaccination also complicate decisions required for best patient care.

The Council on Biologic and Therapeutic Agents (COBTA) has studied the issues of vaccinology and immunology for the past two years. This study included a review of the scientific literature and interactive testimony with four expert groups including academic, regulatory, industry, and practitioner experts. Topics included safety, efficacy, duration of immunity, research and development of vaccines, vaccine licensing, product labeling, adverse events and adverse event reporting, governmental oversight of manufacturers, and legal issues associated with medical procedures.

Vaccines have played a significant role in enabling people and animals to live longer in this world filled with microbial pathogens. Vaccine products vary in efficacy and safety. Modern science continues to learn more about the immune systems and to develop strategies and technology for safer and more efficacious vaccines. Thorough evaluations of the risks of the disease, and those potentially associated with the vaccine, compared to the benefits for the patient, are necessary in crafting optimal health recommendations that include vaccination.

<u>**COBTA concludes that there currently exists inadequate data to scientifically determine a single best protocol for vaccination or revaccination**</u>. Advances in antigen science, adjuvant function, impacts of different vaccine carrier solutions, and the immune system's acute and chronic reactions to stimulation are impressive, but there remain gaps in our understanding. The body of knowledge about the variability of genetics within a breed or species, and the resulting impacts on the individual patient's response to vaccine or associated *adverse reactions*, is increasing but remains insufficient to make

general recommendations. COBTA believes that variation in our patients and their lifestyle, and between the individual vaccine products available, requires a customized approach to vaccination recommendations to best match the variation in the patients presented for immunization.

The practitioner and client must make the best patient-care decisions where there exists a valid veterinarian-client-patient relationship. Vaccine decisions require a thorough and ongoing review of scientific information and expert opinion of this constantly evolving area to properly prepare the customized vaccine recommendations animal patients require.

<u>The one-year revaccination frequency recommendation found on many vaccine labels is based only on historical precedent and United States Department of Agriculture regulation, not on scientific data</u>. Even in those cases where scientific data was submitted to qualify the label claim, the data generated does not resolve the question about average or maximum duration of immunity.

There is evidence that some vaccines provide immunity beyond one-year. Revaccination of patients with sufficient immunity does not add measurably to their disease resistance and may increase their risk of adverse post-vaccination events. Vaccination is a potent medical procedure with both benefits and associated hazards.

It is not currently possible to determine the immune status of a patient relative to all the infectious diseases of concern without conducting a challenge test. Serology does not predict a patient's immune status for most diseases. For those diseases where serology has predictive value of a patient's immune status, the variation within and between laboratories renders the procedure generally unreliable.

Adverse events may be associated with the antigen, adjuvant, carrier, preservative, or a combination thereof. Possible adverse events include failure to immunize, anaphylaxis, immunosuppression, autoimmune disorders, transient infections, and/or long-term infected carrier sites. In addition, a causal association in cats between injection sites and the subsequent development of a malignant tumor is the subject of ongoing research. The role of genetic predisposition to adverse events needs further exploration and definition.

Vaccine program goals include providing optimal immunity against clinically relevant diseases the patient is at-risk to contract, while minimizing the potential for adverse events.

Multiple sources of information can be of value to practitioners in their review of vaccine and infectious diseases, including scientific data and opinion from experts, species and specialty groups, manufacturers and government agencies. All sources of scientific information and expert opinion need to be carefully and critically considered to properly prepare the customized vaccine programs:

1. Vaccination is a potent medical procedure associated with both benefits and risks for the patient. Adverse events, including some that are potentially severe, can be unintended consequences of vaccination.
2. The proper application of vaccines to animal populations has enhanced their health and welfare, and prolonged their life-spans. The risks to animal health from non-vaccination are significant.
3. The goal for a vaccination program is to prevent disease and thereby promote optimal patient, herd, and/or public health.
4. *Different patients require different vaccines and vaccination programs.*

5. Unnecessary stimulation of the immune system does not result in enhanced disease resistance, and may increase the risk of adverse post-vaccination events.

6. Vaccination protects a population of animals by providing a level of resistance to a disease in those individual patients that are able to respond. Vaccination does not protect every individual patient even when they are properly vaccinated.

7. Disease carriers, including animals that shed the infectious agent but do not show signs of illness, are local sources of infection for susceptible animals. Sufficient immunity within a population of animals is an important component of preventing high rates of disease. Programs targeting immunization of unvaccinated animals are critical to disease control.

8. Knowledge of immunology and vaccinology, including associated benefits and risks, and the pathobiology of infectious diseases, are necessary to implement an effective vaccination program. Consideration of exposure, susceptibility, potential severity of disease, efficacy and safety of vaccine, any potential public health concerns, and the owner's preferences are appropriate.

9. Only those veterinarians with valid veterinarian-client-patient relationships are in position to make recommendations **customized to the needs of the individual patient(s) and owner/client**.

(Duh!!! Jds)

10. Revaccination recommendations should be designed to maintain clinically relevant immunity while minimizing adverse event potential.

11. Additional information, including vaccine-specific, scientific data on minimum, average, and maximum duration of immunity is desired to craft optimal revaccination-frequency recommendations.

12. Vaccines, including polyvalent products, should be selected to include only those antigens appropriate for the specific risk needs of the patient, thereby eliminating unnecessary immune system stimulation and lowering potential risks of adverse events.

13. Multiple-dose vaccine vials must be carefully managed to:... Minimize the potential for delivering inappropriate levels of antigen or adjuvant.... Optimize the potential for maximum potency of the antigens present.... And minimize the opportunity for contamination with extraneous microbes or chemicals.

14. Veterinarians should create a core vaccine program, intended for use in the majority of animals in their practice area. Core vaccines are those that protect from diseases that are widely distributed in the region, virulent and highly infectious, thereby posing a risk of severe disease. Core vaccines are efficacious and exhibit patient benefit-risk ratios high enough to warrant their use, and/or are of significant public health significance, or required by law.

15. Veterinarians should consider creating non-core vaccine programs, intended for a minority of animals in their practice area. Non-core vaccines are those that target diseases that are of limited risk in the region, and /or represent less severe threats to infected patients, and/or vaccine benefit-risk ratios

are too low to warrant the use of these products in all circumstances, and/or scientific information is inadequate to evaluate these products. Veterinarians and owners/clients need to carefully consider the benefits and risks of using these vaccine products on an individual basis.

16. *Information about the benefits and risks of vaccination are important in owners' decisions about individual vaccine selection and vaccination program choices.*

17. USDA licensed products have had the manufacturer's claims about vaccine performance substantiated by a variety of testing methods. Careful evaluation of labels and other information is necessary to compare and contrast between the available products.

18. *There is a critical need for more fully developed, scientifically based, and statistically valid evaluations of vaccine products* to provide practitioners with a basis for developing vaccination programs that maximize benefits and minimize associated risks for patients under their care.

19. *Current adverse-event reporting systems in use need significant improvement in the capture, analysis, and reporting of adverse events.* Practitioner commitment to adverse event reporting, and timely access for practitioners to current analysis of adverse event data, are essential to providing optimal patient care.

20. *There is potential legal liability for all medical procedures including vaccination.*

Biological agents are regulated by the USDA, not the Food and Drug Administration, and thus are not subject to those regulations that address extra-label use. *Veterinarians can legally use vaccines in a discretionary manner.*

USDA licensing at the full approval level provides a baseline standard for efficacy, safety, purity, and potency, but the clinical need (relevancy) or usefulness (applicability) of a product are not assured by the licensing process. The USDA must approve labels for biological products. However, current labels frequently contain revaccination interval recommendations based on historical precedence and regulation rather than scientific data, may fail to adequately inform practitioners about the optimal use of the product, and the testing methods may be inadequate to identify rare but relevant safety concerns.

Labels on licensed vaccines make different claims and should be carefully studied when evaluating products. Claims may, for example, declare the product (a) prevents infection, (b) prevents disease, or (c) results in a decreased number or a decreased intensity of clinical signs. Each of these claims represents a different level of performance outcome that might be important in selection of a specific vaccine.

USDA-approved products licensed under the conditional approval process have demonstrated a reasonable expectation of efficacy. Autogenuous vaccines have no demonstrated efficacy.

End of AVMA Executive Board statement of September, 2001

> "The biggest change is: we're taking a considered look at what we are vaccinating each cat for rather than just reacting and giving everyone the same thing. We're looking at what an individual patients' needs are, what risks they are being exposed to, and vaccinating accordingly, rather than just switching to a three-year schedule as the new cookie-cutter paradigm."
>
> *Dr. Margie Scherk, owner Cats Only veterinary Clinic*

Chapter IV
Moolah II – the Economic$

> "Many practices generate 15% to 25% of their gross incomes from vaccination visits. This income is supplemented by fees for additional services generated by the vaccination visit (e.g., dental procedures)...The immediate result of extended vaccination intervals will be the loss of this relatively easily generated income. Some veterinary practices may not be able to survive financially. Those operating on close profit margins and depending heavily on vaccination income will be the first fatalities."
>
> *Gary D. Norsworthy, D.V.M., "Another Perspective on the Vaccination Controversy: Proposed Changes in the Standard Feline Vaccination Protocol," Veterinary Medicine (August, 1999): 731.*

"I agree with everything you said. The vets are too silent about the issue (over-vaccination), perhaps because we are indoctrinated to not criticize our "colleagues" since any one of us may be on the hot seat next for some mistake we made. I could do more, of course, but I have spoken out against vaccines for ten years. I was on the committee in Denver to eliminate the one-year vaccine requirement. (You should have heard the local vets scream.) I stopped vaccinating in my Denver cat clinic and had clients leave my practice because of it. I was called by one "an arrogant stupid bitch" because I wouldn't vaccinate her cat. I estimate I lost at least half a million dollars in practice income...The vets have succeeded in getting people into their doors through the use of fear and that's hard to fight. I actually left practice because I became simply disgusted with what I was seeing.

I am now in North Carolina, and the situation is far worse than in Colorado. I truly believe the vets have gotten together and agreed to stand firm on yearly vaccines. Being such a cohesive group, they are able to refuse treatment (even a dental) unless clients agree to "update" the

vaccinations when they walk in the door. I have spoken to groups here and have plans to get to the vet school to talk to students, but I truly feel like a tiny ant at the bottom of a big mountain. And, as you have seen, some vets are viciously protective of their vaccine income. Ten years ago, there were a small handful of people who even believed vaccines could be harmful. I was one of those, and we were simply ridiculed and ignored.... I continue to thank you because I cringe inside just thinking of the harm that is being done in the name of preventative medicine."
—Email: Dr. L.E., DVM, to JDS, 2/25/2003

"I would like to let you know there are a lot of associate veterinarians who have to have their employment held over their heads for making waves about such an important subject (annual rabies vaccination)... Many of the veterinary facilities boast AAHA status (American Animal Hospital Association) and yet they are not implementing their own Association's recommendations for three-year and core-only vaccines. Also, in areas where there are large populations of immigrants that either don't speak English or are not wealthy enough to own and use computers..they are not being informed

. —P.J., DVM, email to JDS, March 4, 2007

Even former media apologists (who deflected the over-vaccination blame to the manufacturers) have changed their tune from total defense to outright questioning of our trusted veterinarians:

> This (the shots — over-vaccination) can **probably only rarely be accurately attributed to opportunism on the part of the vet.** Most vets use the vaccination schedules they receive with the vaccinations they buy from drug companies
>
> Hot Shots, Nancy Kerns, The Whole Dog Journal, **June, 2005**

> Veterinary medical associations are calling for fewer vaccinations. Are local veterinarians hearing the ring?
>
> Headline, Shots Fired, *The Whole Dog Journal*, **November, 2006**

In **September of 2005** editor Kerns was given a copy of the Hill Research Survey commissioned by the Next-to-Kin Foundation in Colorado showing 79% of vets still giving the annual rabies vaccination. Of course I would like to see this potent argument against her "opportunities" claim appear in her excellent Journal.

> When they say it's not about the money, it *is* about the money
>
> Old cliché

A nationally featured cable vet, said to me about annual shots, "it's our gravy."

In the fall, 1998, issue of *Veterinary Business'* article 'Practice Builder,' Dr. James R. Irwin reveals the course of conduct stating, "from a practical point of view, veterinarians can still use the vaccination 'hook' to get their clients into the clinic."

Other vets have stated that they are "challenged" (oh, the irony of this word) to get the owners to bring in their companion animals for an annual examination without the annual shots – despite the overwhelming and mounting concern about over-vaccination in vet journals! I guess the logic is "let's potentially harm your pets with over-vaccination so they can be healthier." Quite frankly this rationale is a cop-out for these vets' own failure to educate the guardian owners on the absolute importance of the annual exam. The challenge is to convince the guardian/owner that he should not substitute over-vaccination for the vet's inability to inform and persuade him about the benefits of a thorough annual exam and wellness checkup.

According to Dr. Kathleen Neuhoff, DVM, and past-president of the American Animal Hospital Association, "We're now doing 40% fewer vaccinations than five years ago." (Wall Street Journal 7/31/2002)

However, per the American Veterinary Medical Association's 2002 Household Pet Survey, the veterinary office visits for vaccination increased 1.6% from 62.8% in 1996 to 63.8% in 2001 while those vaccination visits for cats increased 13.9% from 61.9% in 1996 to 70.5% in 2001. (Exhibit 7 & 8)

Attempts to get an explanation of this material discrepancy from Dr. Neuhoff in 2002 were unanswered.

In any case, 63%-70% of veterinary visits are still for vaccinations – leading to the conclusion that the small veterinary practice's business model is shot-based, 'co-dependent.'

This chart comes from the 2007 report by the AVMA, "U.S. Pet Ownership and Demographics" page 63, table 2-15:

Service	1996	2001	2006
For dogs:			
Vaccination	62.80%	63.80%	64.40%
Phys. Exam.	61.00%	69.40%	70.20%
For cats:			
Vaccination	61.90%	70.50%	63.70%
Phys. Exam.	59.60%	67.30%	71.30%

Is it obvious that there is a definite overlap between the two services – the shot gets the exam!

The Vaccinators – The Silent Animal Cruelty?

No wonder, in light of the overwhelming evidence in the literature against over- vaccination and the changes in protocols advocated by the vet schools, the AVMA (begrudgingly) now suggests *customization* (rather than the standardized annual shots practiced 50+ years), while the AAHA suggests the three-year protocol. Despite these implicit admissions and guidance to their veterinary members, 79% of the small-animal vets in Colorado, 7 years after the legislation allowing the three-year rabies option, were still giving the annual rabies shot in 2005 – and arguably without *informed consent*, that is, without disclosing potential harm.

Dr. Bob Rogers, DVM in Spring, Texas, estimates that in Texas alone, the unnecessary over-vaccination (not including the annual examination) costs Texans over $360 million a year.

Nationally, the over-vaccination costs (just for rabies) are staggering, without including the economic and emotional costs of *adverse reactions*.

Assume 38,000 small-animal veterinarians (and excluding specialists who may give shots but at a lower rate) each having 2500 dogs and cats per vet under their care or 95,000,000 dogs and cats totally in the US. (This is a conservative estimate as there are 160,000,000 dogs and cats in US, but the average vet typically has 2500 companion animals under his or her care.) If there is but a 50% 'compliance rate' for yearly rabies vaccination – then each year 47,500,000 companion animals are vaccinated. If 2 years of rabies vaccination are eliminated out of every three, then 95,000,000 rabies shots would be unnecessary. At $15 per dose, this amounts to $1,425,000,000 unnecessary cost not including *adverse reaction* costs or the office visit. At $25 average per dose, this amounts to an overcharge potential of $2.375 billion every two out of three-years. These figures do not include the required $35-$48 office visit (another $3,800,000,000 – that's 5.8 billion) nor the costs of *adverse reactions* (astronomical) that result.

Vaccination is not just 'incidental' to the practice of these vets. 47.5 million shots (rabies alone – not including parvo, distemper. et al) divided by 38,000 vets is 1250 shots per vet per year or 4.8 shots a day (5 day week) or a shot every other hour. And that's just for the rabies shot.

40% decline in vaccinations, Dr. Neuhoff?

Maybe it's 30+ years in the finance world, having a major in finance, etc – and being a captive of my own experience, but I can find only one compelling explanation when connecting the dot$: money.

The vast majority of small-animal veterinary practices operate on this shot-based business/economic model.

Exhibit 9 is an economic model I did for the Next-to-Kin Foundation site (www.next2kin.org) in <u>2002</u> (based on data from veterinarian association statistics in 1997), while vaccination revenue was typically 10%-15% of the small-animal veterinarian gross revenue (not including the required office visit for the rabies shot nor the offshoot 'up-sell' or ***<u>adverse reaction</u>*** business from the yearly rabies vaccination protocol). Yet, the vaccination-derived business (not including the 'up-sell' or the ***<u>adverse reaction</u>*** fees and or sales) was 70%-150%+ of gross profit. Why? Then in 2002, the cost of the vaccine for rabies was approximately 60 cents. The shot – the gravy – cost the guardian then $15-$38 with $35 on average for the office visit. In context, at that time, the gross mark-up, using a $25 cost of the shot and $35 for the office visit was 9900%. A $2.25 package of Oreos would have to sell for $223 for equivalence. Of course, this does not include that additional x-ray or blood work, etc., that became necessary with the exam accompanying the required rabies vaccination visit. (Today, excluding shot clinics the cost of the vaccination is about the same, but the office visit is now $40-$48. Thus, the gross markup at $25 for the shot and $45 for the office visit is now 11567% and that package of Oreo would have to sell for approximately $260 using these assumptions!

$223, $260, $290 per package – that's a lot of 'double stuff' for that delicious creamy Oreo filling!

More importantly per Exhibit 9, the single small pet vet's income in the out years (when there would not be the annual shot and without it the vet would not be able to "sell" the annual exam) could drop from an average of $87,000+ to $30,000 or less!

"It's our gravy."

More like the gravy train.

Connect the Doc$.

More on this at Exhibit 9. (Prepared in 2002.)

CHAPTER V
Moolah III

Can Vets Make it without the Annual "hook-shot"?

The irony: articles in the AAHA's Trends Magazine as early as December 1999 illustrated 4 practices that actually thrived weaning themselves off the dependency of the transaction shot-based vaccination business model. Veterinary Business (A Resource for Practical Clinic Management) fall 1998, featured an article "Vaccines Losing Clout as Practice Builder" where the author Dr. Irwin shows that "there are other ways to draw pet owners into the clinic for annual examination and wellness checkups, and at the same time, see their revenue increase.

As Woodward and Bernstein were told, "follow the money!" And yet, we want to believe, "not my vet!"

Progress on Reducing Over-Vaccination, Cover-up, Manipulation of Data??

Per the Economic Report of Veterinarians & Veterinary Practices (2007) published by The American Veterinary Medical Association, between their 2001 edition and their 2007 edition, the Percentage of Gross Practice Revenue in small-animal exclusive practices derived from vaccinations declined from 12.5% to 4.44% or a 64% decline (see charter below) in the 7 years between the 2001 edition and 2005 edition's data. The 2007 book's data was from 2005. Yet, *The Hill Research Consulting Survey, conducted the same year (September, 2005), showed that 79% of veterinarians in Colorado were recommending annual rabies shots for pets.* There is, at best, a disconnect here that deserves explanation because of the veterinarian association's own admission that 63% to 70% (cats and dogs respectively) of all small-animal veterinarian visits are for vaccinations.

Progress? Cover-up? In either case, an explanation is required for this 'disconnect!'

Economic Report of Veterinarians & Veterinary Practices - AVMA
% **of Gross Practice Revenue From Vaccinations**

1999 Edition (stats from **1995**)	12.9% (includes deworming)
2001 Edition (stats from **1999**)	12.5% (no deworming)
2007 Edition (stats from **2005***)	4.44% (no mention of deworming)

- <u>63% and 70%</u> of all canine and feline visits to the small-animal veterinarian per the veterinarians' own statistics are for vaccination
- Next-to-Kin Foundation commissioned Hill Research Consultants to conduct a survey in 2005, *the same year as the stats were taken for the 2007 Edition of Economic Report of Veterinarians & Veterinary Practices by the American Veterinary Medical Association. Results:* <u>79%</u> of vets were still recommending the annual rabies shot to Coloradans.
- Per the same survey <u>62%</u> of all Coloradans, then 6 years after Colorado allowed the three-year option on rabies vaccination and despite the veterinary canon of *informed consent*, were not aware of this option.

Yet, despite the contradictory information above, vaccination revenue decreases 64% in this 5 year period?

Note: in the Financial & Productivity Pulsepoints, 2nd edition, June, 2003, published by the American Animal Hospital Association (AAHA), Vaccination Income as a Percentage of Total Income for veterinarians was <u>14.1%</u> as of 2002.

Thus, from 2002 to 2005 per the AAHA and AVMA respectively the vaccination income dropped from somewhere around 14.1% to 4.4%, or a decline of about 68% per year, while 79% of the veterinarians were still giving the annual rabies shots in 2005 to Coloradoans.

So, what do you think?

- Manipulation of data to show reduction in over-vaccination – while *annual* rabies vaccination is still rampant in reality?

- A disconnect in the data?
- Some other explanation?

Inquiring minds would like an explanation!

Veterinary Ethics & Self Regulation

> The vast majority, if not all, of the North American veterinary schools are currently recommending reduced frequency of vaccination..
>
> *American Animal Hospital Association brochure, 1999*

> Information about the benefits and risks of vaccination are important to owners' decisions about individual vaccine selection and vaccination program choices
>
> *Principles of Vaccination, approved by the AVMA (American Veterinary Medical Association) Executive Board, April 2001.*

> Veterinarians should not allow their medical judgment to be influenced by agreements by which they stand to profit through referring clients to other providers of services or products
>
> *V. B. Influence of Judgment: The Principles of Veterinary Medical Ethics of the American Veterinarian Medical Association (2003)*

> What constitutes *informed consent?* The legal doctrine of *informed consent* arises out of the obligation to obtain consent prior to providing care to a patient. The essence of *informed consent* is that a practitioner informs the client of the material risks of a proposed treatment or procedure and potential alternatives, including the risk of no treatment; the client/patient having been informed, either gives or withholds consent
>
> <u>2006</u> *AAHA (American Animal Hospital Association) Vaccine Guidelines, p.17*

> I'm a licensed mattress professional
>
> *Homer Simpson, The Simpsons*

What constitutes being a professional? Theoretically, the professional possesses an assured level of competency, subordinates their interest to those of the client/patient, and in a timely fashion, discloses any real or perceived conflicts of interest to the client. (Full disclosure is timely, complete – and in plain language; anything less is *FOOL* DISCLOSURE!) Implicit within the disclosure criteria is <u>*informed consent*</u> except under situations where consent cannot be granted (i.e., clear and present danger, etc. In this situation, the professional is granted even greater 'substitute reliance.'

In practice, we have seen the dilution, contamination, and adulteration of this 'professional' calling and concept across 'professions' with CPA's and lawyers blessing the likes of Enron and Qwest, tenured professors plagiarizing (calling it research), revolving doors between state omissioners of insurance and insecurities commissioners between regulating and representing those they formerly regulated. And the financial planners conflicts? I could write a chapter in a book on them (oh, I forget; I did!) What is the common element in this violation of our 'substitute reliance': **betrayal of trust**.

The only distinction between the designations of 'professional' and 'amateur' has become that the former is compensated and the latter is not. The word professional has been devalued becoming, by and large, a self-proclaimed marketing term when, all too often and not in isolation, the professionals are merely guardians skimming the gate — bullies in three-piece suits (and smocks) making the world safe for hypocrisy.

So, yes, systemically, small-pet veterinarians are not alone in this deterioration of calling and reliance but that is no excuse. The argument that everyone is responsible, so no one is responsible, bankrupts trust and accountability — the very essence of professionalism.

Yet one could argue, the over-vaccinating, without *informed consent*, small-animal veterinarians are 'the cream of the crap.'

How? The systemic practice of over-vaccination without *informed consent* makes these vets even more culpable — as they would not only be engaging in fiscal malfeasance but also potentially in concurrent physical harm to our companion animals.

> For evil to triumph, good men need only be silent.
>
> *Edmund Burke*

Worse are those vets, knowing better, who in the name of *collegiality*, are either quiet – or just talk a good game. So these *Vichy Vets* are, in a sense, accomplices to *The Paw Pet Traitors* in the *silent animal cruelty* of systemic over-vaccination.

Over-vaccination is epidemic. I wish these were the acts of a few bad apples, but it appears the barrel is rotten to the 'core' vaccination.

Hypocrisy even cringes when the small-animal veterinarians continue to administer the annual rabies shot without *informed consent* because they are 'challenged' to otherwise get a fee for the annual exam. These veterinarians, in effect, are actually justifying their case on the basis of a dearth of science to prove the duration of the 3-year vaccination (or longer) when there is little or no science underlying the value of the standardized protocol of the *yearly* rabies vaccination! Worse, this practice continues despite up to 10-20 years of writings in vet journals and magazines about the problems with annual rabies vaccination (without even getting into the question of annual parvo and distemper shots) and the availability of the three-year option by law.

> A man is incapable of comprehending any argument that interferes with his revenue
>
> *Descartes*

> It is difficult to get a man to understand something when his compensation depends on his <u>not</u> understanding it
>
> *Upton Sinclair*

The "Science," The Economics, and Veterinary 'Ethics': connecting *The Doc$* = Betrayal of Trust.

Sidebar: Paragons, Putzes and Professionals

I couldn't breathe.

It was 2:00 in the morning

I was 6 and scared to death as my mother comforted me in a grandfather rocking chair with Grandma Buchman's hand-embroidered afghan wrapped around us.

Each breath became harder and harder to take. The wheezing was choking me.

It was my first asthma attack.

Dr. Sam Leiter rushed over to our house. House calls were not unusual then, nor greeted with disdain or a surcharge.

He couldn't have been kinder, more reassuring and quick-acting to "relieve my pain" and fear.

Dr. Leiter was Overbrook Park's (in Philadelphia) "Moonlight Graham." He was loved and revered.

Office visits were in his home. You usually had to wait a while. But few seemed to care – because Dr. Sam would make the house call.

Phyllis Wirschafter was my 11th grade American History honors teacher (before there was grade inflation!).

We all feared her.

She even kept her husband in check, she told us, because her "IQ was two points higher."

Even the Tableman twins wouldn't talk in her class.

She engendered fear. Most of us tried not to be called on and, in her Socratic fashion, be cut to shreds.

Wirtschafter kicked me out of honors history in the 12th grade – not for bad grades or behavior, but because she thought I should be in Advanced Placement (AP) history, even though the advanced placement students already were a year ahead of me.

I didn't want to do it. Enough, though one got four extra points added to their class grade point average for being in AP (before today's grade inflation), I didn't want my grade to suffer to the competition. After all, I needed to get a scholarship. (We were not very well off with my dad dying when I was 15.)

I got an A in AP history that year while receiving 10 college credit hours from my Advanced Placement test. Phyllis Wirtschafter believed in me, even when I didn't.

Dr. Leiter was there at 2 in the morning, comforting a scared 6-year-old.

Phyllis Wirtschafter and Dr. Leiter were professional in competency, putting their patient and student's interest first, and professional in their independence.

Sammy Sosa – "Professional" baseball player

Mark McGuire – "Professional" baseball player

Barry Bonds – "Professional" baseball player

Michael Vick – "Professional" football player

And our kindly vets…..??? Their professionalism is regulated by a board of : *VETERINARIANS*

> The only self-regulation that works is Phillips Milk of Magnesia
>
> *J. D. Schwartz, on proposed self-regulation of financial planners*

I conducted a study of the revocation of professional licenses in Colorado from the latest available statistics for a 5 year period ended 2002. (Exhibit 10) There were **3300** practicing vets. The licenses of **THREE** were revoked by the State Vet Board. The revocation rate of licenses for veterinarians averaged less than 20/100,000ths of 1%. In perspective, this makes the vets virginally purer than Ivory Soap. Our small-animal vets often act not only in the capacity of doctor, but also dentist and pharmacist. The rate of revocation of the licenses of those professionals is *5 times higher*.

When the then Colorado Director of Regulatory Agencies (DORA), Rick O'Donnell, was asked by me: "what percentage of veterinarian licenses were revoked per year," he responded with "1%?"

When I said, "no, try again," he replied with a query, "2%?"

When I told him it was 20/100,000ths of 1% he said he would look into it.

O'Donnell finally responded by e-mail stating that the veterinarians (he meant their Veterinarian Board) are "up for review" in 2011. The implication was there was nothing he could or would do.

Rick O'Donnell chose the interests of 3600 Colorado Veterinarians (2002 numbers) over those of the 2,100,000 dogs and cats in 1,600,000 Colorado households (the 2000 census).

O'Donnell ran, in 2006, for the Republican nomination in the 4th Congressional seat in Colorado. He got creamed. He was succeeded by a former state representative who also did nothing relative to the Veterinarian Board.

No Dog Before His Time

> The task is not for you to complete, but it doesn't exempt you from trying (aka You are not obligated to complete the work but neither are you free to abandon it.)
>
> *Rabbi Tarfon, 1st Century*

> Any jackass can kick down a barn door, but it takes a carpenter to build one.
>
> *Sam Rayburn*

No Effective Legal Recourse to Veterinarian Over-vaccination without *Informed consent*

It's hard to escape this conclusion: of the parties in the Companion-Guardian- Veterinarian triangle only those who are truly inoculated are the veterinarians.

The vets have immunity with impunity because of self-regulation, anachronistic legislation, vaccine manufacturer's indifference, and legal barriers.

The vets are effectively immune from over-vaccination accountability.

Legally, dogs and cats are mere property. Yes, there are cruelty laws and even trusts whereby your companion animal can be a beneficiary (check Leona Helmsley's will) in many states —thus differentiating dogs and cats from one's 52" wide-screen TV.

But for purposes of damages, dogs and cats are mere property – and depreciated property at that unless they have future economic value for stud and or breeding purposes. So, if you would rack up $3,000, $5,000, or $10,000 of unnecessary veterinary expenses due to over-vaccination and subsequent costs from *adverse reactions*, you could easily spend another $10,000 on a lawyer to maybe, maybe, maybe get these legal costs back plus the depreciated value of your 10-year-old Shepherd Lab mix (let's say $100).

One loses in winning.

Furthermore, unlike businesses that are subject to treble damages and legal costs under Colorado's Consumer Protection Act, veterinarians as a "self-regulated profession" (which the veterinarians surely would argue relative to 'The Veterinary Practice Act in Colorado'), are exempted from that very same Colorado's Consumer Protection Act (risking only actual damages and legal fees). Yes, arguably exempt, despite arguments that over-vaccination without *informed consent* causing *adverse reaction* meets the five tests (only one is required by this act) for meeting the standard of deceptive trade practice in light of the financial injury to companion animal owners.

So, if you proved a deceptive trade practice against another business that had actual damages of $5000 plus $7500 of legal fees, you could recover $22,000 ($7,500 of the legal fees and $15,000 for damages as a deterrent to the business' engaging in this activity in the future). However, if a professional, who is perceived to have a higher standard of care, (often fiduciary responsibilities as well as offering substitute reliance, through licensing) engages in a deceptive trade practice as above, and you prove the tests of a deceptive trade practice, the act would exclude you from treble damage recovery let alone legal costs! Furthermore, you would be out your own legal fees! Finally, with the exclusion of punitive damages and the depreciation of companion animals to mere property under the law, there is little or no deterrent for anyone to stop committing these egregious acts.

(It's interesting how the vets, in their white coats, sell their services to us on the basis of protecting our dogs and cats as part of the family for marketing purposes, but for their own legal protection from accountability, the same vets, in white coats, retreat to the theory of dogs and cats as mere property!) (Is the unlucky human surgeon successful in court with the theory that the corpse of his patient is only worth $35?)

In effect, the law is a barrier offering immunity from accountability to these over-vaccinators who violate their own canon of ethics of *informed consent* and disregard, in Colorado, the will of the legislature since 1999 to allow the triennial option for rabies vaccination.

Yes, in rare, rare instances there have been damages awarded for 'emotional distress' to the owner. However, as is, the law is a protective 'guard all' shield for vets offering them barriers to legal recourse.

Of course, one could seek redress at the state veterinary board. The revocation rate, as previously stated, of vet licenses in the state of Colorado 1997-2002 fiscal years was 20/100,000ths of 1%. You'd have a better chance at Churchill Downs, Santa Anita, or the Mirage.

The only perceived profession with a revocation rate rivaling the veterinarians is the certified public accountants – the same profession that brought you Enron, Qwest, Worldcom, etc.

So here's the problem in a nut$Hell: 63%-70% of all visits to a small-animal veterinary practice are for shots. The business model and practice is 'co-dependent' on the shots. Without the shots in any one-year, each vet could see their income reduced from an average of $85,000 to less than $30,000 (2002 study). The vaccination is gravy for the vets and they are "challenged" to get a guardian to bring the pet for the needed annual exam without the annual shots. However, the veterinarians' own journals and associations are finding the duration of the shots to be longer – even much longer than 3 years – up to one per lifetime! And despite the pronouncements of the collegiate vet schools, changes in laws to allow even the three-year rabies shot, and studies showing the adverse and often fatal effects of over-vaccination (in the case of autoimmune hemolytic disease), overwhelmingly these vets continue the practice of annual vaccination and without *informed consent* – with immunity from effective legal or professional accountability, deterrence or recourse.

Realizing that veterinary self-regulation was a crap game of 'irregulation,' and that there was no cost effective legal recourse (save a potential class-action suit which could cost millions), my initial approach to correcting this was a two-fold strategy: (1) increasing guardian awareness to over-vaccination's potential harm, while (2) seeking legislative, regulatory and/or legal redress to veterinarian immunity from accountability. Former Colorado State Senator Hugh Fowler (on behalf of his beloved Zack and the memory of Clinker) has been a true ally in these efforts.

Connecting The Doc$ - Increasing Guardian Awareness of the Potential Dangers of Over-vaccination

> "Men have forgotten this truth. You must not forget it. You become responsible, forever, for what you have tamed."
>
> *The Little Prince*

And what has tamed you.

With Denver being named the #1 city for companion animals, I thought the investigative arms of the Denver local print and electronic media would jump at "connecting the doc$", a local angle with the potential for a national exposé.

I thought wrong.

Despite repeated attempts, the story wasn't turned down – it was ignored with not even a call back until the ensuing 'ratings' sweeps period of 2001 when KCNC 4 (CBS) took an interest.

We would have been better off had KCNC's "crack investigative reporter", Brian Maas and his co-worker Clarissa Scott ignored the story.

Instead of a 'connecting the doc$' hard-hitting exposé – as KCNC had teased for days prior to the airing of the story on over-vaccination, the exposé (and web posting) turned into a softball Valentine for Colorado's veterinarians! (See Exhibit 11)

Following our interview, Ms Scott indicated that the vaccination protocol for her own pets 'would never be the same.' Despite that, and despite Colorado's own CSU admonitions against over-vaccination, and despite AVMA's statement that there was no 'scientific data' to support annual rabies vaccination, and despite the "investigator's knowledge that there had not been a case of pet/human rabies since 1931 per Colorado's State epidemiologist", this is the way that characterization of *adverse reactions* to over-vaccinating came out in KCNC's 680-word story:

- "researchers now believe that common vaccines for rabies, feline leukemia, and other shots can **occasionally** cause a fatal form of cancer in cats. It is believed to occur in about 1 out of every 10,000 shots." *(Heard that before?)*
- "**few** (according to Denver vet Kevin Fitzgerald) have developed cancerous tumors from the shots and died."
- "the benefits of vaccinating (according to Fitzgerald) against potentially fatal diseases far outweighs **the minor risk** of giving a cat vaccine-induced cancer."
- "they (a national task force) are trying to learn what in vaccines is causing those '**rare**' cases of cancer (in cats)", per Veterinarian Robin Starr.
- "some vets are now eyeing vaccines for dogs suspicious that **in rare cases** those vaccines may trigger blood diseases. But there's not much research to definitively establish a link."
- "pet owners are also pressing for more information about vaccination risks, and spreading the word that **in extremely rare cases**, doing what you thought was protecting your animal, could end up with catastrophic consequences,"

Let's set the record straight – as of the time of this so-called investigation and since. First, the 1-out-of-10,000, 1-out-of-100,000 *adverse reaction* statistic quoted by Dr. Fitzgerald had already been proven to have been created out of thin air. All the *adverse reaction* data in that purported study is anecdotal, 'self-reported' by the vets themselves! Incidentally in 2003, this 1-out-of-10,000, 1-out-of-100,000 fairy tale was begrudgingly admitted to by Dr. David Hustead, member-at-large of the AVMA Council on Biologic and Therapeutic Agents (COBTA). In the JAVMA (Journal of American Medical Association) News, Sept. 15, <u>2003</u>, he stated:'…**veterinarians lack the commitment to reporting observations…They might also think an adverse event isn't related so they don't bother to report it."**

Ok, Hustead's comment was 2003, but how could crack investigative reporters Maas and Scott, in 2001, have dismissed the 'independently' reported study mentioned previously of 7.5% to12+% *adverse reactions* at the 99% confidence level within 45 days on 1000 cats and 1000 dogs, information provided to them? How could Maas and Scott ignore published refereed studies by Colorado State University's own Dr. Dennis Macy showing 95% of feline sarcomas (cancers) occur at the vaccination site? How could these investigative reporters ignore the previously stated (and provided) position of the AVMA's own Principles of Vaccination stating, "the practice of annual rabies vaccination is based to historical precedent and government regulation, NOT scientific data"?

Maas and Scott, in my opinion, also committed a 'sin of omission' completely ignoring the economic relationship to and dependency of the small-animal vet practice on vaccinations, preferring to quote a few vets anecdotally rather than investigating documented proof.

To add insult to injury, this investigative story ended with, "Wednesday, vets will be in the NEWS4 Helpcenter at 4, 5, and 6 to answer your questions about vaccinations."

Talk about Dracula (the **pawpetraitors**) guarding the blood bank!

May (ratings) sweep became KCNC's Maas' sweep-under-the-rug!

When I followed up by email with award winning Maas and Scott, Maas' retort was 'while we appreciate your input, we'll stick with the facts.'

His response gives new meaning to 'No Maas!" (my attempt at bow-lingual humor.)

Talk to the paw!

Ok, so one can't be a prophet in one's own home town. So I called on John Emswhiller at the Wall Street Journal with whom I had worked previously on financial planner/financial service exposés. John had me contact the Journal's Rhonda Rundles.

The result was a Marketplace Section front page feature over the fold (with the graphic of dogs on a conveyor belt being shot up by a veterinarian) "Are Annual Shots Overkill?" on July 31, 2002. (It should be noted that the graphic artist, Miss Hewitt, subsequently informed me that the original graphic had dogs falling off the conveyor belt 'dead' but the editors killed that version!)

The story took months to get into the paper. After it was published, Rundles wrote me, "this story was one of the most frustrating experiences of my 18½ years at the WSJ. After the story was edited and waiting to run for many, many weeks, it was cut in half during an 11th hour re-edit. Much of what I originally wrote ended up on the cutting room floor. Even so, the *castrated* version appears to have had a lot of impact, judging from the number of emails and phone calls I received. Most of them were from aggrieved pet owners such as yourself, as well as people who have been fighting their vets on this issue and some enlightened vets who are changing their ways."

But while Rhonda was somewhat unhappy with the final version, nationally, for the first time, the over-vaccination of companion animals issue had at least marginally connected the doc$ - the relationship between the small veterinarian practice economics and over-vaccination (and in the bastion of business reporting – The Wall Street Journal no less). (See Exhibit 6)

Judging from phone calls by purported vets who wouldn't give their name however, a nerve was hit – the dirty little $ecret was out.

It was time to leverage the Wall Street Journal exposé. Foolishly, I thought, now the local Denver media will jump on this national story as it has a local angle. Neither our channels 4, 7, or 9 (the CBS, ABC, and NBC affiliates) even responded. However, Phil Keating of Fox did a piece albeit not the 'follow the money story' which was the thrust of my interview. Editors and writers, with the exception of Rhonda Rundles and Stuart Steers (then at Westword), do not want to believe that there was and still is a systemic compelling economic connection between the business model of the small-pet veterinarian practice and the daily medical practices of these veterinarians, and potential harm to our companion animals. It still is not fathomable to the media. Despite the Enron, WorldCom, Fannie Mae, Qwest, Arthur Anderson, etc., scandals, the media did not want to believe that the small-animal veterinarians are betraying our trust. The media have basically ignored 'connecting the doc$" despite George Bernard Shaw's admonition, "all professions are conspiracies against the laity."

Someone said that insanity is redoubling our efforts after certain failure. Knowing this and disregarding the evidence, I redoubled my efforts to get the media's attention with the placement first in August and then November of 2002 of press releases on the PR Newswire. (Senator Fowler's thinking as well as mine was to leverage the Wall Street Journal article to the attention of the broader media while utilizing these releases as well for our forthcoming attempts at legal remedy in the Colorado legislature.)

Overruled by our marketing consultant on the first PR Newswire release, the piece focused only on over-vaccination rather than on the over-vaccination-and-practice-economics connection. However, the release did include results from a non-scientific poll of journalists. To the best of my recollection, there were over 140 responses to the question of whether the respondents (media) types were informed by their vets of the three-year rabies option. Fewer than 20 (15%) responded that their vet had informed them of the option.

The second release, *Over-Vaccination Alert: Protect Your Pet From Your Vet* drove home the economic connection quoting Vet Bob Rogers of Spring, Texas (who had filed a complaint with the Attorney General of Texas and the State Vet Board against his colleagues for their over-vaccination practices). Rogers stated, "every year the people of Texas spend *$360 million on unnecessary and potentially harmful* vaccinations for their pets. Charging for vaccines that have no benefit and are potentially harmful is theft by deception and cruelty to animals."

There was no media response.

> ...when it comes to science and economics, and putting life's risks in perspective, the media do a dismal job
>
> John Stossel, *Myths, Lies, and Downright Stupidity*, p.1, Hyperion, 2006

Gentlemen's (and Ladies') Agreements: Vichy Vets* & Pusillanimous Politicians

> What men dare do, what men do!
> What men daily do, not knowing what they do.
>
> *Shakespeare, Much Ado About Nothing*

Definition from Encarta: *Collegiality*, n. power-sharing (with power shared equally between colleagues); of college or university (involving loyalty typical of, or belonging to a college or university; (colloquially) "respect for one's colleagues."

Definition from Schwartz: *Collegiality*, n. 'make nice-nice' for one's professional buddies even if it means to cover up questionable acts and protect each other's tushies at the expense of clients and patients.

As Senator and Dr. Tom Coburn mused: "niceness is overrated."

During the interim between the Wall Street Journal article and the press releases, I had many discussions with various veterinarians. These discussions could be broken down into two categories; first, 'stick to financial planning and your own industry – how dare you challenge us – you know nothing – we make very little money relative to other professions'; and second, expressions of support, but gutless (like the kids who stay in the back of the circle during Dodge ball hoping to prevail by avoidance). I classify the latter – Vichy Vets. (*For readers born after 1950, Vichy was the site of the French government which collaborated with the Nazis following France's World War II surrender.)

Talk to the paw.

Could the huge reaction to the WSJ article be turned into some kind of movement among vets who shared our ideas about saving our pets and who had the backbone to stand up to those who wanted us to disappear?

While there were several vets who called with support, none – I mean NOT A ONE would lead the charge to even put together a self-defense fund at $100 apiece to defend vets (those who spoke out against over-vaccination) from suspension and or revocation of their licenses. And yes, according to a few of these vets, reprimands and suspensions have been forthcoming to those who spoke against over-vaccination – let alone questioning the monetary connection for the vet's business model.

Some vets offered to sign a petition, but wouldn't accept a leadership role. Nor would other vets who were pioneers in the science against over-vaccination take the lead. Despite their writings in public, professional journals, and seminars the tyranny of "collegiality" made it impossible for them to publicly make the economic connection. One of the foremost, nationally-known pioneers in this area, who for years on end has been taking an unbelievable amount of abuse from her 'colleagues' on this issue of over-vaccination, found when she was on-the-air (ABC Radio) that she could not connect the doc$ between the economics of the small-animal vet practice and over-vaccination. (Several years later, in an April 25, 2005 email, when 27 vet schools went to the three-year protocol, she wrote: "Some organizations have come up with **A POLITICAL COMPROMISE SUGGESTING VACCINATIONS EVERY 3 YEARS TO APPEASE THOSE WHO FEAR LOSS OF INCOME VS THOSE CONCERNED ABOUT POTENTIAL SIDE EFFECTS.** Politics, traditions, or the doctors' economic well-being should not be a factor in a medical decision." She is now on record, and I am glad that she has found a way to make her public statements consistent with her earlier private views on the connection of money and over-vaccination. Her work in titering for antibodies has saved thousands of pet friends, including my own.

I had conversations with several veterinary school professors during this period. One CSU professor proclaimed himself to be "the Ralph Nader" on over-vaccination issues; but when the media called for a story following up on the WSJ 'he had family matters to attend to.' (Later when "the Ralph Nader of over-vaccination" was requested to appear in support of relevant legislation, he failed to return several calls.) Another discussion with an eminent immunologist (PhD) was heated for almost an hour until he finally said, "Okay. I know it's true. I just didn't want to believe it. We teach our students the three-year protocol. They go on job interviews and report to us that if they are not willing to give the annual vaccination they won't get hired."

It became very apparent to me that *collegiality* plus the fear of economic retribution overshadowed these Vichy Vets' personally-held positions against over-vaccination and its potential harm.

We were out of ideas. By process of elimination, it was time for legislation.

The Fur Flies – Lullabys, Legends, and Veterinarian Association Lies

> (You're) a bunch of gutless worms
>
> *Former Senator Ken Chlouber on pulling House Bill 1260 (Loss of Companionship Damages)*

Realizing the media could not be marshaled, recognizing the vets and their associations were deaf to their own calling, and knowing the insulated vet board cartel acts to protect their own interest rather than clients and companion animals per the statistics related previously, I secured legal review of alternative legal recourse to over-vaccination, the lack of *informed consent*, and consequential (if even reported) *adverse reactions*. Except for the slim possibility of a major class-action suit where the trial lawyers would be fronting millions in cost, there was, and still is, no effective legal response to the constructive silent animal cruelty of over-vaccination and absence of *informed consent*.

Spayed and neutered dogs and cats, whom 96% of the American public include as 'part of their family', who have gone from the backyard to the bedroom (76% sleep in their guardian's bed per the Sealy study), and for whom 67% of Americans (per the Gallup poll) would not take a million bucks, *are mere property*. Not just mere property – depreciated property. And while there are cruelty laws, and 39 states allow our dogs and cats to be beneficiaries of trusts (should we predecease), (think Leona Helmsley), dogs and cats are still depreciated property. Maybe one can recover legal costs and the depreciated value of their pet – but it may cost $10,000+ to get $2000 -$3000 – at best a pyrrhic victory, losing by winning as veterinarians have constructive 'immunity' by law.

Encouraged by then State Senate Leader John Andrews and with the aid of our lobbyist Becky Brooks, HB1260 was drafted to be introduced by Representative Mark Cloer (R-Colorado Springs).

The concept of HB1260 was simple: if an owner gave *informed consent* (already a canon of the AVMA) after being advised about the benefits and risks to pets of vaccination, then the owner could not hold the veterinarian liable for a poor result. This is called an affirmative defense. However, should there be no *informed consent* and *adverse reactions* ensue, the Bill provided for additional damages up to $100,000 for 'loss of companionship.'

The fur hit the fan.

The national media was all over the story. The Next-to-Kin static website's hits went from 150 to 300 a day into the tens of thousands.

The *New York Times*, *USA Today*, etc., interviewed Mr. Cloer.

He was a happy camper.

Second Hand Smokescreen

Not surprisingly, the vet association was against the bill. What was surprising was the extent of deliberate mischaracterizations of the legislation that the vet association employed to deflect the problem (of silent, systemically, economically-motivated over-vaccination and its harm to our pets) and reframe the issue to the elevation of dogs and cats to "human status."

And the media bought it.

The story became "elevation to human status" rather than creating accountability and deterrence against harmful over-vaccination that had become economically institutionalized in small-animal veterinarians' practices. There was no mention of the science (or lack thereof) or the economics (connecting the doc$) let alone the horror stories that motivated this bill.

The vets and their lobbyists framed the debate early. They falsely stated that HB1260 would elevate dogs and cats to human status. They said it would displace monies from children's needs. And be a boon to trial lawyers. (Matter of fact, trial lawyers were not particularly fond of the affirmative defense hurdle nor the cap on loss of companionship damages) (Exhibits 12, 13, & 14). The great hypocrisy was a letter from the association which stated that "it (HB1260) attempts to dictate the practice of medicine," when all the bill did was enforce their own canon of ethics of *informed consent* that the vets systemically violate hour after hour, day in and day out, month in and month out and year in, year out! Further, one position paper holds, relative to the aforementioned charge, "for example, a veterinarian would be precluded from offering a 'safer vaccination option' (e.g., a non-adjuvanted vaccine with a one-year protection) or altering vaccination protocols in response to a public health crisis." As to the offer of a safer vaccination, I have to admit we were totally baffled by an adversary who ignored their very own "science" -- and then offered a "safer" alternative. What basis did they have at that time to call it "safer?" There was/is none. Secondly, "altering vaccination protocols in a public health crisis," was a red herring. If that were really their concern, (and never the intent of the bill), we would have been more than happy to have it amended. They made no attempts to communicate any desire for amendment. As to their charge that the bill was created without input from veterinarians: guilty as charged. The veterinarians had proven they did not wish to clean up their own act.

Their position statement also claimed that HB1260 would:

- Escalate the cost of veterinary medical care
- Contradict efforts in the General Assembly to effect tort reform in human medicine.
- Duplicate remedies already provided under current law, such as redress in cases of non-economic compensation due to willful and wanton conduct (including aggravated cruelty to animals) or those provisions specifically not exempting vets from being disciplined or sued; (or) waivers for certain inoculations already utilized by veterinarians throughout Colorado

There are good reasons, and then there are real reasons. And the real reason for these obfuscations was to avoid connecting the doc$ between money and knowingly harmful practices to guardians' companion animals. So, as I quoted elsewhere: "when you have the facts, argue the facts. When you have the law, argue the law. And when you have neither, attack your opponents, mischaracterize, create straw-men arguments, deflect and change the issue."

As to cost going up, millions and billions of dollars yearly are already shifted to pet owners through unnecessary shots, followed by billions of costs to owner/ guardians in correcting *adverse reactions*.

As far as playing the evil trial-lawyer card (which sometimes has merit), HB 1260 provided for an affirmative defense: a signed *informed consent* form (which the AAHA had published in Wilson's book in three previous editions – but which obviously had not been used – See Sidebar: **Informed consent or Faux Informed consent aka Cover The Vet's Ass**). In addition, the bill required inexpensive non-binding alternative dispute resolution prior to any legal action! Furthermore, damages would be capped at $100,000. Now, rightfully you might ask, why $100,000? And I would ask you, why not? Was it not dogs who saved many of the survivors of 9/11? And isn't it true that the families of those who died in 9/11 were given reparations to make the families whole up to $1,500,000? Are our companion animals worth 6.7% of a human life? Well, in an American Animal Hospital Association study, 40% of the guardians said they would spend anything on their companion animal in a life-threatening illness or accident, and again in a Gallup Poll commissioned by Iams (Procter and Gamble), 66% said they would not take $1,000,000 for their dog or cat. Finally, the duplication of remedies argument is arrogant flagrant baloney both literally and constructively as outlined previously.

The Denver Post ran a story about HB 1260 by Julia Martinez on February 9, 2003, "Fur Flies Over Bill On Status of Pets…Owners could sue for emotional loss." First, the subhead was factually incorrect. Emotional loss is a broader category legally – including emotional distress, etc. Secondly, the story states, "but the proposed law would recognize the emotional suffering that occurs at the death or injury of a pet, <u>laying the foundation for elevating their status to companions,</u> supporters say."

First, the initial part of the article accepted the faulty premise that HB1260 elevated dogs and cats to human status (which was not in the bill) and then later, in the same article, backtracked stating 'laying the foundation for elevating their status to companions.' Furthermore, Ms. Martinez compounded the acceptance of this red herring by quoting Senator Steve Johnson, a licensed veterinarian from Fort Collins. He seemed to accept that "elevation" was implicit in the bill, stating: "If you elevate their (the pet's) status, it will complicate the client-veterinarian relationship. If the pet is elevated, do I then question the owner (about their decisions)? (That would make it) a <u>three</u>-way relationship."

Well, first, I would ask Senator Johnson: since when was the companion animal, owner/guardian, veterinarian relationship – NOT a three-way relationship? Second, Senator Johnson, and Ms. Martinez, bought the false "elevation" premise without seeking comment from the sponsor to affirm or deny it. Third, per Colorado law, if a lawmaker has a personal or financial interest in any bill, he or she shall disclose it and not vote on it. (Article V, Section 43 of the Colorado Constitution, "a member who has a personal or private interest in any measure or bill proposed or pending before the general assembly, shall disclose the fact to the house of which he is a member, and shall not vote thereon.")

Senator Johnson did not get a chance to vote on HB 1260 because the vet's lobby got it killed in committee. But I was disappointed that he did not qualify his opinion to the Post reporter.

Of course, the above provisions do not cover 'collegiality,' or 'being an accomplice to a red herring and mischaracterization' by a conflicted lawmaker.

Ms. Martinez never responded to my phone or emails to clarify these points.

And the vets were successful in reframing the issue. They deflected HB1260's purpose. They labeled the bill 'animal rights.' (Labels are for shirts.) This was not animal rights; this was a bill for companion animal protection. The mere thought of those PETA whackos pairing the treatment of chicken fryers raised for food to Holocaust victims makes me, as a Jew – A Dogged Jew at that – want to drag the PETA President to the Holocaust Museum by her hair.

Mr. Cloer pulled the bill, and Senator Andrews was unable to obtain other leadership approval for a late senate bill reintroduction as our failsafe.

The bill had been originally ordered by the Speaker to go to a committee the chair of which had an election finance committee headed by lobbyist Lynn Young, wife of the past President of the Colorado Vet Association. Get this: he had been featured on the cover of the association's magazine *announcing the three-year rabies option in 1999*!

So, the deck was stacked against us. But to paraphrase Daniel Webster the only causes worth fighting are the lost causes.

But at least Webster got to argue for his lost causes.

We were informed by Rep. Cloer that HB1260 would be killed. But worse, it would be killed without even the possibility of testimony. This rarely employed tactic was allegedly instigated by lobbyist Young and blessed by the Speaker of the house.

Rep. Cloer convinced me of the futility of presenting a bill before a committee that would not even allow testimony. By pulling the bill prior to committee massacre, it could be reintroduced later in the legislative session. To paraphrase Cloer, 'there would be no second bite at the apple should we defy the Speaker.'

So, the choice was either go to the committee hearing only to have the bill struck down without testimony (but with the press present to ask why no testimony – a questionable assumption in light of Martinez's previous coverage) or to pull the bill in the hope of fighting another day in the house. I chose the latter – to fight another day – believing Senator Andrews could arrange a late bill reintroduction. (Incidentally, under the so-called "Gavel-Act," it is unlawful for a chairman not to have a full hearing on *any* bill referred to committee.)

Chlouber, the Senate sponsor, wanted to make the House chairman and vets accountable to the press, forcing the issue of their having cut off any testimony. Cloer prevailed in his reasoning of bringing it back again (which never happened).

I acquiesced.

In retrospect, Chlouber was right.

We were gutless. I was gutless.

I apologize to Senator Chlouber. It might have been fruitless, but I should have done something to encourage them to act on the bill in broad daylight – and, in the words of P.J. O'Rourke "let the critters scamper" answering 'what did they have to hide?'

The vets won this round – but ironically, after the tussle, increasing at an increased rate, more states adopted the optional three-year (non-scientific economic compromise) protocol. Some of our language apparently leaked into laws in other states. The vet associations, the animal hospital association, and the vet schools were begrudgingly changing – but not our friendly, our trusted, small-animal veterinarians.

Side Bar: A Veterinarian's definition of *Informed Consent*

> "...Informed consent is *not* intended to protect the practitioner. It is a process wherein your veterinarian informs you of the risks, benefits and consequences of treatment; tells you about alternative treatment; lets you know when there are practitioners better qualified to treat your dog; and answers questions that you might not yet have enough information or presence of mind to ask. Informed consent is for the client/patient, not the practitioner. It is not, as a vet's lawyers may have indicated, a document *primarily used to cover his posterior* in the event a case heads south."
>
> *Mutual Aid, Richard Lerner, DVM, Bark Magazine, May 2007*

Documentation of Rabies Vaccination

(Recommended legal form per AVMA – 2001)

Client's Name _____   Patient's Name _____

In recent years, rabies has become more prevalent in wildlife populations which means humans and pets are more frequently exposed to this fatal disease. Skunks, raccoons, foxes, and bats are the species that most frequently carry and transmit this disease. Rabies is most commonly transmitted through saliva when infected wild or domestic animals bite humans or other animals.

Some state laws require that your pet be vaccinated annually for rabies; others require it every three-years. This vaccination serves not only to prevent the spread of the rabies virus, but is the primary factor in determining the type of medical treatment bite victims receive and how state health regulators handle your pet after he/she has bitten a human or other domestic animal.

For these reasons, it is **essential** that this practice be able to document the rabies vaccination status of your pet. Acceptable documentation includes a rabies certificate, a valid rabies tag, or a letter, fax, or phone call from your veterinarian with the date of administration, serial or lot number, and expiration date of the vaccine. Please provide the following information, so we can include it as a vital part of your pet's medical record.

Administration date of rabies vaccination _____ Date vaccine expires _____

Method of documentation _____

(rabies certificate, rabies tag, letter/fax/phone call from veterinarian)

If you cannot substantiate the rabies vaccination status of your pet, we must consider him/her to be **unvaccinated** and the following public health regulations might apply:

> 1. If your pet is unvaccinated, bites any person or animal, and **shows clinical signs** consistent with rabies, but does not die and is not euthanized, he/she must be strictly quarantined for ten days at a facility approved by a public health officer **at your expense.**
>
> 2. If your pet is unvaccinated, bites any person, and dies or is euthanized within ten days of the bite, his/her head must be sent to the state diagnostic laboratory for rabies testing.
>
> As evidenced above, the rabies vaccination status of your pet can have serious consequences should he/she bite a human or another animal. If you do not have documentation of current vaccination with you, please provide this information as soon as possible. Alternatively, if your pet has no history of a recent bite wound and shows no symptoms consistent with rabies, you may have your pet innoculated today, so that he/she has valid vaccination documentation.
>
> I hereby request that a rabies vaccine be administered today. _____ (initials)
>
> I hereby decline the administration of a rabies vaccine today and will provide valid documentation of vaccination as soon as possible. _____ (initials)
>
> _____   _____
> Signature of Owner or Authorized Agent   Date
>
> <u>Legal Consents for Veterinary Practices (With Spanish Translation</u>), James F. Wilson, DVM, JD, Priority Press Ltd, 4th edition, 2006 (note 3rd edition was published by the American Animal Hospital Association Press, 2001!)

Please compare this "approved" legal form with the statement immediately above it. Then I ask you, dear reader, where is Doctor Lerner's *informed consent* that is the "process wherein your veterinarian informs you of the risks, benefits and consequences of treatment; tells you about alternative treatment" in <u>this</u> *official* informed consent??????

Where?

Informed consent or legal 'overkill' for the 'overkill' of overvaccination?

And who will take the time to read and digest all this legalese?

Pets as family members – per veterinarian marketing?

Pets as property per veterinary legal actions and seldom used *'informed consent?'*

Talk to the Law NOT the Paw?

Below is the exact text of our (Next-to-Kin's) vaccination *informed consent* card for rabies vaccinations as well as parvo and distemper (small enough to keep in your wallet should you forget it... the card folds over to provide on the front for the Pet/Companion Animal's Name and date of birth.)

VACCINATION ALERT

Prior to immunization of the registered pet, the Guardian and I have discussed the current science of vaccination from three viewpoints:

(1) Current state of veterinary practice, including uncertainty of the safety to the animal of annual vaccination;

(2) State and Local Law, which requires vaccination every _____ years, except for certain circumstances which may or may not be related to age or health of the pet;

(3) Alternative approaches, such as antibody titering, and/or prolonging periods between vaccinations, all in the better health interests of the pet.

The Guardian has made his/her decision about vaccinating this registered pet in accordance with this discussion.

_____   _____

Signature of Veterinarian   Date

_____

Guardian/owner signature

Love Letters

Not to be outdone by the mischaracterization by the Colorado Vet Society, on February 20, 2003, Next-to-Kin Foundation received this message from the e-mail address of a prominent veterinarian in the San Diego area. Skip it if crude language is offensive to you.

Subj: slanderous statements
Date: 2/20/03 3:44:28 PM Mountain Standard Time
To: info@next2kin.org

Dear Next-to-Kin,

I bet Next-to-Kin refers to those you date, right?

I love this internet-it allows the dissemination of any bullshit any one (or a "no one" in your case) wants to put out there on websites. Trouble is weak-minded people believe you non-professionals. The professionals like me have to waste time re-educating with facts vs/ personal opinions you whip out of your ass.

I understand hacks like you wanting to spread your venereal infected thoughts and misinformation. I expect it. We all have read the stories from people like you who owned a dog and so you're an animal expert and know secrets like "it's better to breathe in your dogs farts so they won't be harmed" or "my hamster is a special hairless breed that needs to hibernate in my rectum."

What I will not tolerate is your attack on the dedicated and hard working world of veterinarians like myself.

How dare you morons write about vets needing / desperately depending on vax income. Your head is so far up your bottom you need a snorkel to breathe.

My 1 ½ doctor animal hospital grosses nearly a million a year and vax make up a very small % of that. Many of us are in this situation. How about printing a retraction now that you know the truth? I bet you don't have the guts, and I know you lack the brain power for understanding the facts.

I love that financial guru Jim Scwartzberg. He rails about greedy vets. What did he devote his life to doing? He was a damn bean counter in the business world. He worshipped money. I can picture him erect with excitement rolling around naked in a pile of stocks and bonds. I know about the secret compartment where you carry your quarter rolls. He names his dog Moolah for God-sakes! You should understand what a hypocritical money-changer you are, Jimmy. Vets are greedy? Look in the mirror, you money-monkey, you slave to the dollar. Are the quarter rolls back there at least protected in plastic, James?

So let me understand-Scwartzbaum works in and dedicates his life to money And has a dog named Moolah and others named "Tax loop hole" and "Hidden Fees" and people like me who go to veterinary medical school and dedicate their lives to helping animals are the greedy ones. You pathetic money-grubbing hypocrite. Are you sure Moolah did not die from a fatal immune reaction to the latex condoms you were using with him/her (sorry, I didn't know if Jimbo was a gay or straight money-monkey changer. Anyone calling themselves Next-to-Kin has to be under suspicion for that kind of activity.

Signed/Dr (–)

Attempts in 2003 to get confirmation or denial from Dr. (–) as to the authenticity of this email went unanswered.

Communications about this with the national Jewish Anti-Defamation League, the San Diego regional Anti-Defamation League as well Denver's Anti-Defamation (and in particular, its president Bruce DeBoskey – were not responded to. Furthermore, according to attorney Richard Saul, who serves on the Denver Anti-Defamation League's board (and who secured the not-for-profit tax exempt status for Next-to-Kin), Mr. DeBoskey promised him to call me on this subject on several occasions.

Mr. DeBoskey and Dr. (–) have yet to respond.

Mr. Pape vs. N2K (Next-to-Kin Foundation) – Stacking The Deck

> In fact, the more I watched the regulators work, the more it seemed the real beneficiaries of the regulations were the entrenched businesses, unions, and regulators themselves
>
> *John Stossel, Give Me A Break, p. 30*

> There are three sides to every story: your side, my side, and the true side
>
> *Uncle Louie Schwartz*

Rebuffed and out-maneuvered legislatively, legal options greatly restricted, and the media either disbelieving or bamboozled by the vet associations relative to connecting the doc$ and thereby frustrating the 'discovery' of the real harm of over-vaccination, a different tactic was obviously necessary to inform guardians.

Senator Fowler wrote an ad to run several times in the Denver Post, paid for by the Next-to-Kin Foundation.

But prior to publishing the ad, and on the advice of counsel, we purchased from the State of Colorado a list of all the veterinarians licensed in the state. We sent a copy of the proposed 'ad' to each and every one of these 3600+ licensed veterinarians in Colorado for their comments and corrections. (see exhibit 15)

There wasn't even a mention of the connection between over-vaccination and the systemic economic motivation (the money) of the vets in the ads!

Yet the reactions were the same old – harsh, arguing off the point, attacking, etc. (though none reached the personal character assassination and anti-Semitic level of the email sent either by Dr. (–) or his impostor. There was only one constructive criticism, pointing out our statement in the ad that there hasn't been a case of rabies in Colorado since 1931 as technically incorrect. The statement should have read there has not been a case of *human* rabies since 1931. We made the correction in the ad – PRIOR – to publication.

We ran the corrected ad – "Your pet wants you to read this: Is Your Veterinarian Still Over-vaccinating Your Pet? – several times. (See exhibit 16)

> "The conceit of the anointed"
>
> *Thomas Sowell*

Isidor Rabi, a Nobel laureate in physics was once asked, "Why did you become a scientist rather than a doctor, or lawyer, or businessman, like the other immigrant kids in neighborhood?' Dr. Rabi answered, 'My mother made me a scientist without ever intending it. Every other Jewish mother in Brooklyn would ask her child after school, 'Nu? Did you learn anything today?' But not my mother. She always asked me a different question, 'Izzy,' she would say, 'did you ask a good question today?' that difference – asking good questions – made me become a scientist." (Donald Sheff, New York Times, January 19, 1988)

The Bureaucracy responds to our newspaper advertising

The Chief Colorado Epidemiologist, Communicable Disease Control Program (Mr. Pape – I'm not his publicist) is by his own description "the epidemiologist responsible for rabies surveillance and prevention in Colorado." On June 13, 2003, I received from Mr. Pape a letter of admonition as president of the Next-to-Kin Foundation. His letter was issued without any prior conversation, correspondence, etc., with the Next-to-Kin Foundation, myself, or Senator Fowler to ascertain our side of the story. Furthermore, his prejudicial letter *almost simultaneously* appeared as an article in the Colorado *Voice* (Vet Association Journal), Summer 2003, issue! It was 'Department of Health Corrects Inaccuracies by Opposition Group,' republishing the letter in full – the one he wrote without checking the other side of the story. Please see Exhibit 17, a,b,&c.

His inaccuracies aside, as a Colorado health officer – *"the"* epidemiologist – he failed the basic premise of due process – rushing to judgment – failing to gather all the facts and get both sides of the story. Old Judaic proverb, 'half truth, whole lies.'

And as the great Talmudic scholar, Rabbi Hillel would say, 'the rest is commentary.'

So, first, *"the"* epidemiologist – Mr. Pape – reacts to only one side of the story. Secondly, he utilizes the draft ad copy sent to him by vets – that was NOT the final ad copy – which had he even bothered to call me or Next-to-Kin we could have shown him! Had he even bothered to do investigation 101 and called us, we could have shown him that every vet in Colorado (per the licensing board over 3600) four weeks prior was sent a draft copy of the prepared ad – *for comments and changes*. We received only 11 responses: two were positive and 9 were negative out of 3600! He would have also found out that he was provided the uncorrected ad (by the complaining vets) not the ad which ran in the newspapers. He would have seen the change to "no human rabies" since 1931 from the erroneous "no rabies since 1931." (Exhibit 17) That's why you recheck statistics – to catch errors.

But then again, Mr. Pape is *'the'* epidemiologist – a man of the scientific method.

Secondly, Mr. Pape's letter apparently went unedited into the CVMA's professional journal – without getting our side of the story. The question is whether Mr. Pape's action was a lapse in judgment, grandstanding, or another case of the regulated snaring the regulator? Regardless, could Mr. Pape's action be classified as "negligence of a duty of care" pursuant to Pearsonv Norman, 106. 396, 106 P. 2nd 361(1940)?

Professions and businesses, it seem, are very often successful in manipulating the cry for consumer protection so that regulation becomes instead, legal protection for the profession, business, and regulator!

As to Mr. Pape's inaccuracies in his *Voice* article, one example should suffice. Notice that our ad states, "(the Colorado Legislature changed the rabies vaccination law to permit vets to vaccinate no more often than every three-years." Mr. Pape's take: "This is an incorrect interpretation of this law. In fact, local ordinances are prevented from requiring vaccination more often than required by vaccine label." Mr. Pape's statement misrepresents the law by suggesting that vaccines can either be 1-year duration or 3-year duration and therefore, annual shots could be mandatory.

The facts: Colorado law requires local governments to follow the standard imposed by the "Compendium of Animal Rabies Control." CRS 25-4-615(2), thus:

> "Vaccines used in state and local rabies control programs should have a three-year duration of immunity. This constitutes the most effective method of increasing the proportion of immunized dogs and cats in any population. There is no laboratory or epidemiologic data to support the annual or biennial administration of 3-year vaccines following the initial series."

(An aside. Pioneer Dr. Jean Dodd's response to Mr. Pape's negation of titers (Exhibit 18) on June 23, 2003 states "This situation is complex and reflects inherent bias in accepting titers for rabies – for which acceptable titer levels are already established for purposes of export/import of animals to rabies free countries all over the world, and for import to other countries just to ensure that pet dogs and cats entering these places are adequately immunized/protected. Furthermore, the CDC (Center for Disease Control) and WHO (World Health Organization) have determined what they consider to be protective rabies titer levels for people – namely 1:5 and 1:50, respectively, so – how can anyone say that rabies titers don't reflect immunity. Must be political issues here.")

Mr. Pape, as Colorado's Chief Epidemiologist, *'the"* Epidemiologist also has authority over the West Nile Virus and the Bird Flu.

Pawnote:
> Per 'How Worried Should You Be?' by Dr. Ranit Mishori in the 9/23/2006 edition of Parade Magazine, for the period 1980 thru 2004, (twenty-four years) only "54 instances of human rabies reported in the US."

This is a rate of eleven billionths of 1% of the US population, per year!

Of those, how many involved pets? Answer: virtually none. Dr. Mishori again: "Despite the stereotype of the 'mad dog' foaming at the mouth, canine (and cat) rabies is rare in the U.S. In mice, gerbils, rats, rabbits and squirrels, it's practically nonexistent. The majority of rabies cases now result from exposure to bats."

So what's the annual cost of managing two human (bat) rabies cases?

Assume the following:

1) an average United States population of 200 million during this period to be conservative (we are soon reaching 300 million)
2) a companion animal population on average of 100 million (we are now exceeding 160 million dogs and cats in US households, and in Colorado alone in the 2000 census there were 2.1 million dogs and cats in 1.6 million households)
3) 30,000 small-animal veterinarians (there are 38,000 to 40,000 today) on average
4) a 50% compliance rate on rabies vaccination annually

Do the figures with me:

1) **the incidence of human rabies is 11 billionths of 1% or 2.16 per year and**
2) At 30,000 small-animal veterinarians per year with an average of 2500 dogs and cats per vet - and a 50% compliance rate to just the rabies shot per year for 25 years multiplied by $15 only for the shot per year and only $30 for the office visit - $42,187,500,000 (billion) **has been collected by the vets for 11 billionth of 1% rabies cases.**
3) #2 does not include the cost of *adverse reactions* to the rabies shot alone (not including the cost of parvo and distemper shots and *adverse reactions* to these shots). The vets have admitted that the commonly spoken

1/10,000 - 1/100,000 *adverse reaction* ratio was bogus - and all self-reported! The previously noted independent study of 1000 dogs and cats in Britain showed 7.5%-12% *adverse reactions* within 45 days at the 99% confidence level. Thus, just a 1% *adverse reaction* using but a $200 dollar cost on average (auto immune hemolytic disease which is 70% fatal can cost $3000-$15,000 alone) - would add to the cost of the shot another $1.875 billion. **At 2% *adverse reaction* and $500 average cost, this would add another $9.375 billion for 11 billionth of 1% exposure of 2.16 human rabies cases from bats (obviously not vaccinated)!** PS - This doesn't include the *adverse reaction* to the over-vaccination of Parvovirus and Distemper - which unbeknownst to most owners is voluntary — not legally required — and studies are showing that post-puppyhood Parvo and Distemper shots are a waste of money!!!!

P.S. When was the last time your vet "bundled" the "P" and "T" shot together with an annual vaccination — without bothering to tell you that not one was required?

Back to saving one dog at a time…

We were running out of options — save my still making it a point to talk with at least one dog guardian a day. Pondering our "dog bill" over lunch at Bambino's with Hugh Fowler and me, Senator Andrews suggested increasing 'guardian clout' by changing the composition of the Veterinarian Board akin to what Teddy Roosevelt did in 1903 with the National Coal Board. Basically, the board would be reconstituted to include a majority of vets versus consumers, but the small-animal veterinarians would have only one member and the remainder of the vets and non-consumers on the board would have differing and somewhat conflicting interests, e.g., homeopath, nutritionist, immunologist, etc.

Senator Andrews' idea was a very good one.

But neither Senator Andrews, nor any other legislator had a chance to offer this in the General Assembly – the bill had been pulled from action.

A Hail Mary and A Hurry Moses

It was time for A Hail Mary coupled with a Hurry Moses.

In May of 2003, I read an article on insurance patents co-authored by a patent agent and an actuary, Tom Bakos.

I had vaguely remembered from my discussions with Chubb (huge insurance co.) that they had received a patent on a computer process relative to insurance. However, as I recalled, insurance patents were few and rare.

And insurance related patents in what is called the 706 area (business methods) are very rare; at the time of this writing, fewer than 325 since 1977.

In June of 2004, after continually running into brick walls, it came to me: why not attach a pet-health insurance policy to homeowners' and/or health insurance products through a patent, and seek a second patent to allow a discount for minimum vaccination by law? This would obviously increase the insurers' profits through more sales and higher retention of existing policies, but – more important to us – would save thousands of sick companion animals!

Now, it is not that actuaries don't care, but actuaries make their calculations based on expenses including claims. No actuary would sign off on a proposed minimum vaccination discount unless there were evidence that this would reduce claims. Whether an actuary loves, hates, or is indifferent to companion animals, the actuary would base his or her decision on a discount for minimum vaccination from experience.

And past claims experience allows a discount for a minimum vaccination by law.

With the economic incentive of pet insurance savings if the guardian by law does the minimum vaccination, the pressure would be on the veterinarian to explain why more frequent vaccination is necessary (it rarely is) and to point out the enormous risks as well as the imagined benefits attendant to increased frequency.

Money talks, and just might cause the *informed consent*, ignored by the vets despite their canon of ethics, to be enforced by the owner. Or the vet may just find he has lost clients.

Our insurance actuary calculated that with our contemplated coverage attached to a homeowners and/or health insurance policy, if 15% of today's market were to take this option for their companion animals, in time the 2.7% of small-animal vet visits for euthanasia could be reduced to 1.1%, saving annually as many as 175,000 dogs and cats from 'economic euthanasia' (because without the insurance the guardian couldn't afford the medical costs for a new 'leash on life.') Furthermore, and this is my calculation, if our insured pet's healthy life span is increased but 1 year (due to the minimum-vaccination-by-law discount and more frequent healthcare) – this would 'save' another 1,200,000+ companion animals a year.

The patent on our Heal! Insurance was issued on July 17, 2007.

It is **Patent No. US 7,246,070 B2**

Now the process of securing the direct writer(s) and or reinsurer(s) is taking place. It will take additional time and effort, hopefully not another three years and $100,000++!!

> Certainly the fact that a veterinarian takes his clients' animals, pets often as deeply revered as members of the family, puts him in a position of a bailee for hire and a fiduciary as far as the care and protection of *this personality* is concerned
>
> *Thorpe vs Board of Examiners in Veterinary Medicine*

> A fiduciary is a person having a duty, created by his undertaking, to act primarily for the benefit of another in matters connected with the undertaking
>
> *Tepely vs Public Employees Retirement Ass'n*

The Hail Mary approach to solving our problem would be a class-action suit with a big-time tort lawyer firm, as individual recourse would be at best a pyrrhic victory. Our initial legal research revealed that a class-action remedy for malpractice was excluded by the Colorado Consumer Protection Act.

Now I am no fan of class-action suits despite the protestations, and despite persuasive counsel during this Quixotic battle. In class-actions, I have seen where the aggrieved get bubkus and the lawyers make out. But there is a place for them – a necessary place for class-actions — especially if by process of elimination there is no other recourse — regardless of the imbalance between client recovery and the lawyers' remuneration.

Our excellent counsel helped us to come up with an appropriate theory for a class case to fit this betrayal of trust. However, because of the large front-end monetary expense a law firm would have to put up, animal lawyer after animal lawyer after animal lawyer — demurred.

But the only two options left were class-action or anti-trust.

Save for two large national vet chains, the veterinary business is so fragmented that even proving constructive anti-trust actions via disparate statistics would probably be unwieldy. (By the way, when was the last time you escaped a Vet visit for less than $100?)

So, at this point, the anti-trust approach is not an option, leaving only the class-action alternative, with a reluctant lawyer pool.

Now, for a class-action suit to work (lawyers use the word 'to be certified') the damage must be common to all plaintiffs (owners).

Adverse reactions to vaccination do not share commonality — other than that each was an *adverse reaction*. However, the cost of the shot for over-vaccination without *informed consent* — does constitute commonality for a potential class-action. Furthermore, should the vets try to shift blame to the vaccination manufacturers (who basically have immunity) they would find that a non-starter as they are 'sophisticated users.' Truly, 38,000 small-animal veterinarians each having approximately 2500 companion animals under his or her care with 50% shot compliance is over 47,500,000 shots a year. (And that is just one shot.) This equilibrates conservatively to almost 5 shots a day at a minimum 5 days a week. Thus, vaccination is not 'tangential' to the small veterinarian's practice, whose lawyer would be inclined to use the 'incidental to the practice' defense (despite the fact that 63%-70% of all visits are for vaccination!). Vaccination IS 'common.'

The question turns on fraudulent inducement for over-vaccination especially in light of the veterinarians' canon of ethics for *informed consent* and holding themselves out as 'fiduciaries' upon whom we bestow substitute reliance.

Yet, after over a year of working with a major national class-action firm that has won hundreds of millions annually, and after their initial enthusiasm, and hundreds of man hours on my part (without pay) as their 'consulting expert,' they punted without explanation. End of class-action suit initiative.

Small-animal Veterinarian Continued Defiance of the Law and *Informed consent*

By late 2007, the following has occurred (or not occurred) relative to rabies over-vaccination:

- Most if not all the vet schools are recommending the three-year rabies protocol
- The AVMA is recommending 'customization' rather than 'standardization' of vaccination protocols
- All but one or two of the states now approve at least the three-year option for rabies vaccination.
- The vet association admits that historically the *adverse reaction* reporting is flawed

- A Former AAHA President has called the annual rabies vaccination protocol 'pure fantasy.'

One would think these changes would have filtered down to the small-animal vet.

Not.

Back to step one.

Next-to-Kin Foundation engaged Hill Research Consulting to do a poll – The Next-to-Kin Foundation's First Annual Companion Animal Rabies Survey.

In answer to the question (asked of pet owners), "Does your veterinarian recommend <u>annual</u> rabies vaccination for your pet?"

79% said '**yes**,'

4% were 'unsure,' and

only 17% said 'no' – 7 years after the legislation allowing the three-year option.

A second question was asked about the Colorado State law passed in 1999, now requiring vaccination only every three-years

62% 'were not aware of the law' (the three-year option) 7 years later despite the Veterinary canon of '*informed consent.*'.

So what was the small-animal veterinarian response to the law seven years after it passed, and to their *informed consent* canon?

Talk to the Paw.

The survey's results were statistically accurate ± 3%.

What was the reaction to this survey:

- Pet-owning Colorado legislators were contacted >> indifference
- The Investigative reporters in the print media >> no response
- The crack TV investigative reporters >> nada

> "One doesn't remain silent as his neighbor bleeds."
>
> *Paraphrase: Judaic ethics*

Don't talk to the paw.

Anyway

> ...People favor underdogs, but follow only top Dogs.
> Fight for a few underdogs, anyway
>
> *Kent Keith, Anyway*

> No dog before his time,
> One dog at a time,
> The inheritance of loss –
> To make loss matter, anyway
>
> *Moolah's legacy.*

Recommendations of What <u>You</u> Should Do, remembering: I'm not a veterinarian!

Take Charge in Your Selection and Management of Your Small-Animal Veterinarian – ask / demand the following:

Do you give <u>complete</u> <u>information</u> relative to the costs and benefits of the rabies vaccination as well as any others including the parvovirus and distemper shot? (Even the bordetella – "Kennel-cough" – shot is becoming suspect for *adverse reactions*.)

- Please provide a copy of your *<u>informed consent</u>* form. If you don't have an *informed consent* agreement, how come?
- Do you give a combination rabies, parvo and distemper shot? Why, when these shots given together are referred to derisively as "the wombo combo" in the profession?
- Does your clinic utilize blood titers as an alternative to over – vaccinating for rabies? For parvo and distemper? If not, why not?
- Does your clinic send out an annual reminder for shots? (If so this means that the practice is queued off of shots – beware!)
- Does your practice send out an annual reminder for the annual exam? (in contrast - a good thing!)
- (Here's a test whether lip service is being given: ask an <u>associate</u> vet of the practice if during their hiring he or she was told the policy of the clinic is to do *annual*

rabies shots? Maybe the vet won't answer this, so try having a friend call the front desk inquiring about being a new client and ask if it is the clinic/hospital's practice to give annual rabies vaccination? If no, ask if there is an *informed consent* form which clients sign for the vaccination of their companion animals.)

Have the veterinarian sign off on the consent form provided in the appendix.

Chapter VI
K911©

You are whom you protect
<u>Elle</u>
ELLE "GHIARDELLI"
'15 Minutes of Fame – Daily'

No "bone-ing" up for Ms. Elle – all is 'elle'-mentary to the Elle-quent Excellence of Elle-cution. Ms. Encyclopedia. "El Kvell" Citizen K911 en-ABEL-s sans dog-ma & vanity, "Elle-vating" – scent from Above "the whole kit & caboodle poodle" performs ***Bark mitzvoth,*** daily

> The only whole heart is the broken heart.
>
> *The Kokzer Rabbi*

You can't get a replacement for your forever dogs – but they can have successors.

And, Elle was Moolah's successor.

At the moment I first picked her up, she put her paws tightly on my shoulder, then looked straight into my face with those Betty Davis eyes, finally attaching her face firmly against my cheek (knowing she closed the deal).

Elle uses tools.

As a pup, she used her Nylabone to disengage the expanding fence in the house to meet me at the door.

Elle is discriminating.

Having gotten hold of my wallet, she disengaged not the Discover Card with the $2,000 limit, the Master card with a $5,000 dollar limit, but rather the Visa with the $15,000 limit. No she didn't chew it or the wallet, but rather I found the wallet, and the Visa card, in front of her paws unscathed as if to say: "see what I can do, now write down that 800 number for greenies!"

Ms. Personality.

So, when she wasn't right – I knew it

"I-MAX" – The Kosher "Ham"

MAX-A-$1,000,000

Stay-Free Maxie, once a roamer, is now a homer.
Office Max – Max Headroom – The *Crotch* Potatoe,
Miramax, The Kosher Ham, Maxie's got Moxie.
The Max Factor – makeup artist, a leaner – not a wiener
Max (Not) Mum Security:
I-MAX-IMUS (in the morning)
Max The Knife/ Max Mossad
A Crown **JEW**-el

Even with the addition of Elle, there was still something missing in the house after Moolah's graduation.

I had met Max outside of PETCO a year prior to his adopting me. I commented to his guardian on what a fine-looking standard poodle she had. Immediately, Max leaned into me. The Guardian said: "that's odd, he doesn't like men." I told her I was looking to adopt a third dog, and asked her who her breeder was. She said, "Jill Cole, and her bitch just dropped a litter."

I was flabbergasted, since I had been on Jill's list for a couple of years now – hearing nothing. So, I called Jill. She had forgotten. To make things right – I got the pick of her litter: Moses.

Moses made the house fuller but still there was something missing at Fort Schwartz.

Almost a year to the day later, I got a call from the guardian of Max. 'Things have changed. Max gets loose – has adventures – would you consider adopting both Max and our other standard?'

I couldn't have four where I live, but I told her let me see how Max and I get along over a weekend as well as how he deals with Moses and Elle on a trial basis.

The guardian said he would be no problem: 'won't even get on our bed and we've been coaxing him to do this since a pup to no avail.'

Max was on my bed the first night and ever since – huddled against and protecting me ever since.

The Fort was now complete and the heart whole again…

Like their predecessors, Max, Elle, & Moses are there.

Always, there – for me.

They rely on me and I rely on them.

There is a third rail to this reliance – relying on veterinarians for the medical care – be it the primary care vet, specialists, and in an emergency – the Animal Hospital emergency care vets.

Managed reliance, yes; unfettered trust in the emergency room vets, no.

SUBSTITUTE RELIANCE

We give substitute reliance to professionals. That's what we pay them for.

And with reliance-transference to a professional there is the assumption of a higher standard of care than just *'caveat emptor'* (buyer beware).

Wrong. It's simply unfair to our animal companions to make this assumption.

In my opinion, systemically, (meaning "built-into" the system) the small-animal veterinary 'profession' is just another business. Their actions speak louder than their pontifications and marketing. Furthermore, the veterinary 'professional organizations' are simply trade organizations – protecting the interests of their members despite their brochures and marketing materials – flouting a concern for the guardian/owner and the best interests of their companion animals.'

The Madison Avenue Vets.

Mad Avenue Veterinarians.

> Things aren't what they seem. Skim milk often masquerades as cream.
>
> *Elsie*

The 2% award goes to the American Animal Hospital Association for their flaccid attempt at self-regulation despite their marketing and past web assertions to the contrary. If anything, the AAHA despite assertions of protecting the companion animal and the guardian's best interest from substandard medical care, has utilized, in my opinion, secrecy ('buried mistakes?') to protect offending veterinarians and animal hospitals.

And the self-regulation of vet hospitals as claimed by AAHA is at best porous. Here's an example: that microchip system that you dutifully purchased (which included the chip inserted into your pet along with the plastic identification tag to increase the probability of recovery should your pet become lost) has a major flaw in its total protection reuniting system. My experiences with Elle and Max will illustrate; difficulties aren't the exception, but unfortunately can be the rule. And, if you think your vet association and local and state governments have adequately prepared for Pet Evacuation due to the Federal PETS Legislation in light of the Katrina disaster – think again. (For example one Denver Post article of 10/13/2006 headlined, "Denver Receives F for Evacuation Procedures" – and that's for humans – now think about the preparation for companion animals!)

The purpose of this chapter is to illustrate that these are systemic problems and to offer my opinion as what to do to minimize your potential problems. Again, the era of the Dr.

Sam Leiters is over. *We* must manage our companion animals care. The retort, 'but my vet is different,' 'not my vet,' or 'I like my vet' are abdications of our responsibility. It is on your shoulders regardless of substitute reliance and warm fuzzy assertions by your 'friendly veterinarian.'

(Protect Your Pet from the Emergency Room Vet)

> Do not stand idly by at the blood of a neighbor"
>
> - *Judaic proverb*

I should have known better.

We had major screw-ups relative to an urgent care situation with Max by the CVES emergency animal hospital. To again utilize the same animal hospital was a big mistake on my part. Central Veterinary Emergency Service's owner/manager, in the prior incident, did refund over $400 for unnecessary/uncalled-for procedures – in an explicit admission of fault. And subsequently, the offending vet, though it will be denied or euphemized as 'personal reasons or other opportunities' left the practice (or was dismissed?).

The emergency vet failed to follow the protocol desired by my regular vet, which incidentally ran up huge additional costs. Evidence of culpability was a subsequent visit by this now-departed vet to apologize to my regular vet. It should be noted, another vet at my usual vet hospital indicated to me, 'and this was not the first time (difficulty with the veterinarian in question).'

The Situations in Question: The Failure To Supervise & The Course of (Mis)conduct?

In the wee early morning hours of 12/31/2005 I took Elle into the ER at CVES.

Elle was not herself. The presentational symptom was her back (she has mild dysplasia). However, she was quite okay – nothing acute. Unlike prior visits, the ER was empty: no triage was going on. There didn't seem to be a security problem. Nevertheless, I was not taken to an exam room. Rather, Elle was taken to the back and I was to stay in front reception area. (I didn't even get a 'biscuit' for my good stay.) Waiting and waiting, I finally buzzed. They stated they were not done with Elle's exam.

Now how can the ER vet do an exam without my detailed input? I know of Elle's history of eye problems, spay incontinence (rarely), her mild dysphasia and her medication protocol (though I wrote on the intake form her medications) This was contrary to past practices at the same ER room when they did not have triage, etc., going on. This protocol was unlike anything in my prior 20+ years of experience with dogs and emergency rooms.

Finally, I asked the vet to come out to the reception area. When questioned about this procedure she stated that she "has been at this practice for 2 months and it is always done this way." This was confirmed by another owner a few days later to Dr. Kris Abbey at Hampden Family Vet Hospital. So there is no question that this was not an isolated event but rather a standard of practice – or an alleged violation of standard-of-practice that the owners of this ER failed to supervise. (Proof: since this incident, the head of the ER, stated this practice was not the standard at the ER unless there was an acute situation or triage going on (none of which were happening during Elle's visit to my knowledge.)

Bad practice management (standards and procedures) often becomes mis-diagnosis/ mistreatment whether Vet Medicine, financial planning, CPA work, etc. Just because one makes a good marina sauce doesn't mean the restaurant will succeed.

The erstwhile ER doc (Dr. "D") had indicated that Elle had a 103.9 temp. She not only wanted to do x-rays (which I agreed to) but thought we ought to do joint taps for poly- arthritis which would have required anesthesia, plus lots of money. I could not understand her. I had that bad feeling. So, I agreed to come back in an hour after they were done with the x-rays ($340 with visit). In the interim I called another ER room to make provisions to get a 2nd opinion. (See page 147 –Email to Dr. Abbey)

Dr. "D" reiterated that Elle had a 103.9 temp (although again, I did not see the temp being taken). She gave me the x-rays and Elle and I went to The Animal Hospital ER for a second opinion.

Now typically a dog's temp will go up due to anxiety. So, if anything with another car ride – Elle's temp should have gone up.

At the animal hospital, Dr. Michaels, in the presence of a vet tech and me – took Elle's temperature.

101.9.

Without my presence: 103.9 at the CVES's ER room. In my presence at another hospital – just a half an hour later: 101.9.

Of course, the treatment prescribed was dramatically different. The point this anecdote makes: questionable practice management standards and a failure to supervise can become mis-diagnosis, mistreatment, and costly harm.

Subsequent Follow Up – "I've done all I can (will) do"

"Due to a breakdown in communication," I called the CVES owner to give him the chance to remedy the situation (failure to supervise and resulting negative effects on other dogs and cats) that may have occurred at his ER.

He indicated that he had sent a memo to all his vets and staff that the practice is to bring the patient <u>and owner</u> into the exam room – unless there was a triage situation. He indicated sometimes the vet "for their convenience" may not have done this (not allowed the owner with the pet) but no vet other than Dr. "D" was involved in this practice.

I made the Judaic proverb point above. And I suggested he do a sampling of outcomes relative to CVES ER's patients over the past 2 months. He refused saying that he couldn't do it and "I've done all I can do." He offered no alternative to follow up on Dr. "D's" patients (or others) during this period. He even refused a "phantom shopper concept" to audit the practice.

I consulted a known rehab vet in another state for her take on this situation (she had copies of the exhibits prior to discussion). The consultant wrote, "I would never personally do an examination without a medical intake first. Owners typically have enough intuition about the problem to help and can also help gauge a pet's response to painful stimulus during the exam. That is the first problem. The second one is Dr. "D's" attitude that this is the only way it is done. Medically I have to say that if she was given the information from a tech that Elle's temp was 103.9, and then on her examination she found multiple swollen joints, she could warrant the diagnostic plan she outlined, but the reality is, a Polyarthritis case is not emergent. She (Elle) should be treated for pain, and then referred to the primary care doctor. At least, that is what I expect of my local ER. I want the ER docs to make my patients comfortable, and to save their lives. Diagnostics to accomplish those are great, but not for non-emergent things. So for the ER doc to take hip rads and joint rads is ridiculous, as neither area is going to cause the immediate demise of a patient."

Lack of Recourse

AAHA's (The American Animal Hospital Association – located in Lakewood, Colorado) on its website relative to "pet owner complaints" states…"The Association strongly encourages pet owners and the directors of accredited practices to engage in constructive dialog regarding their concerns. In some cases, it may be appropriate to seek the assistance of trained mediators to facilitate such discussions. Again based on experience, client complaints to regulatory agencies (i.e. The Veterinary Board – jds), better business bureaus, or other organizations often do not resolve problems or result in a satisfactory outcome for either party."

This statement corroborates the ineffectiveness of the Colorado Board of Veterinary Medicine – which has a rate of license revocations averaging 20/100,000ths of 1% over the past 10 years.

According to the Colorado Consumer Protection Act, when "regulated professions" lose a lawsuit they are merely subject to damages – not even legal expenses. (Businesses are subject to treble damages plus legal for deceptive trade practices!) Veterinarian practices (including Vet Emergency Rooms) are "regulated professions."

Going To AAHA for Recourse:- Per AAHA's website and talks with their representatives, the AAHA is NOT an investigative body. Furthermore, AAHA refuses to release to the public its standards of accreditation to determine compliance or deviation from standards of practice and procedure. Thus, should one make a complaint, the results will be kept private by AAHA. Furthermore, AAHA states, "the number and or/nature of complaints against an accredited member that may be received, or even the existence of any complaint, <u>is a matter between AAHA and its members and is **not** made public</u>…A copy of a signed written complaint will be forwarded to the medical director of the accredited member practice. The original complaint will be placed in the file of the accredited member and will be available to AAHA's on-site evaluation staff at the time of the next regularly scheduled evaluation.'

So AAHA, the accreditor, judges in private, keeps the findings private, asks for complaints without making available the standards of care - and yet holds itself out as the Good Housekeeping Seal - so people can rely on its accreditation? Is this accreditation or veterinary hospital protectionism – a trade association masquerading as a professional organization?

Legal Action Resource: As stated previously, companion animals, by law, are property. They are depreciated property to boot, unless a show animal or stud animal. Thus, a lawsuit could easily cost often $10,000+ to realize maybe a few hundred dollars challenging this course of "professional" conduct. This is the principal argument for a law awarding serious money for loss of companionship damages. We are going after this (again) in Colorado in the 2008 session.

Substitute Reliance & Accreditation (Accruditation?)

> Choosing an AAHA accredited veterinary practice for your pet's medical care *assures you* that the practice you have selected has the facilities, equipment, staff, and *medical protocols* that AAHA believes are important for the delivery of high quality care. Further, voluntary commitment to the AAHA Standards and the Accreditation Program demonstrates that the practice has chosen to have itself measured by an outside organization against the most rigorous published Standards in the industry.
>
> *AAHA Accreditation taken from AAHA website www.healthypet.com*
> *1/4/2006*

Most lay people have come to the false perception that accreditation is an assurance of competency. And with this assurance of competency one can delegate with greater confidence – thus, substitute reliance.

And accreditors do little to dispel this false notion – implicitly encouraging accreditation to be akin to 'A Good Housekeeping Seal' of approval and competency.

But accreditation is *not* competency and thus, in reality, a *false basis* – for substitute reliance. Accreditation is about facilities and ingredients. (Inputs, not outputs; incomes, not outcomes). The assertion is that if an institution has the proper facilities and procedures (ingredients) the desired outcome will occur.

However, *just because one makes a great marinara sauce doesn't mean the meatballs and spaghetti platter will be palatable let alone get 4 stars*. Furthermore, just because one makes a great marinara sauce doesn't mean one can run a restaurant. A terrific engine is not, alone, reliable transportation.

The American Animal Hospital Association (AAHA), the accreditor of Animal Hospitals, refuses to even disclose the recipe for the marinara sauce (the ingredients, and procedures) relative to their accredited ER rooms.

In some cases (*of dispute between owners and the veterinary practice*), it may be appropriate to seek the assistance of trained mediators to facilitate such discussions. Again based on experience, client complaints to regulatory agencies, better business bureaus, or other organizations **often do not resolve problems or result in satisfactory outcomes for either party**.

AAHA Accreditation, Pet Owner Complaints from website
www.healthypet.com/about_complaint.aspx 01/04/2006

This from the AAHA, the trade organization of Veterinary Animal Hospitals, is an explicit indictment of the lack of value – worthlessness of the state Veterinary Boards!!!

So, while the AAHA encourages that it be the recipient of complaints from consumers if the parties can't agree (though, on the other hand they are not 'an investigative body'), they are discouraging using the Vet Board or other consumer complaint resources. However, they keep private the findings even from those complaining. The complaints and possibly findings merely go into the accused hospital's file until its next accreditation review — which may be up to three-years hence.

Furthermore, AAHA's site on 01/04/06 stated, 'the Association also reserves the right to conduct on-site evaluations of accredited practices at intervals shorter than three-years if, in the Association's sole judgment, circumstances warrant such action.'

Justice delayed is companion animals and their guardians denied??

The Emperor's Association has no clothes.

Or, as the Wendy's commercial went: 'where's the beef?'

> The number and/or nature of complaints against an accredited member that may be received, or even the existence of any complaints, *is a matter between AAHA and its members and is not made public*
>
> *AAHA Accreditation taken from AAHA website www.healthypet.com*
> *1/4/2006*

So, was Elle's incident an isolated anecdote or just another example of a systemic failure of accountability in the veterinary 'profession?'

Accreditation or Accruditation?

AHHA!! No laughing matter.

AAHA and not in the eureka sense!

Accreditation — assurance of competency, assurance of ingredients or merely a marketing, business development fluff, and protectionism for Vet Hospitals who pay their trade organization for the charade?

What to Do:

Before going to the ER vet:

1. Have a list of all medications the companion animal is presently taking

2. Have a prepared list of all the companion animal's illnesses and conditions

3. Take a note pad or tape recorder to the ER room with you (if not another witness) **Remember, we tend to do what is *in*spected not *ex*pected**.

Accreditation – assurance of competency, assurance of ingredients or merely a marketing and business development fluff for Vet Hospitals who pay for the charade?

One Canadian vet, Dr. Andrew Jones, (www.veterinary-secretsrevealed.com) has had the guts to offer e-books and multi-media courses to companion animal owners to (I hate this word) empower guardians in preventative care – which hopefully minimizes unnecessary ER visits. I look at Dr. Jones' work as useful to our companion animals and unfortunately necessitated by an insulated, smug, unaccountable small-vet business protecting its own. Of course, the vet association is now taking him to task and trying to shut him down! (This is what business cartels involved in collusion do – 'in the consumer's best interest' is the spin – not what professions ideally do. Follow the money!)

I hope other veterinarians will join Dr. Jones. (Our attempts to get even those vets who agreed about overvaccination protocols to put together a mutual defense legal fund met polite indifference (even from the Vets who have spoken out). There were no John Hancocks among <u>these all-talk-no-walk-our-talk vets.</u>) And sadly, despite their brave and vociferous complaints, even the holistic vets' modus operandi has been appeasement and collegiality at the end of the day. Deeds not words are what count, Vichy Vets!

The root, systemic problem is: little or no effective recourse to veterinary malpractice (including overvaccination, and the failure to supervise) as outlined in Moolah's story. Compounding the lack of accountability are the insulting, arrogant, deliberate pontifications by the e$tabli$hment veterinarian community about its own accountability (which is all hat and no cattle) whether it be the vet board, legal standing, or in this case the American Animal Hospital Association. And of course any attempts to create accountability for the e$tabli$hment veterinarian community are met with the standard deflection of: "you will increase veterinary costs due to increased litigation" – (overlooking the multimillions in unnecessary costs just due to over-vaccination, the physical harm of *adverse reactions*, and plain old heartbreak!!).

Pickin' A Vet & Minimizing & Preventing ER Room Problems

I wrote a personal financial life planning book, *ENOUGH*. In it is a chapter about picking a financial planner titled "Lullabys, legends, and lies" after the Bobby Bare song. This title was a compromise with the editors as I wished initially to title the chapter: "Pickin' a Planner or Pickin' Your Nose."

Now the typical advice in picking a vet – Credentials, Convenience and References – are the standard fare offered by pet writers. Not discounting these factors there are caveats. First, credentials are not necessarily an assurance of competency. As a fee-only financial planner, I had the tickets: magna cum laude in finance, MBA, writings, etc. etc. etc. Credentials are a proxy for competency and often a very weak hanging chad. (Schwartz theory – there is an inverse relationship between competency and elected position in professional organizations.) That aside, I gave my riff on my tickets. But, in time, when clients asked me about my credentials, my answer became, "my results."

Convenience is important but not at the expense of competency. The real question becomes then competency and availability (and not in the emotional availability per Dr. Phil.) (I've often thought that Eli Lilly, to bring Prozac back on patent, should buffer it with 'emotional bio-availability' but that's another story.) As you have seen from the ER episodes, although it is always available, ER is your last alternative. So the next question after competency (and possibly Prevention – see Dr. Andrew Jones' course website – www.veterinarysecretsrevealed.com) is: Availability – even in a non-acute emergency – rather than hours of operation.

When referencing a vet, people typically don't like to say negative things (even if they would like to.) So, a better first question might be: "would you recommend this vet?" (of course they would). Then your follow-up to the affirmative response: "how many people, then, have you referred to this vet?" "How many have you referred in the past year?"

Numbers speak louder than words.

So if we have gotten through Credentials, Convenience and Referrals, let's get to the questions Parade Magazine wouldn't ask, keeping in mind 65%-70% of all small-animal vet visits are for vaccinations, "the gravy of our practice" as one famous vet remarked to me.

Veterinarian Candidate Survey

Questions my pet wants to ask about your practice(s)

Yes No

1. Do you require my *informed consent* relative to the costs and benefits of the rabies vaccination as well as the parvo, distemper, and other shots?

    (This is a 'kill shot' question. In financial planning, I suggest people call the planner and say, "I have $10,000, or $100,000 or whatever to invest. What should I do?" If he gives a direct answer, hang up – he is not a planner – he is a stock, mutual fund, whatever jockey. Same goes here and with question #2)

    a. May I see a copy of your *informed consent* form?. If you don't have one, how come? (If the candidate does have one, compare it to the one provided in Moolah's chapter – that will tell you quite a bit about bedside manner versus legal liability!

    b. Do you give the rabies, parvo and distemper shot all at the same time? Have your colleagues, when these shots are given together, referred to the battery derisively as "the wombo combo" as do others in the profession? Have you wondered why? Would YOU like to be vaccinated in this way?

    c. Does your clinic utilize blood titers as an alternative to over-vaccinating? If not, why not? Do you have a clear understanding of the immunology involved?

Yes No

2. Does your clinic send out an annual reminder for shots? (If so, this means that the practice is cued off of shots – beware!)

3. Does the practice send out an annual reminder for an annual exam (in contrast - a good thing).

4. Does the practice have a formal wellness/preventative care program? Please provide a copy of the steps, etc., that this entails. (It is one thing to say they practice wellness/preventative care - another thing in reality. My experience is that most who say they have a wellness program are merely providing ear candy. If they show you a 3-ring "Wellness" binder marked with each pet's name – see if there is anything in the binder – no kidding!)

5. Do you feel your vet-school courses in nutrition equipped you adequately?

6. Have you taken post-grad for-credit nutrition courses?

7. Does your practice have a quota relative to any of the dog foods they sell in order to be able to get prescription dog foods from the manufacturer?? Please provide the answer in writing. (In the past, it is rumored that a certain 'over the hill' brand required a quota!!!)

8. What has been the turnover rate of dog and cat patients the past three-years? How does this compare to the turnover rates in other practices? (If they don't know their turnover rate, then there is a question of businesslike practice management.

SCHWARTZ'S LAW (whether it be a vet, legal, CPA, financial planning, etc., practice): BAD OR INEPT PRACTICE MANAGEMENT EVENTUALLY BECOMES BAD MEDICAL, FINANCIAL PLANNING, CPA PRACTICE...

Yes No

9. Do you offer holistic vet modalities (acupuncture, homeopathy, Chinese herbs etc)? If not, have you referred? To whom have you referred and what kind of cases? If not, why not? (This is to see how closed-minded the vet is - my way or the highway or you can have any color Ford you want as long as it's black.)

Tough – maybe – but your companion animal can't speak and you have little recourse after the fact. Remember the revocation rate average of vet licenses in Colorado over the last 10 years was less than 20/100,000ths of 1%. To put this in context, small-animal vets often act as doctors, pharmacists, and dentists. The revocation rates in these professions is 200%-300%-400% higher. There is one variable – your companion animal can't speak. You must be his mouthpiece.

You want to be liked or you want your companion animal to be given the best?

What happens when you don't have time to carefully "vet" your vet?

Elle's anecdotal ER experience

A story in e-mails

Date: Sat, 31 Dec 2005 04:28:55 -0800 (PST)
From: "james schwartz"
Subject: URGENT FROM JIM SCHWARTZ: ELLE POODLE
To: Kris Abbey, DVM, Elle's regular Vet

Kris:

Elle was whimpering around 1:30 AM. Unusual.

She was sitting down a lot.

So I gave her a coated aspirin and did the Equilight (low emission photon therapy) for 20-25 minutes.

While the whimpering stopped - she did not go her usual place on my bed and was restless.

So I took her into the CVES emergency room (with trepidation after my last go-round with them)

I DON'T HAVE ALOT OF CONFIDENCE IN DR. "D".

1) unlike my previous visits - they would not allow me to be with Elle during Exam.

when I asked if this was for security reasons, the answer I got was, "I've only been here 2 months and that's the way it is."

2) She did the full exam without a medical intake. It was only after I waited and waited that I called them in the back. Then she took the intake - but again I was not allowed to be with Elle.

3) I gave her the intake of the following besides the presentations symptoms:

Medications - 1/2 ppa at night for spay incontinence (which they first treated her for as a pup!)

- *1000 glucosamine*
- *1 drop right eye cyclosporine daily, 1 drop twice a week left eye*
- *one del-immune*
- *I brought the fatty tumor medication we talked about to show her*

I told her of Elle's mild dysplasia

4) finally she came back and said Elle had a 103.9 temp - that hadn't gone down.

She said the right hip showed discomfort and in the lower part of her back.

She said there appeared to be a bit of fluid in some of the joints - but that this is subjective

5) Dr. "D" then went through a litany - without stop - of considerations

As I write I have ok's 4 x-ray shot front and whatever
But she also wants to consider after the x-rays for poly-arthritis - joint taps that would require anesthesia - and blood work.

I AM NOT CONFIDENT IN HER AND I AM UNCOMFORTABLE HAVING ELLE UNDER ANESTHESIA WITH HER, KRIS. I DON'T HAVE A GOOD FEELING ABOUT THE VET.

I was going to wait till Saturday morning to take Elle to Hampden Family - but I got the recording saying you would be closed on the 31st

I will call you around 7 AM - I am so sorry - but I appreciate your giving me your number for an emergency like this. I'll get the x-rays as well.

Please advise. I'm going back to CVES now - it is 5:30 am...I just want to get Elle through till I can see you or Melanie Monday. I would even be glad to take her to another emergency place - I just don't have confidence in this Vet.

jim schwartz

Date: Sat, 31 Dec 2005 07:08:26 -0800 (PST)
From: "james schwartz"
Subject: FOLLOWUP ELLE FROM JIM SCHWARTZ 7:44 AM
To: "Kris Abbey2"

Kris:

I went with my gut - and transferred Elle for a second opinion over to Animal Hospital Center.

Upon discharge at CVES - even Becky the receptionist was perplexed at why I couldn't go into the exam room with Elle. She thought maybe they took her right back to back. I asked her if it was a security question. She didn't know of any security problem to let an owner into an exam room.

Also, Kris, there were no other patients at my intake time.

So to recap, she was taken to exam - without me - examined at first without any intake from me on her medicals - until I rang the bell to ask what was going on - asking for the vet (who then in the reception area took down the medicals- and then went "back" to finish the exam.

Dr. "D" reiterated since she had been there (two months) it had always been that way.

The bill was $340 with xrays. She reiterated <u>that Elle's temperature was 103.9 and had not gone down</u>

After scaring and confusing the Hell out of me, her instructions read "the x-rays show moderate hip dysplasia and arthritis in both hips.. There are no changes in the spine or the carpus. I am still concerned that the fever may indicate another underlying problem such as polyarthritis. Further diagnostics would include a complete blood count, chemistry panel, urinalysis and joint tap (**Kris, she wanted to anesthetize Elle). If you decide not to pursue any further diagnostics at this time then I would consider placing Elle on pain medications and an antibiotic called doxycycline. You can discuss this with the veterinarian at Animal Hospital Center and/or your regular veterinarian."

I saw Dr. Michaels at the ER of Animal Hospital Center.

She was great.

I watched as they took Elle's temperature (rectal) - in the exam room as they examined Elle.

101.9 - taken anally - NOT 103.9 - (not more than 30 minutes later).

She did a very thorough exam moving joints, etc., while I was there. She did suggest possibly upping Elle's glucosamine to 1500. And thought acupuncture would be a good idea.

So Dr. Michaels was another $100 versus what $500-$800 for all these other things Dr. "D" wanted on the basis of 103.9 (which I was not allowed to be in the exam room to see...)

I think (the owner) needs to know. I will say the receptionist who came on when I came back for Elle – (Becky) was excellent.

As you recall the episode with Max two years ago - the care of ER over there was questionable and they made good reimbursing on Max.

I had an overwhelming feeling in my gut - relative to Dr. "D" - and that I had to get a second opinion. And for once I listened to my gut.

I think (the owner) needs a talking to - not just from me (though this is the second unpleasant experience - that both have a common element too - lots of dollars - in Max's case unnecessary - and in this case avoided though the 'initial exam' in my opinion was worthless - or thermometers are off. But as far as excitement - Dr. "D" said no because a) "if anything the aspirin should have lowered the temperature" and b) the temp was taken "and didn't go lower" at least 1 1/2 hours later.

Because they previously made good, I gave this ER a second chance. I was wrong. I shall not use them again...

jim schwartz

Date: Sun, 1 Jan 2006 16:58:26 -0800 (PST)

From: "james schwartz"

Subject: Information Request To Register Complaint about Member Hospital's ER Policies & Procedures

To: info@aahanet.org

AAHA

Please advise of the procedures to register a complaint relative to the course of conduct of a member's ER services and protocol.

What is the procedure - as well as the procedure for auditing the ER's adherence to policies and procedures relative to standards?

What are the avenues of recourse within AAHA relative to it's standards for certification.

Thank you.

Subject: ER & CC AAHA Standards

Date: Tue, 3 Jan 2006 12:30:20 -0700

From: "Elise Atkinson" <elise.atkinson@aahanet.org>

To: manofdog01@yahoo.com

Dear Dr. Schwartz,

I received your email about the ER & CC standards. We are putting the finishing touches on the new versions. As soon as I have them available I will send them to you. Do you have a copy of the latest AAHA Standards of Accreditation CD with the sled team on the cover? That new CD will be a part of any specialty accreditation evaluation. I would be happy to send you the CD now if you do not have it already.

Sincerely,

Elise Atkinson, BA, CVT
Practice Accreditation Coordinator
AAHA

Date: Tue, 3 Jan 2006 13:56:59 -0800 (PST)
From: "james schwartz"
Subject: RE: ER & CC AAHA Standards
To: "Elise Atkinson" <elise.atkinson@aahanet.org>

Ms. Atkinson

No, I am not a member.

But I do have a complaint to register relative to standards of practice in an emergency room - and need to know the criteria for accreditation - to be sure of the complaint's validity

The VCES has yet to respond to a request - which I find of some concern as well.

Please let me know if AAHA does or does not make available standards of practice in accreditation for Emergency Room practices.

jim schwartz

Elise Atkinson <elise.atkinson@aahanet.org> wrote:
Hi Mr. (or is it Dr.) Schwartz,

Are you currently a member of AAHA? I could only find you listed in our data base under J D Schwartz and Co. We currently only send our AAHA standards CD to practices scheduled for an evaluation. I am sorry that I automatically assumed you were an AAHA member. If you are a veterinarian or practice owner I need to direct you to our Members Services Center and they will send you a more comprehensive packet. I am sorry to sound confusing.

Sincerely,

Elise Atkinson, BA, CVT

Practice Accreditation Coordinator

AAHA

Subject: RE: AAHA complaint process - Clarification needed from Jim Schwartz

Date: Thu, 5 Jan 2006 14:59:03 -0700

From: "Mary Brussell" <mary.brussell@aahanet.org>

To: "james schwartz"

Jim:

While AAHA does have standards for our members, many of the procedures and protocols that a hospital follows are individual to that hospital. What works for one hospital may not work for another hospital.

If you wish to file a complaint it is then AAHA's job to process the complaint per our protocol and determine whether a standard has been violated.

While AAHA is a voluntary association, the CVMA (Colorado Veterinary Medical Association) is the regulatory agency in Colorado. If you have not already done so, you may wish to contact them.

Mary

Date: Thu, 5 Jan 2006 14:35:39 -0800 (PST)
From: "james schwartz"
Subject: RE: AAHA complaint process - Clarification needed from Jim Schwartz
To: "Mary Brussell" <mary.brussell@aahanet.org>
Ms. Brussell

Your response seems inconsistent - contradictory.

On one hand you indicate that

"While AAHA does have standards for our members, many of the procedures and protocols that a hospital follows are individual to that hospital. What works for one hospital may not work for another hospital."

So it appears that AAHA does have ER standards of practice but you have not forwarded these to me as requested.

This is not an acceptable response to me. I would be complaining in a vacuum - why would AAHA not provide the standards relative to the question I posed???

Then you state "What works for one hospital may not work for another hospital." This would indicate a voluntary relative nature - rather than a standard of practice.

The vet board (your recommendation) is of little value. As I hope you know, Ms. Brussell, in the past 10 years, the average revocation rate of vet licenses in Colorado has been 20/100,000ths of 1% - making vets 8300% purer than Ivory Soap. Furthermore the revocation rate of human docs, dentists, and pharmacists (all capacities vets operate as) are 400%-600% higher.

So, I would prefer to exhaust the process with AAHA - in light of AAHA being one of the leading lights in the question of overvaccination and three-year protocol - rather than pursuing my other options.

Thus, I ask you to reconsider and provide the standard of practice for ER and or Critical Care for accreditation - relative to intake of a patient - in a situation that is without trauma, where the clinic is not busy, nor there is a security issue.

In this case, the ER - which was empty, the dog was not in any trauma - would not allow me to go with the dog into an exam room - to give background info. Furthermore, I had to buzz - to get the vet to come out to take the information. The vet commented that she was not done with her exam. (This dog had several problems and medications she needed to be made aware of). Since in previous visits to this ER room, I had been taken with my dogs to an exam room to wait for the vet, I asked, "was this a security problem?" The vet answered, "no." Furthermore, I reiterated past experience, and this vet indicated, "I've been here 2 months - and this is the way it has always been done since I've been here."

(My own vet has had another owner corroborate that this is the practice of the ER - and the other owner was furious.)

Now this statement "I've been here 2 months - and this is the way it is," indicates a standard of practice by the ER Practice - unless the vet on duty has unilaterally imposed her will - without the knowledge of the practice (which would also indicate a failure of the duty to supervise.)

Furthermore, she indicated a 103.9 temp - which in picking her up an hour later was per the vet 103.9. (She was prescribing besides x-rays which I approved - doing anesthesia to do joint taps).

I took her from this ER to another ER for a second opinion. They did their exam with me there with the dog. If anything, 30 minutes later - a new ER etc - the temp should have gone up. The temp was 101.9. I was there.

Questionable practice management - whether in law, accounting, medicine, financial planning - too often becomes bad medical, financial planning, legal, accounting, and ER veterinary misdiagnosis.

There would have been a whole lot of unnecessary work up - costly - and possibly at risk for the dog - had I not got a second opinion.

Therefore the standard of practice per AAHA standards of practice for ER and critical care - is critical to know about.

I ask for the specific code and standard detailed.

I hope you will reconsider.

If you choose to not forward the standards of practice I request, I would like to know the reasoning for having these standards - which are unavailable - and a complaint process that hides the standards from the public. After all, what good is a good housekeeping seal of approval - or being one of the select 14% that receive AAHA accreditation - if the minimum standards of practice are hidden unavailable to the public - the accreditation supposedly seeks to protect?

jim schwartz

Tel/con with American Animal Hospital Association

1/9/06 AAHA BS

Automated message from AAHA. "Thank you for calling—all lines are busy at this time. If you know the extension of the person you are calling please press 1". Another automated message: "The mail box you have dialed is inoperative. Please hold for the Operator." Background music plays. A live operator answers, "American Animal Hospital Association, Mary speaking, how may I direct your call?" JS: Yes, Mary Brussell? Operator: Okay, one moment. JS, Thank you.

MB: This is Mary may I help you.

JS: This is Jim Schwartz; we've been in correspondence by email. Yes, Mary I was a bit confused by your letter in that you would not provide the standards of practice for the ER that you go through. May I ask how come?

MB: Well, the standards are for the veterinarians industry only, for the veterinarians and veterinarian hospitals.

JS: But how can you judge—when I read your complaint process, whether I have a valid complaint relative to your standards—if I don't know what the standards are to check them to begin with?

MB: Well, as I mentioned in my letter if you submit a complaint then it would be up to the protocol to then see if there was a standards violation.

JS: But that's in a vacuum. Why—I still don't understand? By the way, I've gotten a hold of them through a third party and they are in violation, but that is not usual and typical in associations that they will not provide their standards of care for minimum accreditation. Can you tell me why?

MB: Umm—that's just how the protocol was set up here with this association. No, I can not tell you why, I didn't create the protocol; the board of directors did.

JS: Well, this will make very interesting reading. So, in your website, you state, you suggest that you do not go to the vet board, which is useless or the other places, yet you suggest going to resolve it if you can't with the vet, to your board and then you won't make known the protocols for which to judge if they have been violated or not. That seems like a catch 22. Am I incorrect?

MB: Well it is all there. If you want to submit a complaint, it will be handled by protocol. It would just need to be in writing. I don't know what else to tell you. I didn't come up with this protocol; it was the board of directors.

JS: Who is the head of accreditation overall and for the ER rooms now?

MB: Excuse me?

JS: Is there a section head, for example, head of accreditation and then a subsection head of accreditation for ERs?

MB: Well, all the standards accreditations were created by a taskforce by other veterinarians.

JS: OK so they're—MB interrupts

MB: Well the taskforce—they're no longer, I mean they've been unsettled because the standards have been in effect.

JS: OK so there is no standing committee at this point. Is that correct?

MB: Yes.

JS: Okay–That's disheartening. What your telling me because– you read the situation; it's been corroborated and it's been going for on at least two months at this veterinary hospital.

MB: Well, again you can submit a complaint in writing and I don't even know who the hospital is so I can't even look to see if they are accredited.

JS: They are accredited.

MB: Again, I don't even know who it is so I can't tell you anything.

JS: Yeah if–MB interrupts

MB: If you want to submit something in writing then you've got–JS interrupts

JS: Who does it go to Mary?

MB: Everything's in that website, it goes to our membership audit and control committee.

JS: Audit and control committee?

JS: Well, it seems that it's more of a cartel to me than it is to protect the public when you won't release the standards. I have the standards but other professional organizations don't do that and—

MB: I can't answer for other organizations.

JS: You can't answer for anything is what you're telling me. Appreciate your time. Thank you. Hangs up.

Now, changing the subject –

as problematic as is the professional accountability of the

veterinary emergency room –

disaster preparedness

for your companion animal is much worse

Disaster Dissing-Preparedness

(PETS – The Pets Evacuation and Transportation Standards Act signed in October of 2006 by President Bush)

> So far (only) <u>11</u> states including Florida, Illinois and New Hampshire have reworked their disaster plans to accommodate this new law which requires municipalities to include companion animals in their disaster plans
>
> **OR RISK LOSING FUNDING"**
>
> *Dog Fancy,* **<u>June, 2007</u>***, p.43*

> <u>44%</u> of Hurricane Katrina's victims were those who chose to stay behind because they were not willing to abandon their animals
>
> *The Not for Profit Fritz Institute Study*

> <u>2/3rds</u> of American Households have dogs and or cats – <u>2x</u> as many as have kids.
>
> *Bob Vetere, President of the American Pet Manufacturers Association, Newsweek, 'The Pets We Love & Drug,'* **<u>April 16, 2007</u>**

In light of Katrina and the then-recently-passed Federal PETS Act (Pets Evacuation and Transportation Standards Act ((S.2548)) passed in large part due to Katrina and people staying with their companion animals), I made over 16 calls to local authorities in **<u>July of 2006</u>** as to where to take my dogs in case of a natural disaster.

As of this writing in **early 2008**, I still don't have an answer as to where the provisional locations for shelter or 'co-location' (where both companion animals and humans) should go in a natural emergency. Furthermore, Denver's crack TV 'investigative reporters,' all made aware of this situation, have chosen to ignore it. One, whom I tolled the days -20, 40, 60, 180, 360 days with no answer, continues to email me back with 'thanks for keeping me up to date' but no action.

The Denver TV local media indifference continues despite a Denver Post article of **October 13, 2006** which headlined 'Denver Receives F for Evacuation Preparedness.'

The rating was *59.8 out of 100* by the American Highway Users Alliance's 2006 Emergency Evacuation Report Card.

59.8% is 'partial proficiency' for the wretched Denver Public Schools', but 59.8% is an abysmal flunk for disaster preparedness for humans.

If disaster preparedness is this inept for humans, then what is it for companion animals?

59.8%?????

> As some day it may happen that a victim may be found
> I've got a little list, I've got a little list
> Of society offenders who might be underground
> And who never would be missed
> And who never would be missed
> *Gilbert & Sullivan, The Mikado 'I've Got A Little List' (KoKo)*

The PETS Act requires 'the provision of essential assistance for individuals with household pets and service animals, and themselves, following a major disaster' according to the Humane Society of America's reporting of the Act. And in particular, local and state authorities must submit these plans in order to qualify for grants from the Federal Emergency Management Agency (FEMA).

All I wanted was a list – which I recognize could change depending on the nature of the disaster at the time – of the provisional locations to which I might take my dogs.

In a two minute web search in <u>**July of 2006**</u> I found that Jackson County, Wisconsin, posts their plan (see Exhibit 19) – and locations. California, after the Northridge disaster, posts their plan of <u>1997</u>. Furthermore, California's CARES (California Animal Response in Emergency System) plan states that such animal preparedness is necessary because:

- Up to 25% of pet owners will refuse to evacuate because of their animals; this represents 5%-10% of the total population directed to evacuate.

- The individuals who refuse to evacuate, or attempt to return to the evacuated areas because of their animals, risk injury, exposure to hazardous materials, and their own lives, as well as those of emergency response personnel who must rescue them.

- *Animals that are not cared for by their owners during a disaster may become a public health and safety risk.* Loose and displaced animals are possible carriers of disease and can become a nuisance or danger to people.

- Another public health and safety risk is the presence of animal carcasses. Decaying carcasses can contaminate water sources or lead to <u>*outbreaks of diseases such as cholera or anthrax.*</u>

And what has been the local, county, and state response in Colorado since <u>July of 2006?</u>

Talk to and talk to and talk to – blame each other, blame lack of funding, blame the legislature, finger point, and finger point.

All I wanted was two damned locations.

I've called Arapahoe County Animal control (remember them?). They said they are working on it, blamed everyone else, but said they are working on it. I called the Arapahoe Sheriff's office. They referred me to animal control (who had provided Centennial City Councilperson, Betty Ann Habig, with a 40-page document – without any lists of locations!) I talked with Centennial's city manager who referred me to Denver Dumb Friends League – who had no idea. I called the American Humane Society and couldn't even get past the automated phone system. I chatted with a Dr. Heckendorf (these people blend into each other in a sea of red tape) who was either with the state or the state vet association – and his comments made red tape blush. And on and on and on – 'and see and see and see – it's not in my authority…'.

Finally, I got a hold of Emily. Emily works for a Dr. Kevin Dennison of Colorado SART (Colorado State Animal Response Team). Ever notice the <u>more</u> acronyms, the <u>less</u> achievement and (com-PET-ency)?? (Exhibit 20)

Emily was 'understanding' of my frustration but was a blamer par excellence – blaming the legislature, the state, the localities, the Red Cross – and of course, lack of resources. Finally, after 30 plus minutes she stated a couple of salient points:

- They won't designate places to locate or co-locate humans and companion animals as the nature of the disaster will dictate those locations.
- However, most probably, the locations would be fairgrounds and shelters
- All the Federal government requires is a plan which can be a sheet of paper that says we have a plan....

At least 30, maybe 40, man hours, and now over a year, and this is the state of preparation?

In my erstwhile calling as a professional business and personal financial planner, the theory of "we have no provisional planning" would get one fired. And the foolishness of not having provisional locations is accentuated by the fact that in a disaster, without preplanning, the increase in phone calls would jam lines, increasing frustration – right when anxiety should be calmed, not increased. Furthermore, why has Jackson County, Wisconsin, have deemed provisional places of importance (in <u>July of 2006</u> when I Googled) but the City of Centennial, Arapahoe County, the State of Colorado and the Colorado Vet Association feel provisional locations are not necessary?

Talk to the paw, latte swilling paw-PET-traitors

Well, Dr. Dennison did call after my 30 minute call with Emily (Emily at one time asked if I was a reporter – to which I responded in the negative – but maybe that's what finally got Dennison (who wasn't 'available' previously) to call, 20 minutes later.) He did the same old soft shoe – playing the victim, blaming, finger pointing. And just 'coincidentally' Ms. Thea Thompson of Arapahoe County then called after failing to return 4 or more of my previous calls. <u>July 24, 2006</u> must have been my lucky day. I should have bought a Powerball.

But still no list.

And still no media response to this situation despite emails which tolled the days since inquiry and no response now over one-and-a-half years.

> There are good reasons and then, there are real reasons
>
> *Ellis Schwartz*

Then, in late January of 2007 , I took an emergency-care course for companion animals. The <u>following</u> <u>email</u> explains the real reason behind the lack of preparation in providing provisional locations and co-locations for humans and their companion animals. To prevent retribution I have removed the teacher's name…

Date: Mon, 22 Jan 2007 11:47:36 -0800 (PST)

From: "*james schwartz*"

Subject: *Systemic Veterinary Malpractice Overvaccination: Katrina Proof*

To:

Systemic Veterinary Malpractice Overvaccination: Katrina Proof

Saturday, I attended an emergency first aid class taught by 10-year veteran of animal disaster response, who has worked with state and national disaster planning committees

I was the only attendee.

XXX, who is either on the S.A.R.T. board which 'coordinates' disaster relief for companion animals or consults with it, revealed the real reason now – almost 8 months later, why S.A.R.T. still has not provided me with two locations for my dogs to go to (whether co location or not) and despite the passage over a year ago of the Federal PETS act.

The reason: SART's policy is that they won't know where to send the companion animals until the disaster hits.

> *(Now I have spent thirty years in planning – whether business planning or personal financial planning –and it is true, the best laid plans often go astray. But the alternative, no plan in place – is a default to chaos as there is no basis line. This <u>non</u>-approach to planning is a prescription for chaos and reaction rather being proactive and prepared.*
>
> *This is pure reckless systemic stupidity and incompetence with absolutely no justification.*
>
> *Of course, if this is the status of companion animal disaster 'preparation' and planning, one can only wonder about the state of <u>human</u> disaster planning in Colorado.)*

The same CVT, CPDT also related her experience relative to her hands-on vaccination experience during Katrina relative to companion animals.

If a dog or cat did not have a current vaccination tag, they were immediately hit with a combination shot for rabies, parvo and distemper.

Now, the course of conduct in non-emergency veterinary vaccination (to which we are vehemently opposed) has been to give the same dosage to small dogs as large dogs. Thus, the Taco Bell Chihuahua at 6 lbs gets the same rabies dosage as Scooby Doo (at 90 to 120 lbs) during normal non disaster veterinary vaccination practice!

Yet, during disaster, the standard of practice – during Katrina – was to give full dosage to Scooby Doo but only half dosage to the Taco Bell Chihuahua! One might argue that this practice was due to a lack of adequate supplies. But if anything, this would make the point that for regular vaccination protocol, where there is no disaster, only half dosage is required.

In effect, like the vet's changing their protocol to 'customization' two or three-years ago under pressure, would not this half dosage protocol (like 'customization') be an implicit admission of normal, daily, hourly standardized harmful malpractice – compromising the health and life of companion animals for over 20 years? And per the Hill Consulting Research study in 2005 showing 62% of the public not aware of the three-year option on rabies and 79% of veterinarians still giving the annual rabies shot despite legislative passage of the alternative 7 years prior, compounded by veterinarian's canon of ethics requiring informed consent, is this not additional prima-facie proof of small-animal veterinarian deliberate, systematic malpractice due to the profession's addiction to shots to economically sustain their practice?

Semper Fido

Jim Schwartz, *A Man of Dog*

So we see how even the lack of emergency preparedness compounds the overvaccination issue!!!

And I still have no list – 18+ months later.

But, I am making preparations for having a place at least 20 miles from where I live – in case of an emergency – be it friends, a shelter, or a fairground.

And that is not comforting, PAW-PET-TRAITORS....

> FURTHER RESOLVED, that the American Bar Association supports the principle that emergency preparedness plans should take into account the needs of individuals with household pets or service animals as an essential part of the response to any disaster or emergency situation.
>
> *ABA-TIPS Animal Disaster Relief Network*

American Kennel Association Recommendations for Disaster Preparedness

Proper emergency planning can help save the life of your pet. The American Kennel Club has prepared the following checklists to help pet owners pack a portable pet first-aid kit and prepare for an emergency evacuation. Preparedness is important in any disaster situation and these checklists can be applied to any emergency that calls for evacuation from your home.

Evacuation Checklist for Pets	Portable First Aid Kit for Pets
Dog medicine(s), i.e. heart worm, flea, ear mite medicine, etc.	Water-proof storage container for kit
	Antiseptic/anti-bacterial cleansing wipes/Alcohol prep pads
Dog Bowls	Eye wash
Dog Food (1-week minimum, 2-week suggested), dog treats, etc.	Eye and skin wash in one
	A sock (foot wrapper)
Can opener	Latex surgical gloves
Leashes: walking leash, short leash	Electrolyte powder (add to water on hot days)
Harness (to attach to seat belt)	Emergency space blanket
Extra dog tag, (masking tape, laundry pen) Cell #, Hotel # and Room #	Small flashlight
	Bottled water
Pet records stored in waterproof container or plastic sealable bag	Medicated balm
	Leash and collar
Crate	Soft muzzle
Dog bed/blanket/toys	Speak to your vet about what to pack in case your dog has a sudden allergic reaction
Supplies/Paper towels, rug cleaner, toilettes, towels, flash light	Flexible bandage
Current dog photograph(s) with your notification information: useful for fliers should your dog go missing or must be left at shelter	Gauze roll
	Bandage scissors- to cut gauze and to clip hair around wounds
	Wood splint
	Paper towels
Dog friendly hotel listings/ telephone lists	Plastic baggies
Shampoo	Small cold pack and hot pack (self activating)
Litter/portable litter pan	Cotton swabs
Duct tape	Antibiotic ointment/packets
Bottled water	Tweezers
Pet First Aid Kit	Space for copy of dog's papers & vet records (sealed in plastic bag

More important information may be obtained online from the following very reliable sources: The Humane Society of the United States (www.humanesociety.org) and the American Red Cross (www.redcross.org/services/disaster/0,1082,0_604_,00.html).

A Final Word From the Red Cross

If you must evacuate, do not leave your animals behind. Evacuate them to a prearranged safe location if they cannot stay with you during the evacuation period. (remember, pets are not allowed in Red Cross shelters.) If there is a possibility that disaster may strike while you are out of the house, there are precautions you can take to increase your pets' chances of survival, but they are not a substitute for evacuating with your pets. In a statement of understanding, The American Red Cross recognizes The Humane Society of the United States as the nation's largest animal protection organization responsible for the safety and well-being of animals, including disaster relief.

Identification – life-saving necessity for your pals

All of the preparedness information we have provided – and you accomplish – is pretty much worthless if during an emergency your pet is not in your custody or cannot be identified. There are several ID products on the market but the micro-chipping system you may be relying on might just let you down.

Micro Chipping – Worthwhile but A Materially Flawed System

A lost companion animal is a guardian/owner's nightmare.

Accordingly, we tag our pets for identification. There are even USB tags (www.**toptagpetid.com**) which can be purchased today that will not only give the typical contact information, but medications as well as other relevant information about our pets.

But tags get lost.

People go on vacation and the phone number of tags may not be useful in that event.

Some use tattoos. But many people who find a lost companion animal don't know of tattoos except on Carmelo Anthony – to locate info to reunite the dog or cat with its guardian.

So the advent of the microchip (inserted under the anima's skin) was a godsend – as, unlike the tag, it couldn't be lost, negating the potential for identification. And, if one prevails on the microchip service, one can change the phone number relative to the tag when on vacation and then change it back.

Typically, an addition to the information on the microchip, to be placed on the companion animal's collar, is also provided.

In my case, the provider's (HomeAgain) number is molded into the tag (1-800-252-7894).

(Point of note: there is some spotty evidence of harm such that one should not insert a chip at the time nor site of vaccination.)

However, the inked identification number of the pet on the tag rubs off or wears off easily – rendering this part of the identification system worthless.

Why is the plastic tag on the collar important when there is a chip already?

Obviously, people finding the lost dog or cat first, have to know about the chipping system, AND have a clue that the pet might have one. Then, secondly, they have to have the presence of mind to find a shelter or an animal hospital which can check out the chip. Otherwise, this blurred back-up tag is worthless to the good Samaritan in locating the pet owner.

Upon inspection, all of my dogs' microchip tags were blurred beyond recognition. And upon surveying some friends who had the microchip implanted in their pets, we found not one of the tags was legible.

Not one.

Nor do I nor any of those I surveyed recall being told by the installing veterinarian of an option to buy an optional "stainless" steel identification tag that would not smudge. The plastic collar tag with microchip kit was standard.

Home Again advertises on their website that it has over 4 million companion animals chipped and that over 363,000 pets have been recovered.

Chipping is admirable and worthwhile, but it turns out the total delivery system could be easily improved, greatly increasing the probability of recovery.

The real concern is that the good Samaritan who recovers a pet with an illegible chip ID tag will do the right thing. Those finding may or may not know to go to a shelter or vet's office to scan the chip for identification. The odds are intuitively overwhelming that the vast majority of people finding the pet are not vets or shelter people. By providing a collar tag with indelible data (even at a higher cost, ±$8 additional which would come down with volume and being the standard kit), the odds are the recovery rate would be higher.

How to enhance the probability of pet recovery for your "chipped" companion animal:

First, it turns out, that these chips can burn out. *Therefore, yearly, at your pet's annual physical have the chip scanned to determine its functionality.*

Secondly, double check the chip service's data base. It turned out Home Again couldn't locate my dogs per their numbers and had the dogs' names misspelled. Also, tag each pet's chip input with any medications and medication alerts if possible.

Third, order the stainless steel tags imprinted with your pet's chip ID number (thereby minimizing the illegibility factor.) Home Again has advertised that this option is available but the vets I've contacted were not aware of this option from Home Again until very recently.)

Fourth, consider a separate tag that has an 800 number to allow you to change phone numbers, cell numbers as the circumstances warrant – as a backup especially in light of my not isolated experience with HomeAgain's data base. Yes, the tag could be lost – but this is a backup anyway.

Chapter VII – Ricki

Re-calling

SLICK 'RIC'
A Pisser and A Privilege (1986 – 2001)
She was 'a lot of me.'

Known for putting on the dog, Ricki specializes in dog earring limited partnership prospectus'. The 'Uptown Pooch' has a face you could write checks to. 'The Maltese Fashion-Hound' never doggie bags it. Motto: It's not the height of the dog, but the fight in the dog

> Though she be but small, she was fierce
>
> *Shakespeare*

6'4", 220 lbs of twisted steel and sex appeal in an 8 lb Maltese body.

Named for "Slick" Ric Flair – 16 time, 16 time, 16 time World Wrestling Champion (considered the greatest professional wrestler of the modern era)

Stylin' and profilin' yet she had a face you could write checks to!

(Or, she would gladly accept –Visa, MasterCard, and American Express!)

Ricki was defiant: "you talkin' to me?...talk to the paw... have your people talk to my people."

Her website: www.biteme!.com

She was a master of 'the stink eye' (metaphorically speaking).

My father would have called her a 'shtarker' – a 'Susie Brent.'

Ricki was a pisser and a privilege.

The same compliment a NY Times columnist gave me.

Ricki would rear up her tuchass in a game of Frankenschwartz with me. With paws down, she'd challenge me with a soprano guttural "aggrrrhhh" (making Captain Morgan's utterance sound weeniesque). I'm told, when younger she'd get on my top desk howling when I was gone, only to walk away from me upon my return.

I was her staff.

She had me on a short leash.

Forget Croce's 'Don't Mess With Jim," – you don't tug on superman's cape, you don't spit into the wind, and you don't pull down the mask of the Lone Ranger – and you don't mess with Ricki.

Trachea, patella, back problems along with increasingly frequent 3-4 second seizures, and advancing age finally took their toll – but not without a fight with the Roberta Duran of dogs. It took 2 dosages of enough valium for a 70-pound dog to finally sedate her, before I helped her soul graduate from her body.

Ricki, the Maltese That Roared – a pisser and a privilege.

Ricki was a lot of me.

Ricki was a mind reader.

She knew when she was going to the vet's office.

She would shake.

Not the wet shake coming in from the rain (effected typically within a foot of my presence – talk to the paw!) but an indisputable nervous shaking (even Superman had his kryptonite.)

Regardless of route to the vet, direct, indirect, circuitous – somehow she knew.

And she would shake.

She knew.

And they say dogs don't know!

And now, I know, with good reason.

> ## MAJOR PREMISE – OR, WHAT RICKI TAUGHT ME
>
> To satisfy the revenue requirements of their prevailing, systemic economic model, the small-animal veterinarian community (including those vets who ever-so- faintly raised their voices, choosing to maintain solidarity with their colleagues rather than raising Hell) continue knowingly and deliberately to harm companion animals by over-vaccinating due to their prevailing economic model.

She shook.

She knew.

The small-animal vets knew and have known.

I guess it was from the anaphylactic reaction she had (before I knew of the problems of over-vaccination) back when she was a puppy! (She would, subsequently, require a shot before the annual rabies shot!!)

Yet, the violating small-animal vets have had economic amnesia forgetting their ethics, oaths, and that first spark or calling when, at an earlier time, they knew they wanted to become veterinarians.

And Ricki, the Robert(a) Duran of dogs, pound for pound, regardless of route to the vet, would shake.

Memo: Last Call: The Re-calling

To: The Small-Animal Veterinarian Business

> I got principles. You don't like these principles? I got other principles.
>
> *Groucho Marx*

Once upon a time...

Each had it...

Each veterinarian-to-be, had it...

The calling...

The calling probably started with his or her first pet

That dog he or she will always remember

That forever dog – the per-pet-tual kitten....

... that gave them the itch to scratch

To become a veterinarian

(despite the math and science requirements!)

But after 4 years of college, four years of vet school, there were:

- college loans,
- getting the first job as a vet – and enduring the older, bored veterinarian
- and then opening the practice and overhead - $5,000, $10,000, $20,000 or more per month for a receptionist, equipment, insurance, supplies, etc
- before he could even pay himself let alone the college loans

And of course, these costs didn't include the exigencies of a family.

Taught in vet school of the horrors of rabies, parvo, and distemper, the veterinarian-to-be learned that vaccinations were a good thing for the companion animals and their guardians. But, he would become frustrated by the lack of caring by many owners. Like other vets, he would state that he was "challenged" to educate the guardian to get his dog or cat in for an annual exam. The required-by-law (prior to 1997) annual rabies vaccination shot reduced (though it didn't eliminate) this 'challenge.'

Vaccinations were not only a good thing for the dogs and cats but also good for the practice. Often the vet was giving away services to those who couldn't afford them, and the shots (the required annual rabies shot in particular) became "our gravy" as one nationally known TV veterinarian stated to me. With a markup of up to 14,000% (the cost of a rabies shot is approximately 60 cents, retailed at $20-$40 + $35-$45 for the required office visit), that shot covered a substantial if not all the overhead and the give-aways, being as much as 70%-150% of the gross profit.

So, the dogs and cats needed the vaccinations, and the small-animal vet needed the vaccination business model to sustain his practice.

Vaccination appointments now constitute 63%-70% of all the visits to the small-animal veterinarian. The appointment solicitation is queued into the computer system, tickling the reminder card to be sent annually to owners.

But then 15 – 20 years ago, the question of over-vaccination of rabies shots and the growing incidence of *adverse reactions* started infiltrating the veterinarian professional literature.

Ignored at first as the ramblings of crazies, the incidents of *adverse reactions* to vaccination increased as well as the drumbeat against this practice – first with collegial dignity by other vets between themselves and then by angry owners. Controversy became denial which became "because I and the state said so" defensiveness. In reaction, faulty statistics were employed purporting to show that only 1 in 10,000 pets had an *adverse reaction* to the annual rabies shot – stats which were all self-reported by the vets. Finally, a few vets came out of the collegial closet ever so gently and then, years later, begrudgingly, veterinarian schools, associated veterinarian institutions, etc., began invoking questions of companion animals' health and the carte blanche advisability of the annual rabies shot (admitting that there is no <u>science</u> to support the annual rabies shot.)

In response, veterinarians and their veterinarian associations often became shrill in disagreement with ad hominem attacks on those proving the adverse effects of overvaccinating (especially with the annual rabies shot.). Independent studies of 1000 dogs and 1000 cats showing 7.5%-12%+ *adverse reactions* within 45 days at the 99% confidence level – were dismissed as the work of kooks. Even when veterinary schools suggested a compromise (the three-year protocol), the tenured professors were attacked.

And the defensive, ad hominem pejorative responses continued despite articles published in veterinary-practice management magazines. They showed how practices had not only survived but also throve without the vaccination shot model. But these alternative practice models were by-and-large ignored – just like the *adverse reaction* statistics (one reaction in 10,000 vaccinations, etc.) which now even the American Veterinarian Journal's findings cite as faulty at best.

And at the end of 2005 in Colorado, almost 6 years since the rabies statute was amended to allow a three-year option for the rabies shot, a survey conducted by a nationally known polling organization showed that 79% of Colorado vets still administered the annual rabies vaccination. And they did so without *'informed consent'* – violating an ethical canon of their own American Veterinary Association.

Vaccination, thought once to be a good thing, became a practice of harmful over-vaccination, defiance of the spirit of the law, and a violation of the canon of ethics of *informed consent*.

What was the vet, faintly remembering that forever dog or cat, to do?

> Reasons create laws and then the reasons change but the laws don't
>
> *(Faulkner, I think)*

Change.

We love change – we just hate to be changed.

"And, the only people that like to be changed are wet babies," said Don Robinson.

But change cannot be denied – even by mischaracterization, pejoratives, words of mass deflection and changing the subject.

Change is inevitable.

And the changing of the prevailing small-animal veterinary business model from that of a shot-transaction-model is a must – for the health of companion animals, to restore trust in and reliance on the professional veterinarian, and for the long-range economic viability of the veterinarian's practice.

Better the over-vaccination dollars (and the consequential costs of *adverse reactions*) be spent on a preventive care and wellness business model for companion animals. These veterinarian business models exist and have been described in vet practice literature for 10+ years.

> "Between the idea and the creation, falls the shadow,"
>
> *TS Eliot.*

The shadowy practice of overvaccination must end.

It is time to re-call that original calling.

It is time to re-call that forever dog or cat's memory.

It is time to remember the calling of why one became a vet.

Already introduced to the Colorado General Assembly is new animal protection legislation, **"The Companion Animal Act of 2008"**, House Bill 08-1308, based on the myriad of information to which I've tried to expose you.

Politically, the most important information is probably that there are, as of 2006, more than THREE MILLION dogs and cats in 1 ½ million Colorado households. The pets can't vote, of course, but their guardians CAN VOTE. And that's the political force up against a group of veterinarians numbering fewer than 3,500 – who DON'T WANT CHANGE!

Veterinarians must accept that they can no longer promote expenditures of time, money and emotional energy by owners (on care), and then when something goes awry simply say, "Oh well, tough luck Mrs. Jones. It's just an animal under the law.

> Animals are merely personal property; therefore, you may not collect damages for your loss, other than the market value of your pet.
>
> *James Wilson, DVM, author of 3 editions of Legal Consents for Veterinary ctices*

Changing the legal status of licensable companion animals and assistance animals from "mere property" to "living property" makes the law consistent with today's mores and recognizes the sea-change in our nation's cultural attitude toward the treatment of our pet animals. It also brings forth recourse and protection akin to other professions, and reinforces the veterinarian's duty of care.

The veterinarian associations have fought any reclassification of companion animals. The AVMA in a statement by its executive board (May of 2003) wrote the following resolution:

"The American Veterinary Medical Association promotes the optimal health and well-being of animals. Further, the AVMA recognizes the role of responsible owners in providing for their animals' care. Any change in terminology describing the relationship between animals and owners *does not strengthen this relationship and may, in fact, diminish it. Such changes in terminology may decrease the ability of veterinarians to provide services and, ultimately, result in animal suffering."*

I kid you not. This means that the vets believe that if pets are called "companion animals" or their owners are called "guardians", the vets won't be able to take care of the pets any more and the pets will thus be harmed. I'm wondering how many clients, knowing their vet is committed to this kind of thinking, would even WANT his pet to be seen by such an "professional"?

More: Ralph Johnson, was the Executive Director of the Colorado Veterinarian Association in 2003 and still is. After 'dodging the bullet' of Colorado HB1260 (killed in committee – would have provided up to $100,000 of loss of companionship damages), on July 20, 2003, in his presentation "Legislation Regarding Recovery of Non-Economic Damages in Veterinary Malpractice Suits" to the American Veterinary Medical Legal Association in Denver, Colorado, stated:

"(The profession needs) to lead the way in developing a resolution to the issues…A proactive approach has its risks, certainly, but so does an approach that is solely reactive… (our group has) made no decision yet about formulating and advancing a specific bill (but) we're doing our homework."

Johnson's dog must have eaten his homework in 2003 as the 'homework' has yet to be found since or as of this day in early 2008 – <u>almost 5 years later</u>

Justice demands that the small animal vets cannot be "like a pediatrician" professionally protecting "the human-animal bond" on one hand, and then plead when it comes to liability that they are akin to a garage mechanic. (No offense to garage mechanics.)

If they have no more fiscal responsibility than garage mechanics, who really do deal with your "mere property" – then professional status should be lifted making the veterinarians subject to the Colorado Consumer Protection Act; that law provides treble damages and legal fees as relief to the aggrieved, versus mere damages and no legal fees where the negligent party is a member of a "regulated profession."

Disengenuousness.

Betrayal of the trust of substitute reliance.

Contempt of the law.

Contempt of their own canon of ethics (informed consent).

Our bill, the Animal Companion Act of 2008, sponsored by Representative Deborah Stafford, provides for damages up to $100,000 for loss of companionship when a pet is harmed, reclassification as 'living property' (in the sense of 'duty of care'), and full disclosure of all subsequent malpractice awards (just like we have for physicians in Colorado).

The law would also provide:

- Holding harmless a vet who, based on experience and education in immunology, and in the best interest of the animal, refuses to vaccinate any given companion animal, and reports to any animal licensing authority that such vaccination is contraindicated; such authority shall accept such a report in lieu of vaccination.

- Re-composing the Vet Board to 4 Veterinarians (1 traditional, 1 integrative, 1 academician, 1 nutritionist, for example) and 3 consumer reps (representatives to replace the "vampire-guarding blood bank.")
- AN AFFIRMATIVE DEFENSE in the case of overvaccination if the vet can prove that the procedure was done with the *informed consent* of the guardian.
- Calling for Mediation or Arbitration of complaints before going to court.

Political Ramifications of such a bill:

- 3,000,000 dogs and cats in 1,500,000 Colorado households versus 3,500 veterinarians – the animals can't vote – will their guardians?
- 65%-70% of all Colorado households have a dog or cat (TWICE as many as have children!) – 48% have multiple dogs and cats – certainly enough voter/guardians to influence a close election.
- Our proposal is for Animal Protection rather than "animal rights" ala PETA whackos – will legislators get the difference?
- Confers a "kinder, gentler" persona upon lawmakers seen as unsympathetic or uncaring (pets have always been darlings of public policy)

What would Ricki (whom her vet continued annually to vaccinate, despite her annual response of anaphylactic shock) – what would my Ricki do?

She'd shake, give them the stink eye, then squat, pee on their shoes, and say, "talk to the paw."

The fate of HB 1308 will not be known before this book goes to press, but previous experience suggests that supportive legislators will have their work cut out for them. There are no or few precedents in other states, but Colorado has been cutting-edge on some subjects – perhaps this will be one of them. The un-enfranchised pet companions hope so.

I miss you, Ricki.

It's time to remember that fur-ever dog....

(Incidentally, Ricki's last weeks were so difficult that I promised myself to work up some kind of planning device which would help you to make that final decision. The result is Exhibit 21) .

Chapter VIII
Caller ID: Holy Moses – My Youngest K9 Star of David

Moses Buchman.

My maternal grandfather whom I never got to know.

He died at the age of 56.

I wasn't even one yet.

Lore, family legend has it that Moses (Moe) was to be a rabbi succeeding his judge rabbi father and grandfather in Lithuania.

But America was calling.

Moe became a shopkeeper (Buchman's) on Main Street in Indiana, Pa., catty-corner from Stewart's Hardware (as in Jimmy Stewart fame.)

Lore/legend has it that he had a green thumb – even growing Kentucky blue grass in Western Pennyslvania.

Lore/legend aside – both sides of the family spoke well of Moe. (The ninth miracle.)

Moe Buchman.

Well, that really wasn't his given name.

When Moe came through Ellis Island the registrar asked his name. Moe didn't quite understand him and said, "Moses, bookman."

The scribe, piercing Moe's Yiddish. wrote 'Moses Buchman.'

Only recently did I find out his name was Halperin.

Lore and legend.

I hated Hebrew School – in particular, Har Zion's Hebrew School in West Philly. There were only two good parts to Sunday school. First, my dad would take me to Linton's for breakfast. We would talk about the Phillies with Paul the waiter. And second, being picked up after school by my father and going to Aunt Martha's and then Bubbie and Poppie's. The tour was always good for a dollar – and another 50 cents if I would sing 'Oh, My Papa' imitating Eddy Fisher. (At 6 I gave up the song when they would not meet my price of $1 – due to inflation.)

That's about all I remember and got out of my Hebrew school education including my Bar Mitzvah at Har Zion.

We went twice a year to High Holiday Services (aka The Fashion Show.) I didn't understand the services, they were boring as Hell, and I'd rather look at my Richie Ashburn baseball card.

My father always wore to services his good Hamilton watch, the one with the cover. As the services dragged on, I would alternatively ask him the time and how much longer or pull up his watch from his wrist, opening the lid to find out what time it was. I am probably responsible for the first recorded incident of carpal tunnel syndrome.

When I asked my mom why one has to go to services and Hebrew School to be a Jew, she replied, "You don't. As your Grandpa Moe used to say, 'Judaism is in your heart, your home, and how you conduct yourself.'"

I was 8.

One Sunday afternoon, almost 45 years later, I was going into Petco and saw these two standard poodles on leash, one white and the other black: Max. Turned out Max' breeder was Jill Cole, in Larkspur. And Jill's champion girl had just dropped a litter of standard poodle puppies.

Now I had been on Jill Cole's list for three years – so I called.

Because of the oversight and my Jewish guilt embellishment, Jill gave me the pick of the litter – Moishe (Moses) named for Grandpa Moe.

I gave Jill a couple of my shirts to give to Moses so he would know my smell when I would come to get him in six weeks. When my friend Senator Fowler and I arrived at Jill's fence, the puppies – three white and one black – were in the yard. The black one turned around and ran to me, circling my legs, running back and forth between my legs, and finally into my arms as the others watched.

That was Moses.

(And he still runs between my legs at 75 lbs to this day!)

Every day Moses, Max, and Elle teach me Judaism is in one's heart and actions. Especially 4 years ago when I was going through radiation for T1 larynx cancer. (I never smoked.)

Before retiring nightly, the bed lineup is as follows: Elle – right side bottom (where Moolah would always situate herself – must be a female thing), Max – by my left side, and Moses lying velcro against my right side with his head snuggled initially against my shoulder. Once the radiation treatment commenced, Moses would lay his head ever so gently on my neck.

Not every night – but seemingly on the nights with the most discomfort.

And when the radiation treatment was over, he stopped laying his head on my neck. (In the morning after going out, Moses and Elle jump back on the bed, both laying their heads across my chest – facing me. Max waits his turn!)

They say that Moses Buchman – Moses Halperin – had a green thumb. He could grow blue grass in Western Pennsylvania

– my relatives and his former neighbors would say as if it was a minor miracle.

Just a dog?

Or furry miracles.

Ambassadors from God.

My dog, Holy Moses –- another K9 Star of David – worthy of Moses Buchman, Moses Bookman, Moses Halperin – the grandfather I never met.

No dog before his time.

Semper Fido(c)

Epilogue

> I am I because my little dog knows me
>
> *Dorothy Parker*

Unlike Rocky, Hoosiers, October Sky – there is no heroic triumph to conclude these stories. There is no small-town team winning the Indiana State Championship, nor a former bone-breaker down on his luck becoming the heavyweight boxing champion, or a rocket boy from a depressed coal town in West Virginia breaking out to become a NASA scientist.

This is where we are:

- There is still rampant over-vaccination without *informed consent*
- Guardians are generally unaware of vaccination risks
- The legislatures are still unwilling to recognize a new cultural status for pets
- Pet's cemeteries are still not giving back your pets remains
- You still can't buy really affordable, convenient major medical pet health insurance without games
- There still remains an overall lack of accountability in the profession supposedly protecting our Ambassadors from God.

I wish that were not the case.

My dad (Ellie Schwartz) died when he was 60. I was 15. Though a very smart man, he had but an 8th grade education. After being a very successful shoe salesman rep for Sundial shoes, he got the entrepreneurial urge. Unfortunately, unlike his shoe endeavors – nothing went as well for him. Finally, he settled down being a part owner, with his brother, of D.E. Regan Co. Regan was a regional distributor for Young's Rubber Co – Trojans.

It sounds more glorious than it was. He worked his tuchass off. He was up at 5, on the road at 6:30 AM and not home till 6 PM every evening including Saturdays as a traveling salesman. And then on Sundays – it was time to do the books. And then the cycle began again.

I could tell when he was coming home. It was three backups into the space in front of our row house on Brentwood Rd. And then he would drag in, bring in 'the books,' read the Evening Bulletin with dinner and fall asleep on the couch, except on Sunday.

On Sunday, ritually, he and I would watch *Meet the Press* with Lawrence Spivak. And weekly, he would point out to me what today we call spin, half truths / whole lies, and reiterate over and over again, "don't be a 14-carat phony, don't be a 14-carat phony!." And then my mom, Rhea, would chime in, 'have the power of your convictions.' These were their 'drive by' naggings.

5 AM to 6:30 PM 6 days a week, coaching me via the *Meet the Press* on Sunday, all so his sons could have a better life – and the college education and the choices he didn't.

To paraphrase a Judaic parable, it seems another man daily dutifully dragged his tuchass doing his chores. Balancing two pails of water across his shoulders, each day he went down to the well to fill these buckets. Yet as he returned to his house after this routine, day after day, he would notice to his chagrin that one pail was full and the other empty.

Finally after a couple weeks, in disgust he realized there were tiny holes in the right pail. "Shmendrick, (pisher – someone of no importance)," he said condemning himself. His pail had failed. Worse, he felt he had failed.

The next day, instead of balancing both pails on his shoulders, he just walked down to the well. He noticed something odd. On one side of the road down the middle of which he walked daily were just grass and some dandelions. On the other side, there was lush greenery and every flower imaginable.

That side of the road…had been watered by his 'faulty' pail.

In Judaic thought, the question is asked: who is a hero? A hero is one who overcomes his limitations, restrictions. It is claimed that if you move 1/8" against your limitations, restrictions, the Almighty will move the other 7/8". The Judaic Exodus from Egypt (mitzraeim in Hebrew which means 'restrictions, limitations, narrow places') is also a metaphor today for each of us to leave our slavery of habits, restrictions, limitations, narrow places – 1/8" at a time.

The flowers on Shmendrick's path are the 1/8" – one dog at a time.

For more than 15 years, the collegial debate between a few vets and the majority of vets about vaccination has been going on – in journals, in meetings and their associations, etc., with little progress at best or to little-or-no avail at worst. And with the caution of not confusing correlation with causation, it just seems when we at Next-to-Kin Foundation

A. connected the doc$$ relative to over-vaccination and the vet's economic business model, and
B. pushed for landmark (though defeated) legislation, and
C. built a website "hit" by thousands of pet pals, and
D. did some local advertising which caught the attention of the *Wall Street Journal* in a front-page article,

NOW,

E. many states (49) have the three-year (economic compromise) vaccination option,

F. all twenty-seven vet schools prefer the three-year protocol and the AVMA is begrudgingly pushing 'customization' (vet discretion) of shot protocols, and

G. there is even a movement to 5 to 7+ years on parvo and distemper vaccinations, and some say they are good for a lifetime, despite denials to the contrary and statements that the 'changes were already in the works.'

BUT, to date, there is no Seabiscuit beating Man o' War in the match race of the century, no Cinderella Man (James Braddock) recapturing the heavyweight crown rising from the depths of the depression and welfare.

NEVERTHELESS, there are a few more flowers on the roadside – and 1/8" at a time – saving one dog at a time - from our leaky pail.

It's now up to the small-animal vets to move the other 7/8", recalling their own 'fur-ever' companion animals.

***

Shalom, Dad and Mom for your drive-by naggings on Judaic ethics.

Shalom, my co-pilots of the 'Rider of the Heavens,' Moolah, Buddy, Nicki, Ricki: thank you for giving my soul a way: to make loss matter - no dog before his time.

> Dogs are not my whole life, but they make my life whole.
>
> *Roger Caras*

EXHIBITS

Exhibit 1

RABIES VACCINATION CERTIFICATE

Owner: Schwartz, Jim   Pet's Name: Moolah
         Englewood   , CO 80111

Canine, Male, Yes   Pet's Birthdate: 09/01/89
Breed: Poodle, Standard   Color: Black

Date of Vaccination: October 29, 1999

1 Year Vaccination

Vaccination Type: Pfizer   (Defensor I)

Rabies Tag No.: 99-216005

Vaccinated by: ......*Earl C. Wenngren DVM*............ DVM

              Wenngren DVM, Earl

(Rabies Vaccination Certificate)

Exhibit 2 –Moolah Health Record

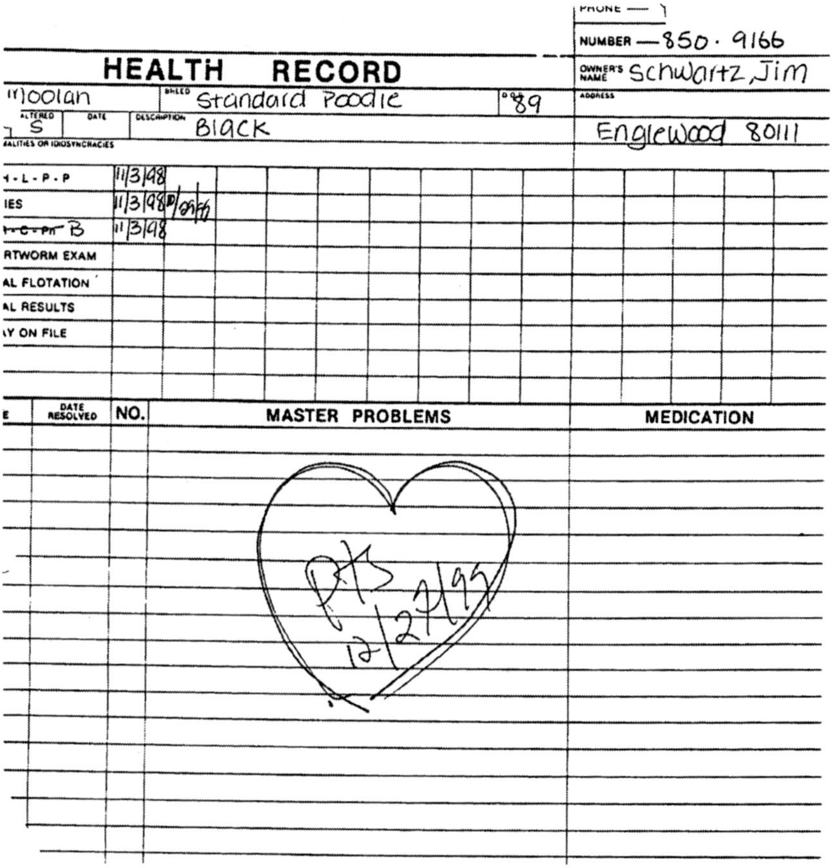

PHONE NUMBER — 850 · 9166

HEALTH RECORD

OWNER'S NAME Schwartz, Jim

Moolah — BREED Standard Poodle — '89

ADDRESS

ALTERED S — DATE — DESCRIPTION Black

Englewood 80111

…ALITIES OR IDIOSYNCRACIES

…-L-P-P	11/3/98	
…IES	11/3/98	
~~…-C-PI~~ B	11/3/98	
…RTWORM EXAM		
…AL FLOTATION		
…AL RESULTS		
…Y ON FILE		

…E	DATE RESOLVED	NO.	MASTER PROBLEMS	MEDICATION
			PTS 12/27/95	

Exhibit 3a – Mayor Pye letter, pg 1

Centennial
Colorado

Randy Pye
Mayor

Doug Milliken
City Treasurer

Claudia Cygnar
City Clerk

CITY COUNCIL

Dr. George Gatseos II
Ward I

Betty Ann Habig
Ward I

Becky Lennon
Ward II

Bart Miller
Ward II

Jack Forhan
Ward III

Andrea Suhaka
Ward III

Alan Fletcher
Ward IV

Betty Wotring
Ward IV

April 3, 2001

Mr. Jim Schwartz
Centennial, CO 80111

Dear Mr. Schwartz:

In regard to your many emails and the recent ads you purchased in the Centennial Citizen about animal vaccinations, specifically dog vaccinations, and their possible over-use I have spent considerable time investigating the facts so that I may respond in a prudent and responsible manner.

Let me first say that I too am a dog owner and take the concerns you have stated very seriously.

In researching this matter I visited with a number of people and organizations. I have come to the belief that your actions while well intended might be misdirected.

The Colorado Department of Public Health and Environment was very helpful in pointing out that under Colorado law, 25-4-607 C.R.S. 1973 as amended they clearly delegate the authority to enact mandatory rabies vaccination laws to local jurisdictions and the responsible **Public Health Officer** for those jurisdictions. In Arapahoe County and Centennial it would be the Tri-County Health Department.

I spoke with Mr. Bruce Wilson at Tri-County Health and he referred my attention to their Regulation II-99, Section 2 that states that animals shall be inoculated in accordance with the provisions of the "Compendium of Animal Rabies Control". In reviewing that document, under Part I, titled **Recommendations for Parenteral Immunization Procedures, Part B – Vaccine Selection**, it states in part "only vaccines with a 3 year duration of immunity should be used". I asked Mr. Wilson if under those guidelines it is required that only 3-year vaccines be used? He clearly stated that these were only **recommendations** and that it was up to each veterinarian to make the choice between 1 and 3 year vaccines or using both.

I then asked him how veterinarians were notified of the recommended change to 3-year inoculations since it is Tri County Health's charge to oversee the program. I was told that it was done through a variety of different venues. They are as follows:

City of Centennial
7777 East Arapahoe Road, Centennial, Colorado 80112
303-734-4567 FAX 720-488-0933
www.centennialcolorado.com

Exhibit 3b, Pye ltr, pg2

1. State-wide contact through the "Compendium of Animal Rabies Control" as published by the National Association of State Public Health Veterinarians, Inc. This is the compendium accepted and used by all veterinarians.

2. Through their office, Tri-County Health which notified:
   a. Colorado Veterinarian Medical Association
   b. Denver Area Veterinarian Medical Society
   c. Colorado Association of Animal Control Officers
   d. Colorado Federation of Animal Welfare Agencies

All legitimate veterinarians are members of one or more of the above and it is Mr. Wilson's belief that all were notified by at least one of the above and all are well aware of the recommendation for a 3-year vaccine.

I also inquired if it was harmful to inoculate a pet with a vaccination on a yearly basis? I was told that it was not *if* it was a 1-year vaccine which many veterinarians still use. I was also told that while the verdict is still out, because of a lack of scientific data, there is increasing concern of using a 3-year vaccine annually.

I then contacted Ms Thea Thompson at Arapahoe County Animal Control Department and asked their procedures for issuing licenses and what they required of vaccinations. Ms. Thompson told me that they accept 1 **or** 3 year vaccinations. In order to get a license you must present a current vaccination certificate. If your veterinarian has inoculated with a 3-year vaccine it must be stated on the certificate or in a letter from the veterinarian. She stated that this is the only way they can track which vaccine was used.

I have asked both Ms. Thompson and Mr. Wilson how I would know if a veterinarian was inoculating my pet with a 1 or 3 year vaccine? Both told me that since both vaccines are legal, it is up to the pet owner to inquire if they have a concern.

I also asked what to do if I only want my pet inoculated with a 3-year vaccine and only every 3 years, but my Veterinarian insists on inoculating annually? I was told that as a responsible pet owner and a consumer of services, that I should change to a veterinarian that is willing to follow my wishes but also under any circumstance I should still have my pet examined annually.

I believe that both agencies, Tri-County Health and Arapahoe County Animal Control have done what their agencies are required to do and I believe it would be impossible for either agency to notify every veterinarian in and outside of Arapahoe County as you have suggested. I believe that Mr. Wilson has used prudent judgment in notifying the variety of associations and societies in order to get the word out.

In regards to the responses you received from both Council Members Lennon and Miller. Your use of their responses out of context is detrimental both to your credibility and to their attempt to convey the reality of the current situation within the city. As elected

Exhibit 3c, Pye ltr, pg3

officials we don't have the luxury of responding to an issue with widespread impacts without at least doing some investigation on both sides of the issue.

I suggest that your time and attention might be better directed to veterinarians, since that clearly seems to be the ultimate decision maker on what vaccine is used. You might wish to continue your emails and any advertising media you feel appropriate that will also notify the public in general. That is where I believe it will do the most good.

As for myself, I will be inquiring of my veterinarian as to the vaccine he uses and how often. I believe that is what is incumbent upon myself as a responsible citizen and pet owner.

Thank you for your correspondence on this matter and I wish you the best on your quest.

Sincerely,

Randy Pye
Mayor

Cc: Council
Tri-County Health – Mr. Bruce Wilson
Arapahoe County Animal Control – Ms. Thea Thompson
file

Exhibit 4- Arapahoe County Animal Control Statement

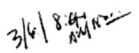

3/6/1 8:44

Here is the list of Vets that Arapahoe County Animal Control has contacted reiterating that we do indeed accept 2 and three year rabies vaccinations for licensing and bites.

Date	Vet	Phone	Contact
02/28/01	Animal Hospital Center	740-9595	(strictly a hospital/no longer gives rabies shots)
02/28/01	Alameda East	366-2639	(Connie Roberts/Director)
02/28/01	Broadway Estates	795-2584	(Lori)
02/28/01	Evans East	757-7881	(Holly)
02/28/01	Heritage Place	770-3320	(Cindy)
02/28/01	Seven Hills	699-1642	(Caralee)
02/28/01	Smoky Hill	693-2020	(Diana)
02/28/01	Tenaker	850-9789	(Lori)
02/28/01 *	Tendercare	689-9500	(Penny)
02/28/01	Wingate	771-8620	(voice mail)
02/28/01	Woodlawn	795-5065	(Shauna)
02/28/01	Southeast Area	751-4954	(Danelle)
02/28/01	Animal Clinic at the Festival	850-9393	(T.J.)
02/28/01	University Hills	757-5638	(Brittany)
02/28/01	Homestead	771-7350	(Tina)
02/28/01	Pet Palace	699-0477	(voice mail)
02/28/01	Piney Creek	693-3133	(Sara)
02/28/01	Rocky Mt. Small Animal	347-2637	(Michelle)
02/28/01	Cherry Hills	730-3248	(Dawn)
02/28/01	Columbine	979-4040	(Karen)

- Tendercare Vet Clinic is the clinic Unincorporated Arapahoe County contracts with to provide medical treatment for our stray and injured animals.

If I may include one last thought, Unincorporated Arapahoe County Animal Control does not and has not (to my knowledge) ever insisted that a dog be vaccinated. We have many animal owners in our jurisdiction that have provided us with a letter from their vet advising us that the dog for whatever reason cannot receive a rabies shot and we license their dog. Back in '99, we, as in years past and to date, only request the dog have a current rabies vaccination to license a dog. Those people who were new to our license program at that time were requested to have an attachment on their rabies certificate that stated that the vacine that was given was a two or three year vacine so it would be duly noted.

Exhibit 5 – McKelvey, DVM, letter

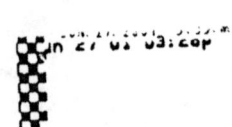

Date: 6/25/2001
To: Sabra L. Chandler
From: Rocky McKelvey D.V.M.
R/R: Rabies Vaccinations in Colorado

I would like to respond to the questions you submitted to Dr. Winton last week. The issue of not only rabies, but all vaccinations is a hotly debated topic in the profession at this time. Every journal article that you read has a different "expert" suggesting a different protocol and frequency of vaccination. The recommendations you cited in your questions are just that, recommendations. The stance of the AVMA has been to get more solid research under our belts before we make sweeping changes in vaccine protocol. We fully expect those changes to be announced at the upcoming AVMA meeting this July. As a company we have chosen to "err" on the side of conservative medicine until we can see some solid evidence to change our recommendations. In Colorado the recommendations for vaccine frequency are actually on a county-to-county basis so that blurs the issue even more.

Traditionally veterinary medicine has marketed itself by recommending yearly "shots". We as a company have been getting away from that philosophy and putting more emphasis and cost on the exam and less on the vaccine itself. We are in the process of changing the wording on the annual reminders to reflect this change in philosophy. Unfortunately at this time most reminder systems track when it is time for your pet to come in for it's annual check-up based on when vaccines were given. The thing we want our doctors to be stressing is the overall health and well being of your pet through things such as routine pain management procedures, pre-anesthetic lab testing, Senior Wellness exams, and more thorough diagnostic medicine. I am sure you will be seeing changing in vaccine protocols in the near future to reflect AVMA guidelines, but remember the overall focus will be on preventative medicine through a yearly physical and needed lab tests for your pets.

Thank you for your questions,

Rocky McKelvey D.V.M.

Regional Medical Director Southwest Region

6/25/2001

Exhibit 6a – Wall Street Journal Article – pg 1 of 2

Are Annual Shots Overkill?

THE WALL STREET JOURNAL. 7/3/02

For Some Pet Diseases, Yearly Boosters Are Based On Tradition, Not Science

By RHONDA L. RUNDLE

Testing Animals' Immunity Level

AFTER RECEIVING a reminder in the mail from his veterinarian, Jim Schwartz took his 11-year-old poodle, Moolah, for her annual rabies shot. A few weeks later she fell ill and was diagnosed with an autoimmune disease. As her suffering worsened, Mr. Schwartz put her down.

There's no proof that the rabies shot killed Moolah and Mr. Schwartz didn't immediately suspect any link. But when the retired financial planner learned that some veterinarians are vaccinating pets less frequently because of possible fatal side effects, he was furious. "No dog should have to go through what Moolah did," he says.

Evidence is building that annual vaccination of dogs and cats—performed for diseases such as rabies, distemper and parvovirus—may not be necessary and could even be harmful. Vaccines licensed by the U.S. Department of Agriculture are tested to ensure they protect pets against disease, usually for

Please Turn to Page B4, Column 3

OWNERS anxious about annual vaccinations can ask their veterinarians to check their pet's immunity to certain diseases.

In the past, most such tests were costly and had to be sent to an outside laboratory. If they indicated that a dog or cat wasn't protected, the owner had to bring the pet back for vaccination.

But a new 15-minute blood test, called TiterChek, can help determine if a dog is protected against two of the most common, life-threatening diseases: canine parvovirus and distemper. The test, made available in May, is the first of its kind to be approved by the U.S. Department of Agriculture, which licenses animal vaccines.

The kit is made by Synbiotics Inc., a San Diego veterinary-products company. It includes a total of ten tests that detect antibodies against both diseases and is being sold to vets for $125, or $12.50 per test. Synbiotics says it plans to develop immune status tests for cats, probably for feline leukemia and rabies vaccines. Just as vaccines don't bestow 100% protection against disease, tests like TiterChek aren't 100% accurate.

Still, Michael Dutton, a veterinarian and owner of Weare Animal Hospital in Weare, N.H., says the new TiterChek can help him and his clients determine which pets need a booster.

"There's been a lot of discussion about whether we are over-vaccinating a certain population of pets," he says. "We really don't know how long the vaccines work."

Dr. Dutton says he is charging clients $30 for the new in-office TiterChek test. That's less than half his $64 charge for the lab tests, which take 10 days and require mailing specimens overnight in ice packs. That's still more expensive than a $10 vaccination, so Dr. Dutton thinks demand will be small, at least initially. "Most clients have opted for the vaccine because the chances of having an adverse reaction are very, very small," he says.

Older kinds of lab tests can also determine whether pets need a booster. (For a list of major vaccine titer tests available go to www.antechdiagnostics.com)

— *Rhonda L. Rundle*

Exhibit 6b – WSJ article, pg 2

Vets Rethink the Need for Annual Pet Vaccinations

Continued From Page B1

one year. But the tests don't detect long-term side effects, or measure the duration of a vaccine's effectiveness. Recent and continuing studies at several universities suggest that protection from vaccines may last for years, which would make annual shots for some diseases a waste of money—at the very least.

Fears of vaccine-induced diseases date back more than 40 years. But a sharp increase during the past decade in cancerous tumors among cats, between the shoulder blades where vaccines typically are injected, has spurred studies. Some have found a higher-than-expected incidence of side effects. "We see health problems in dogs for which we have no explanation. The classic one is autoimmune disease," says Larry Glickman, professor of epidemiology at Purdue University's School of Veterinary Medicine in West Lafayette, Ind., who is studying possible links with vaccinations. "We see an epidemic of hyperthyroidism in cats today, and we suspect that these are happening because we're over-vaccinating our pets."

Dr. Glickman and his colleagues theorize that repeated vaccination causes dogs to produce antibodies against their own tissue. The antibodies are caused by contaminants in the vaccine introduced in the manufacturing process. While the amounts are minuscule, they gradually accumulate with repeated vaccinations over the years. But Dr. Glickman cautions that more research is needed before a clear link can be established between antibody levels and autoimmune disease.

Vaccination recommendations for cats and dogs vary around the country. Most states require rabies vaccinations every three years, while a handful of states—as well as some individual cities and counties—have mandated annual shots due to local problems with rabies in wild animals. Some other vaccinations are given only when a pet's lifestyle or environment exposes it to a particular risk, such as Lyme disease.

Pet diseases other than rabies aren't a threat to people, thus vaccinations aren't required by law. But veterinarians and vaccine makers have traditionally recommended annual booster shots against potentially fatal diseases such as distemper and parvovirus in dogs and herpesvirus in cats. In a policy statement last year, the American Veterinary Medical Association acknowledged that the practice of annual vaccinations is based on "historical precedent" and "not on scientific data."

The emerging evidence of health risks is prompting some vets to change their practices. "We're now doing 40% less vaccinations than five years ago," says Kathleen Neuhoff, a veterinarian in Mishawaka, Ind., and president of the American Animal Hospital Association, Lakewood, Colo.

"My own pets are vaccinated once or twice as pups and kittens, then never again except for rabies," Ronald D. Schultz, chairman of the University of Wisconsin's Department of Pathobiological Sciences, wrote in the March 1998 issue of Veterinary Medicine.

Some critics of annual shots accuse some vets of ignoring research about vaccine risks for financial reasons. "Vets are afraid they will go broke" without regular vaccines, which account for about 20% of their practice income, says Bob Rogers, a Spring, Texas, veterinarian and outspoken critic of current practices.

Other vets deny that financial motives are involved. ("No one who is motivated by money would ever become a veterinarian," Dr. Neuhoff says.) "The concern is that if we move too quickly to decrease vaccine frequency across the board, we may be opening the door for some animals to become infected when we could have prevented the problem," says Todd R. Tams, chief medical officer of VCA Antech Inc., in Los Angeles, the nation's largest owner of veterinary hospitals.

No one truly knows how long protection from vaccines lasts. Vaccine makers say that proving their duration would be expensive and would require large numbers of animals to be isolated for years.

One company, Pfizer Inc., decided to test its one-year rabies vaccine on live animals and discovered it lasted for at least three years. It sells the identical formula simply packaged under different labels—Defensor 1 and Defensor 3—to satisfy different state vaccination requirements.

Exhibit 7 – TITER report for Max

ANTECH DIAGNOSTICS 17672-A Cowan Avenue Irvine CA 92614 Phone: 800-745-4725

Hemopet/Hemolife
11330 Markon Dr
Garden Grove, CA 92841
Tel: 714-891-2022
Fax: 714-891-2123

Client # 20073
Chart #

Accession No.	Doctor	Owner	Pet Name	Received
IRBC85065160	ABBEY	SCHWARTZ Jim	MAX	04/08/2004
Species	Breed	Sex	Pet Age	Reported
Canine	Std. Poodle 61.5 lbs	CM	7YRS 7 mos	04/21/2004 02:21 PM

Test Requested	Results	Reference Range	Units
RABIES			
Rabies Antibody Titer	1:1800	EXTREMELY HIGH	

- - - - - - Rabies Interpretive Comment - - - - - -

Although there is no established protective rabies titer for dogs or cats, the CDC considers 1:5 to be adequate in people. Some countries use titers to qualify animals for reduced periods of quarantine.
Refer to state guidelines for rabies vaccination requirements in animals.

- -
TEST PERFORMED AT KANSAS STATE UNIVERSITY

HEARTWORM SPECIAL
Heartworm Antigen   Negative   Negative   4/21/04

Dear Kris: Rabies titer is extremely high. Jean

☒ Serologic/vaccine titers for _Rabies Virus_ show ~~adequate~~ extremely high humoral immunity indicating that this dog should respond with a boosted anamnestic response to afford protection against these agents upon exposure.

☒ Recheck serologic/vaccine titers annually, or as required by law.

cc: By FAX to 303-850-0171

W. Jean Dodds, DVM

Page 1   FINAL   04/21/2004 02:21 PM

Exhibit 8a – Vet visits by service, pg 1

Detailed Tabulations

Table 20. Percentage of veterinarian visits by cat-owning households involving purchase of service or product, 1991, 1996, 2001

	1991 (%)	1996 (%)	2001 (%)
Alternative therapies	*	*	0.2
Behavior counseling	*	0.5	0.3
Dental care	4.9	4.7	3.5
Deworming	10.4	7.3	8.0
Drugs or medications	22.8	18.8	18.0
Emergency care	13.6	11.8	9.4
Euthanasia	2.6	3.1	2.6
Flea or tick products	9.5	12.4	15.5
Food	6.7	5.2	4.3
Grooming/boarding	3.5	3.2	2.7
Hospitalization	5.5	4.2	3.6
Laboratory tests	12.5	12.5	13.5
Microchip/tattoo	*	*	0.3
Other surgery	6.2	5.4	4.3
Physical exams	58.6	59.6	67.3
Spay/neuter	19.6	14.0	13.8
Vaccinations	64.4	61.9	70.5
X-rays	3.2	2.9	2.9

*Not available.
Source: AVMA Household Pet Survey.

Exhibit 8b, pg 2

Detailed Tabulations

Table 19. Percentage of veterinarian visits by dog-owning households involving purchase of service or product, 1991, 1996, 2001

	1991 (%)	1996 (%)	2001 (%)
Alternative therapies	*	*	0.4
Behavior counseling	*	0.4	0.3
Dental care	4.9	4.4	5.8
Deworming	12.6	8.8	8.2
Drugs or medications	32.6	29.4	31.3
Emergency care	12.6	11.5	10.5
Euthanasia	2.6	2.9	2.4
Flea or tick products	13.5	16.7	19.8
Food	4.4	3.7	3.7
Grooming/boarding	6.9	6.7	7.5
Hospitalization	4.2	3.3	2.6
Laboratory tests	17.4	15..9	18.6
Microchip/tattoo	*	*	0.6
Other surgery	4.9	4.2	4.3
Physical exams	62.0	61.0	69.4
Spay/neuter	8.4	7.6	6.1
Vaccinations	66.6	62.8	63.8
X-rays	4.1	3.4	3.8

*Not available.
Source: AVMA Household Pet Survey.

American Veterinary Medical Association

Exhibit 9 – Shot-Based Practice Analysis
(courtesy of www.next2kin.org)

The vast majority of dog owners vaccinate yearly. There is an arguably safer choice –the three-year rabies vaccination option – but many, many in the veterinarian community are not informing the guardians (pet owners) of the potential danger to their animal companions' (pets') life, health, and longevity.

Could economics be a factor in this lethargic effort on the part of many vets to provide their clients with an opportunity for *informed consent*?

Yearly rabies vaccination is big business and materially impacts the small-animal vet practice!

We can make these assumptions based upon various surveys and studies printed by animal association groups and trade associations.

- Average vet has 2,500 dogs and cats (45% dogs).
- Cost of vial of rabies vaccine is 61 cents.
- Cost of inoculation is between $15 and $38 yearly not including office visit.
- Cost of office visit is approximately $35.
- Price markup on rabies vaccine: 2400% to 6200% and again, this does not include the required by law office visit.

If 100% of the dogs in the average one-vet practice are annually given the rabies vaccine= 2,500*.45 (dogs per practice) or 1,125 dogs.

The gross operating profit (after cost of goods, 61cents per shot) equals:

@$15 per shot, a net of $14.39 = $16,189.
@$38 per shot, a net of $37.39 = $42,064.

If the three-year option is exercised (versus a yearly vaccination for rabies), then each vet loses between $32,000 ($16,000 x 2 years) and $84,000 ($42,000 x 2 years) of operating profit in each three-year vaccination period.

Adding office visits (1 a year for 2 years x 1,125 dogs x $35 per visit) = $78,800 of potential lost revenue.

(Note: The guardian should see that his/her companion animal receives a wellness exam at least yearly, which would extinguish this loss.)

Now, consider these figures. The:

- Median number of transactions per vet per year in 1997 was 5,102.
- Median gross income per vet in 1997 was $305,000 for a one-person practice.
- Net-income median for a one-vet practice before owner's compensation as a percentage of gross income was 26.8%. Assuming $305,000, that would be $87,300 for the average 1-vet practice.
- Average transaction charge is $58.41 per vet in a one-vet operation.

If 1,125 transactions for rabies vaccine were lost, here is the impact on the one-vet practice for the two years the dog doesn't get a rabies vaccine (assuming no replacement revenue):

- Transactions go from 5,102 to 3,887 or a 22% decline.
- Gross income falls (at $20 per shot plus $35 for an office visit) by $62,000 from $305,000 to $243,000.
- Net median-income per vet in a one-vet situation could drop from $87,000 to $25,000 or by 71%!

And this is only if dogs were inoculated for rabies on a three-year cycle. The impact magnifies with cats going three-years on the shot.

Source: "Financial and Productivity Pulse points: Comprehensive Survey and Analysis of Performance Benchmarks: Vital Statistics For Your Veterinary Practice," published by the American Animal Hospital Association, 1998.

The Small Vet (Non-emergency, non-specialist) Shot Model's Systemic Dependence on Transactions Assumptions:

- That a $25 rabies shot is eliminated for 1,000 dogs only in one-year. (Cats are not considered and parvovirus and distemper shots would still be administered annually).
- Profit on the shot is $24.39 (the cost being 61 cents).

 26% is the net profit margin.

Result: Instead of 1,000 transactions (shots) yielding $24,390, the vet would have to gross $93,807 from other areas of the practice to replace that net revenue. Furthermore, using a $54 average per transaction, the vet would have to conduct 70%

more transactions - 1,737 instead of 1,000 - which would mean a 15% increase in workload (the average vet has 5,100 transactions annually) just to be at the same place. Then consider the loss of office-visit revenue and take out cats, and parvo/distemper annually, and the Small Vet Shot-Based Model indicates red ink for the practice.

Exhibit 10 – Revocations of Professional Licenses (1997-2002)

	#FY97-98	Revoc's	%	#FY98-99	Revoc's	%
Veterinarians	3479	0	0.00000%	3389	1	0.02951%
Doctors	16249	19	0.11693%	16991	14	0.08240%
Pharmacists	6847	2	0.02921%	7118	10	0.14049%
Dentists	7103	1	0.01408%	6900	3	0.04348%
Accountants	12580	3	0.02385%	13524	2	0.01479%

	#FY99-00	Revoc's	%	#FY'00-01	Revoc's	%
Veterinarians	3614	1	0.02767%	3386	0	0.00000%
Doctors	16501	14	0.08484%	14124	10	0.07080%
Pharmacists	7243	2	0.02761%	7642	7	0.09160%
Dentists	6579	2	0.03040%	7536	8	0.10616%
Accountants	13085	1	0.00764%	1386	2	0.14430%

	FY01-02	Revoc's	%	#'97-'02	5Yrs #	%	%toVet
Veterinarians	3642	1	0.02746%	3	17510	0.0001713	
Doctors	14449	13	0.08997%	70	78314	0.0008938	521.703%
Pharmacists	7452	9	0.12077%	30	36302	0.0008264	482.343%
Dentists	7416	3	0.04045%	17	35534	0.0004784	279.235%
Accountants	13917	2	0.01437%	10	54492	0.0001835	107.111%

Exhibit 11a – Transcript, Channel 4 Vaccination coverage

www.NEWS4Colorado.com - Top Stories

5/2002

www.NEWS4Colorado.com / Top Stories

Vaccinations May Put Your Pet At Risk

(KCNC) Apr 30, 2002 10:22 pm US/Mountain

If you automatically take your cat or dog to the vet every year for vaccinations, you may be unnecessarily putting your pet at risk. NEWS4 Investigator Brian Maass reports on a link between some pet vaccines and cancer.

"She was our soul mate, she was just a cuddler, a regal lady,"

So when Sylvia, a short haired tabby died of cancer, it left her owner Jeff Kremer, heartbroken and looking for answers about what caused Sylvia's cancer. What he learned serves as a lesson for other cat owners, a common vaccine used to keep cats healthy is suspected of causing Sylvia's cancer, a vaccine given to cats every day.

Researchers now believe that common vaccines for rabies, feline leukemia, and other shots can occasionally cause a fatal form of cancer in cats. It is believed to occur in about one out of every 10,000 shots.

Denver vet Kevin Fitzgerald says of the thousands of cats vaccinated at his clinic, a few have developed cancerous tumors from the shots and died. Devastating for cat owners, and the vets who gave the shots.

Fitzgerald believes the benefits of vaccinating against potentially fatal diseases far outweighs the minor risk of giving a cat vaccine induced cancer.

Doctor Robin Starr is a Denver vet now working with a national task force funding research to investigate the links between cat vaccinations and cancer. They're trying to learn what in vaccines is causing those rare cases of cancer.

"As a profession it's horrifying to think that something you do that you thought was helping the animal that was preventing disease turns out to sometimes cause this condition. It's just horrifying,"

http://news4colorado.com/topstories/StoryFolder/story_1382679099_html   4/30/02

Exhibit 11b, Channel 4 transcript, Page 2 of 2

www.NEWS4Colorado.com - Top Stories

said Starr.

Horrifying not just for cat owners, some vets are now eyeing vaccines for dogs, suspicious that in rare cases those vaccines may trigger blood diseases. But there's not much research to definitively establish a link)

Jim Schwartz, an Arapahoe County financial planner suspects a vaccination for his dog Moolah triggered an auto immune disease, that cost Moolah her life.

"I'm not an expert; I lost a dog without doubt in my opinion to unnecessary over-vaccination. This should never, never happen to another dog or another cat," said Schwartz.

Many are now trying to make sure that's the case. Vets should no longer automatically vaccinate animals every year. And vets should talk with pet owners before vaccinating, weighing the potential risks and known benefits of vaccination. The vet should give the owner enough information for a good safe decision.

Pet owners are also pressing for more information about vaccination risks, and spreading the word that in extremely rare cases, doing what you thought was protecting your animal, could end up with catastrophic consequences.

The next time you get your cat or dog, vaccinated make sure you talk it over with your vet. Factors to keep in mind are your pet's age, its vaccination history and its environment. For instance if your cat never goes outside and is never exposed to other animals, it may not need vaccinations nearly as often as cats that spend time outside.

Wednesday, vets will be in the NEWS4 Helpcenter at 4, 5 and 6 to answer your questions about vaccinations.

For more information click on the link below:

American Veterinary Medical Association

More Top Stories Stories:
- Four Colorado Football Players Surrender To Police Apr. 30, 2002 2:17 pm
- Afghan Tribal Fight Has U.S. Troops In Middle Apr. 30, 2002 8:50 pm
- Defense Argues For New Trial In Case Of Lisl Auman Apr. 30, 2002 12:52 pm
- Vaccinations May Put Your Pet At Risk May 1, 2002 12:22 am
- Buy Avs Playoff Tickets For The Second Round Apr. 30, 2002 7:10 pm

http://news4colorado.com/topstories/StoryFolder/story_1382679099_html 4/30/02

Exhibit 12 – CVMA Position Paper on HB 03-1260

Colorado Veterinary Medical Association

POSITION STATEMENT ON HOUSE BILL 03-1260

Veterinarians support and promote the significance and benefits of the bond between people and their pets. Indeed, veterinarians spend their professional lives providing high quality care that improves the health of animals – and the humans that own and love them. The Colorado Veterinary Medical Association is concerned that House Bill 03-1260 could diminish that level of care because:

- <u>HB03-1260 will escalate the cost of veterinary medical care.</u> Veterinarians will have to pass on to consumers the increased costs of doing business, including time spent responding to frivolous lawsuits and additional diagnostic tests that will now be required to practice defensive medicine. This is likely to result in:
  - More cases of animals being relinquished to animal shelters.
  - More cases of animal neglect due to failure by animal owners to provide veterinary medical care.

- <u>HB03-1260 was created without input from – or consideration of implications to –stakeholders</u> such as veterinarians and veterinary healthcare professionals, animal shelters, humane organizations, animal control agencies, rescue groups, breed clubs, law enforcement, service animal organizations, etc. This bill may restrict the care that can be provided by these agencies.

- <u>HB03-1260 contradicts the logic being applied in the General Assembly to effect tort reform</u> in human medicine. Further, the bill tries to obtain non-economic damages for negligence, while in human medicine the standard of proof is much higher – gross negligence.

- <u>HB03-1260 duplicates remedies provided under current law.</u>
  - Current law provides redress for cases of non-economic compensation due to willful and wanton conduct such as aggravated cruelty to animals.
  - Veterinarians are not exempt from being disciplined or sued under current law.
  - Waivers for inoculations are already utilized by veterinarians throughout Colorado.

- <u>HB03-1260 attempts to dictate the practice of veterinary medicine.</u>
  - The Veterinary Practice Act regulates veterinarians in Colorado, as administered by the State Board of Veterinary Medicine – which is charged with protecting the public interest.
  - The bill could increase the case load within the Department of Regulatory Agencies, with attendant fiscal implications in a time of severe budgetary constraints.
  - It legislates professional judgment on the part of veterinarians. For example, a veterinarian would be precluded from offering a safer vaccination option to a client or altering vaccination protocols in response to a public health crisis.

For these reasons, the **Colorado Veterinary Medical Association** opposes House Bill 03-1260.

Exhibit 13 – CVMA legislative lobbying alert

Colorado Veterinary Medical Association

TO: Members represented on the House Committee on Business Affairs and Labor
FROM: Christopher J Morris, DVM, president
DATE: February 5, 2003
RE: **URGENT legislative alert and action request**

Your help is needed. Legislators need to hear from veterinarians – NOW! Here's why. On Friday, January 31, Representative Mark Cloer (Rep. – El Paso County) introduced House Bill 03-1260. The bill has many worrisome components, such as:

- It allows dog and cat owners to seek non-economic and economic damages from a veterinarian for negligent practice that causes injury or death to the animal. <u>An award for loss of companionship damages could go as high as $100,000.</u>
- It requires a signed informed consent agreement prior to performing or prescribing any veterinary service "that involves a substantial risk to the life or health of a companion dog or cat" and sets forth specific requirements that constitute informed consent.
- It instructs counties and municipalities that a companion dog or cat may not be inoculated against rabies any more frequently than what is recommended by the Compendium, or triennially – whichever is less frequent.

For these and many additional reasons, and after consultation with our lobbyists and with animal welfare organizations (that would also be impacted by this legislation), **CVMA is opposing House Bill 03-1260**. A copy of the CVMA position statement is enclosed for your review. To make it easy for you to read the whole bill, we've posted a copy on our Web site at www.colovma.com – just click the link right on the home page.

Also enclosed is a list of members of the committee that will hear this bill. The list is arranged by county to make it easy for you to identify your representative. A phone number at the state capitol is provided for each representative, along with an e-mail address if available.

A tip sheet on contacting your legislator is also enclosed. The key points you might want to emphasize in your contact are:

- HB03-1260 will escalate the cost of veterinary medical care.
- HB03-1260 was created without input from – or consideration of implications to – veterinarians and other stakeholders.
- HB03-1260 attempts to dictate the practice of veterinary medicine.

Please contact your representative TODAY to express your views about this bill. The committee hearing could be called within hours, because this bill must be heard no later than February 13. Time is of the essence. Nothing beats personal contact, and you are the best person to help your representative make an informed decision on this bill.

---

789 Sherman Street, Suite 550
Denver, Colorado 80203
303.318.0447 fax 303.318.0450
info@colovma.com www.colovma.com

Exhibit 14 – CVMA Tips on Contacting your Legislator – HB 03-1260

Colorado Veterinary Medical Association

GRASSROOTS LEGISLATIVE NETWORK
Tips on contacting your legislator

I've never contacted a legislator before. How should I do it?

Your legislator can be reached by telephone, e-mail, postal service, or through a personal visit. Whichever way you choose to make the contact, here are a few pointers:

- Be yourself – Communicate in your own style, and project a friendly tone. Identify yourself as a practicing veterinarian who would like to express a viewpoint.
- Simplify – Your communication should carry one message that is simple, consistent, and positive. In this case, the message is to oppose House Bill 03-1260.
- Clarify – Like consistency, clarity is paramount in conveying ideas. Many policymakers have little time to sort out details. Make your message understandable.
- Stay in touch – Volunteer to stand by to answer questions from this legislator as our bill goes through the legislative process. Be sure to provide your contact information (i.e. your phone number and e-mail address) to this legislator.
- Remain civil – A legislator may have an opposite view on an issue, but it doesn't pay to be anything less than civil and professional in any contact. Most elected officials are good people who want to help and who are seeking your guidance. While today they may bitterly oppose you, tomorrow they may be your staunchest ally!

What are the main points that I should make?

House Bill 03-1260 should not become law because:

- <u>It will escalate the cost of veterinary medical care</u>. Veterinarians will have to pass on to consumers the increased costs of doing business, including time spent responding to frivolous lawsuits and additional diagnostic tests that will now be required to practice defensive medicine. This is like to result in more cases of animals being relinquished to animal shelters, and more cases of animal neglect due to failure by animal owners to provide veterinary medical care.

- <u>It was created without input from – or consideration of implications to – veterinarians and other stakeholders</u>. While we can appreciate that the bill is well intentioned, it has severe unintended consequences. This bill may restrict the care that can be provided veterinarians, veterinary healthcare professionals, animal shelters and other animal welfare organizations.

- <u>It attempts to dictate the practice of veterinary medicine</u>. It legislates professional judgment on the part of veterinarians. For example, a veterinarian would be precluded from offering a safer vaccination option (e.g. a non-adjuvanted vaccine with a one-year period of protection) – or altering vaccination protocols in response to a public health crisis.

789 Sherman Street, Suite 550
Denver, Colorado 80203
303.318.0447 fax 303.318.0450
info@colovma.com www.colovma.com

Exhibit 15, letter to veterinarians

Next-to-Kin

Next-to-Kin Foundation
Box J-197 8547 E. Arapahoe Road
Greenwood Village, CO 80112-1430

March 31, 2003

<u>An Open Letter to Colorado Veterinarians and other pet caregivers:</u>

Greetings from this small but rapidly growing organization of pet custodians.

You may be one of the hundreds of local pet professionals who was disappointed -- as we were -- about the shabby treatment given by the State Legislature to the recent bill dealing with over-vaccination.

The original purposes of the act were: to clarify Colorado law on vaccinations, to improve the legal standing of pets in cases of animal abuse, and to protect those veterinarians who have chosen to opt for less frequent inoculation or the use of alternatives such as titering.

Thoroughly intimidated by misrepresentations about the act and threats from his own leadership, the bill's sponsor removed it from committee consideration causing its procedural death and denying the idea appropriate deliberation and possible amendment.

Our feedback having shown strong public support for this idea, we were disappointed that an attempt to save pet companions from dangerous sequellae would be defeated by some of the same people who have taken an oath to protect these animals.

We know that this action was not supported by all the members of your professional organization, because there are hundreds of responsible Colorado vets who have already changed their practice protocols to conform to the ideals of our proposed changes.

To give voice to these heroes and heroines, we are going to run the enclosed ad in as many Colorado papers as we can afford in the near future. We invite you to add your name to the list of professionals who have agreed to subscribe to this call for mercy to our pet companions.

There is no cost -- simply write us (N2K Foundation) a signed note on your letterhead authorizing us to use your name and title in the list which will appear below the copy.

Thank you.

James D. Schwartz
President
www.next2kin.org

Exhibit 16 – Newspaper advertisement

Your pet wants you to read this:

Is Your Veterinarian Still Overvaccinating Your Pet?
You can protect your pet companion(s) from this potentially life-threatening procedure!

<u>Check out the Law</u> — Pets of Colorado are being needlessly overvaccinated —

The Colorado Legislature (1999) changed the rabies vaccination law to permit vets to vaccinate no more often than every THREE years (CRS 25-4-615). The law was enacted **July 1, 1999.**

The Colorado Vet Association notified its membership of enactment with a front page story in its late spring-early summer edition (1999) of its magazine *Voices* — featuring past president John Young, DVM. Denver vets were notified in their summer & winter (1999) newsletter *Pulse*.

<u>Check out the Research</u> — Pets of Colorado are being needlessly overvaccinated —

CSU Vet School and The American Veterinary Medical Association (AVMA): "The practice of annual rabies vaccination is based (only) on historical precedent and government regulation, <u>**not on scientific (pet health) data.**</u>" AVMA Journal, 9/01

Colorado State University Small Animal Vaccination Protocol: "Our adoption of this routine vaccination program (three-year vaccination) is based on the <u>lack</u> of scientific evidence to support the current practice of <u>annual</u> vaccination and increasing documentation showing that overvaccination has been associated with harmful side effects. Of particular note in this regard has been the association of auto-immune hemolytic anemia with vaccination of dogs, and vaccine-associated sarcomas in cats — BOTH OF WHICH ARE OFTEN FATAL"
(Why is this information no longer on CSU web site?)

Titering of a pet's blood is a simple, relatively inexpensive way to determine whether vaccination is appropriate. The procedure is becoming less expensive as more vets use it.

Why are Veterinarians in Colorado still doing ANNUAL VACCINATIONS??

(As a matter of fact, since there hasn't been a human rabies event in Colorado for over seventy years (1931 — Colo. Health Dept.) why are Veterinarians NOT calling for REVIEW of this dangerous vaccination requirement? Smallpox and polio inoculation were stopped for children years ago!)

<u>Veterinarians must honor their own ethics oath – they must stop ignoring Colorado's 1999 law – or they will continue to harm our companions, and cause unnecessary death and illness of Colorado dogs and cats – at needless expense.</u>

Discuss this with your vet now!
Contact us online for simple informed consent card.
Next-To-Kin Foundation • www.next2kin.org
"We Salute Responsible Veterinarians"

Exhibit 17a – Colo Dept of Public Health letter 6/13/2003, pg 1

STATE OF COLORADO

Bill Owens, Governor
Douglas H. Benevento, Acting Executive Director

Dedicated to protecting and improving the health and environment of the people of Colorado

4300 Cherry Creek Dr. S.
Denver, Colorado 80246-1530
Phone (303) 692-2000
TDD Line (303) 691-7700
Located in Glendale, Colorado

http://www.cdphe.state.co.us

Laboratory and Radiation Services Division
8100 Lowry Blvd.
Denver, Colorado 80230-6928
(303) 692-3090

Colorado Department
of Public Health
and Environment

June 13, 2003

James Schwartz, President
Next to Kin Foundation
Box J-197
8547 E. Arapahoe Rd
Greenwood Village, CO 80112-1430

Dear Mr. Schwartz,

I am contacting you in reference to an open letter to veterinarians dated March 31, 2003 and an accompanying notice concerning pet vaccinations. Several veterinarians contacted me regarding this notice and several incorrect statements that it contained. As the epidemiologist responsible for rabies surveillance and prevention in Colorado, I wanted to take this opportunity to discuss the information contained in the notice.

A reference was made to the Colorado Department of Public Health & Environment (CDPHE) rabies statute (25-4-601 C.R.S., 1973 as amended) in the statement: "The Colorado Legislature changed the rabies vaccination law to permit vets to vaccinate no more often than every THREE years (CRS 25-4-615)." This is an incorrect interpretation of this law. The statute amendment, which was proposed by the Colorado Veterinary Medical Association, prohibits local ordinances from requiring vaccination of animals more often then required by the vaccine labeling. Thus, if a veterinarian and owner decide to use a three-year vaccine, a local ordinance cannot require annual or biennial vaccination, nor could the owner be cited for an unvaccinated animal. The law, however, does not preclude a veterinarian from using one-year vaccines.

In enacting the law, I have advised local jurisdictions to remove the time interval from their rabies vaccination ordinances and replace it with language that the animal must be currently vaccinated against rabies as recommended by the vaccine labeling or the Compendium of Animal Rabies Control and Prevention. Essentially this prevents the law from dictating veterinary practice, while insuring public health goals to prevent rabies are met. In response to concerns about vaccine reactions, a new generation feline vaccine has been developed to eliminate the vaccine-associated fibrosacroma tumors. But due to reduced potency, this vaccine is only labeled for annual use. Mandating three-year only vaccines would eliminate this and future improved vaccines from being used. At written, Colorado law allows veterinarians and pet owners to decide what vaccine is best for the animal.

Another statement reads, "Titering of a pet's blood is a simple, relatively inexpensive way to determine whether vaccination is appropriate". The presence or absence of antibody does not correspond to the level of protection an animal has against exposure to rabies, it only shows that an immune response to the vaccine occurred. When challenged with rabies virus, vaccinated test animals with high antibody titers have succumbed to disease, whereas animals without a measurable titer have survived due to anamnestic (memory) response of the immune system. The duration of vaccine protection is established by rabies challenge studies that are required the U.S. Department of Agriculture to get a vaccine licensed. CDPHE does not recognize measuring rabies antibody titers an acceptable substitution to vaccination.

Exhibit 17b, Colorado Dept of Public , pg 2

The notice incorrectly states the occurrence of rabies in Colorado. The last human case of rabies occurred in 1931. Enclosed is a table documenting the rabies positive tests in Colorado over the past ten years and the occurrence of the last rabies cases in certain animal species. Although bats have been our only endemic rabies host in Colorado, for the past thirty years, spill over from bats to terrestrial species has been documented including a bobcat last year. We are faced with numerous rabid bat/pet exposure incidents every summer. I would hope your campaign does not result in owners forgoing rabies vaccinations for their pets.

Finally, the notice states "...polio inoculations were stopped for children years ago!". This is incorrect. Polio vaccination is still required under the Colorado School Immunization law and national public health and medical associations still recommend polio immunizations for all children.

I wanted to bring this information to your attention so your group can provide accurate information in its educational efforts. While the overuse of vaccines in pet animals is an important issue, it is also important to remember that the use of rabies vaccines has almost eliminated the occurrence of rabies in dogs and cats in the U.S. Yet we continue to spend millions of dollars annually in this country on post-exposure rabies treatment of people bitten by dogs and cats. Worldwide tens of thousands of human deaths from rabies occurs annually, most from exposure to rabid dogs. The CDPHE would support efforts to reduce unnecessary vaccination of pet animals, provided these efforts do not adversely impact public health rabies prevention efforts.

If you have any questions concerning this letter, would like to discuss the matter further or want additional information on rabies, please contact me at 303-692-2628 or <john.pape@state.co.us>.

Sincerely,

John Pape, Epidemiologist
Communicable Disease Control Program

Cc: Colorado Veterinary Medical Association

Exhibit 17c – CDPH Letter published in CVMA *"Voice"* Summer 2003

of note

Department of Public Health Corrects Inaccuracies By Opposition Group
by John Pape, Colorado Department of Public Health and Environment

The following is a letter from John Pape, epidemiologist from the Colorado Department of Public Health and Environment to James Schwartz, president of the Next to Kin Foundation, providing clarification of a letter the organization recently distributed to veterinarians.

Dear Mr. Schwartz,

I am contacting you in reference to an open letter to veterinarians dated March 31, 2003 and an accompanying notice concerning pet vaccinations. Several veterinarians contacted me regarding this notice and several incorrect statements that it contained. As the epidemiologist responsible for rabies surveillance and prevention in Colorado, I wanted to take this opportunity to discuss the information contained in the notice.

A reference was made to the Colorado Department of Public Health and Environment (CDPHE) rabies statute (25-4-601 C.R.S., 1973 as amended) in the statement: "The Colorado Legislature changed the rabies vaccination law to permit vets to vaccinate no more often than every THREE years (CRS 25-4-615)." This is an incorrect interpretation of this law. The statute amendment, which was proposed by the Colorado Veterinary Medical Association, prohibits local ordinances from requiring vaccination of animals more often then required by the vaccine labeling. Thus, if a veterinarian and owner decide to use a three-year vaccine, a local ordinance cannot require annual or biennial vaccination, nor could the owner be cited for an unvaccinated animal. The law, however, does not preclude a veterinarian from using one-year vaccines.

In enacting the law, I have advised local jurisdictions to remove the time interval from their rabies vaccination ordinances and replace it with language that the animal must be currently vaccinated against rabies as recommended by the vaccine labeling or the Compendium of Animal Rabies Control and Prevention. Essentially this prevents the law from dictating veterinary practice, while insuring public health goals to prevent rabies are met. In response to concerns about vaccine reactions, a new generation feline vaccine has been developed to eliminate the vaccine-associated fibrosacroma tumors. But due to reduced potency, this vaccine is only labeled for annual use. Mandating three-year only vaccines would eliminate this and future improved vaccines from being used. At written, Colorado law allows veterinarians and pet owners to decide what vaccine is best for the animal.

Another statement reads, "Titering of a pet's blood is a simple, relatively inexpensive way to determine whether vaccination is appropriate". The presence or absence of antibody does not correspond to the level of protection an animal has against exposure to rabies, it only shows that an immune response to the vaccine occurred. When challenged with rabies virus, vaccinated test animals with high antibody titers have succumbed to disease, whereas animals without a measurable titer have survived due to anamnestic (memory) response of the immune system. The duration of vaccine protection is established by rabies challenge studies that are required the U.S. Department of Agriculture to get a vaccine licensed. CDPHE does not recognize measuring rabies antibody titers an acceptable substitution to vaccination.

The notice incorrectly states the occurrence of rabies in Colorado. The last human case of rabies occurred in 1931. Enclosed is a table documenting the rabies positive tests in Colorado over the past ten years and the occurrence of the last rabies cases in certain animal species. Although bats have been our only endemic rabies host in Colorado, for the past thirty years, spill over from bats to terrestrial species has been documented including a bobcat last year. We are faced with numerous rabid bat/pet exposure incidents every summer. I would hope your campaign does not result in owners forgoing rabies vaccinations for their pets.

Finally, the notice states "...polio inoculations were stopped for children years ago!". This is incorrect. Polio vaccination is still required under the Colorado School Immunization law and national public health and medical associations still recommend polio immunizations for all children.

I wanted to bring this information to your attention so your group can provide accurate information in its educational efforts. While the overuse of vaccines in pet animals is an important issue, it is also important to remember that the use of rabies vaccines has almost eliminated the occurrence of rabies in dogs and cats in the U.S. Yet we continue to spend millions of dollars annually in this country on post-exposure rabies treatment of people bitten by dogs and cats. Worldwide tens of thousands of human deaths from rabies occurs annually, most from exposure to rabid dogs. The CDPHE would support efforts to reduce unnecessary vaccination of pet animals, provided these efforts do not adversely impact public health rabies prevention efforts.

If you have any questions concerning this letter, would like to discuss the matter further or want additional information on rabies, please contact me at 303.692.2628 or john.pape@state.co.us.

Sincerely,
John Pape, Epidemiologist
Communicable Disease Control Program

> "I would hope your campaign does not result in owners forgoing rabies vaccinations for their pets."

Exhibit 18 – Message from leading immunologist re:CDPH letter

Subj:	Re: From Jim Schwartz - Dr. Pape's Statement 6/13/2003
Date:	6/23/03 3:40:36 PM Mountain Daylight Time
From:	ChasBerm
To:	UPTRODDEN

Dear Jim: This situation is complex and reflects inherent bias in accepting titers for rabies – for which acceptable titer levels are already established for purposes of export/import of animals to rabies free countries all over the world, and for import to other countries just to ensure that pet dogs and cats entering these places are adequately immunized/protected. Furthermore, the CDC and WHO have determined what they consider to be protective rabies titer levels for people – namely, 1:5 and 1:50, respectively, so – how can antone say that rabies titers don't reflect immunity. Must be political issues here. Jean

Exhibit 19, Pet Evacuation, Jackson Cty, pg1

ANNEX E (EVACUATION AND SHELTER)

The Pet Sheltering Plan below was developed from guidelines of the Humane Society and American Red Cross. Writing the Plan was simple. Getting permission to use the County Fair Grounds was simple. Getting pet shelters to agree to take pets at the onset of an event is difficult. Pet shelters do not like to take in animals that may spread disease. The best solution for a family is having a reciprocal agreement with a friend in a nearby area willing to care for your pets.

APPENDIX 1 (Sheltering Pets)
to ANNEX E (Evacuation and Sheltering)

I. **Purpose**

   To establish guidance and procedures to facilitate the basic safety and care of domestic pets and farm animals, in Jackson County, during an emergency or disaster while leaving primary responsibility with the owner.

II. **Situation and Assumptions**

   A. Natural or technological emergencies and disasters occur which require citizens to evacuate their homes.

   B. Many citizens own domestic pets, such as dogs and cats.

   C. Farmers and other animal owners have a responsibility to deal with potential problems with them prior to, during and following disasters.

   D. Shelters for citizens do not permit pets other than those used for special needs assistance.

   E. Unattended pets may be at risk to themselves and to the general population.

   F. Pet owners and farmers are responsible for any costs incurred as State and Federal disaster programs do not provide funding.

   E. Historically, less than 20% of evacuees utilize public shelters.

   F. Many of evacuees may now bring their pets with them.

III. **Concept of Operations**

   Jackson County residents are encouraged through public education to pre-arrange reciprocal pet (foster care) agreements with relatives and friends prior to the onset of disaster situations.

   For those, who do pre-arrange animal care or when time and circumstances do not allow owners time to move pets and farm animals, it may become necessary (if it can be done with reasonable safety) for a decision to be made to help find shelter and care for

Jackson County EOP

Exhibit 19b, Jackson Cty Evac, pg 2

ANNEX E (EVACUATION AND SHELTER)

household and farm animals. These animals may be taken by owners or designated personnel to designated kennels, animal shelters, boarding facilities, veterinary hospitals or other appropriate facilities.

A. Pre-Incident:

    1. Jackson County Animal Shelter, Public Health and Emergency Management will maintain a pet sheltering plan.

    2. Keys to planning:

        a. Estimate population of domestic pets within the jurisdiction based on the formula provided (see attached "Estimated Pet Population" worksheet):

Municipality	Estimated Number of Households	Estimated Number of Dogs	Estimated Number of Cats	Estimated Number of Birds
Black River Falls	1128	356	308	64
Alma Center	142	45	39	8
Hixton	138	44	38	8
Melrose	163	52	44	9
Merrillan	183	58	50	10
Taylor	161	51	44	9

        b. Coordinate, develop and maintain, with appropriate government agencies and private organizations, a resource network, with lists and contact information for kennels, boarding facilities, animal shelters, veterinary hospitals, or other resources, which will participate in the sheltering of domestic pets during emergencies and disasters. Identify animal disposal resources. Identify outlets for unclaimed pets.

        c. Establish guidelines and procedures in conjunction with participating groups for the:

            1) Emergency medical care

            2) Sheltering of farm animals and pets.

        d. Coordinate public education activities relating to animal evacuation with the media and other groups publicizing emergency care for pets. (This could include outreach activities, such as brochures, news articles and public service announcements for veterinary offices, kennels, pet supply businesses, etc. and the general public.) Special consideration should be given to special needs groups.

B. During Incident:

Exhibit 19c, Jackson Cty Evac, pg 3

ANNEX E (EVACUATION AND SHELTER)

    1. Jackson County Animal Shelter, Public Health, Emergency Management, Local Veterinarians, Animal Hospitals and County Fairgrounds (Agricultural Animal Care).

        a. Coordinate response and public information activities with adjacent counties and appropriate support organizations to provide resources and mutual aid, if necessary.

        b. Follow procedures for emergency actions as developed in preparedness activities.

        c. The Jackson County Animal Shelter Supervisor (or designee) will report to the County EOC to coordinate appropriate animal rescue activities.

C. Post Incident:

    1. Jackson County Animal Shelter, Public Health, Emergency Management, Local Veterinarians, Animal Hospitals and County Fairgrounds (Agricultural Animal Care).

        a. Coordinate transition to normal operations.

        b. In cooperation with the providers, track the disposition/reunification of the pets.

        c. Notify participating boarding facilities, appropriate agencies and local media of cessation of emergency activities.

        d. Review and evaluate, with all participating groups, the effectiveness of procedures during emergency response and recovery.

IV. Organization and Responsibilities:

The Jackson County Animal Shelter, working through local jurisdictions and resources, to develop the network of pet care participants available to respond in emergencies.

A. Animal Owners:

    1. Maintain primary responsibility to develop plans to care for their animals.

    2. Encouraged to pre-arrange emergency animal care with friends, neighbors (not necessarily near neighbors who may be equally effected by a disaster.

B. Jackson County Animal Shelter to:

Exhibit 19d, Jackson Cty Evac, pg 4

ANNEX E (EVACUATION AND SHELTER)

1. Maintain a list of participating kennels, boarding facilities, animal shelters, veterinarians, veterinary hospitals and other pet resources in the County, provided to Jackson County Emergency Management and updated annually.

2. Designate a representative(s) to coordinate with the respective kennels, boarding facilities, animal shelters, veterinarians, veterinary hospitals and pet disposal resources to the extent possible.

3. Coordinate public information about pet disaster issues.

4. Designate representatives to implement plan. These individuals shall oversee and designate shelter requests and coordinate and track pet placement to the extent possible.

5. Advise Wisconsin Emergency Management of any problems that develop in implementing the plan. Include information on the status of pet evacuation in situation reports that are submitted to the state.

C. The following agencies/organizations have an advisory or support role:

  1. Wisconsin Emergency Management (WEM)   800-943-0003
  2. Wisconsin Veterinary Medical Association   888-254-5202
  3. Wisconsin Federated Humane Societies   414-728-6822
     800-227-4645 Toll Free
     303-748-1140 Pager
  4. Dept. of Agriculture, Trade & Consumer Pro.   414-473-3757
  5. American Red Cross   608-233-9300
  6. Dept of Health and Family Services   608-275-5472
  7. American Humane Association (AHA)   800-227-4645
     Dick Green 303-885-2179 or Samantha Bradley

Exhibit 19e, Jackson Cty Evac, pg 5

ANNEX E (EVACUATION AND SHELTER)
Attachment 3 (Reception Center and Shelter Map)

APPENDIX 2 (Statement of Understanding)
to ANNEX E (Evacuation and Shelter)

Statement of Understanding
Between the

_____

and
Jackson County Emergency Management

PURPOSE
This statement defines an agreement between the
_____ and
Jackson County Emergency Management in caring for pets during disaster situations.

HAZARDS IN WISCONSIN
Wisconsin is vulnerable to a wide range of hazards, both natural and technological. Periodic disasters result from tornadoes, floods, winter storms, drought, hazardous material accidents, terrorism and other events that can cause injuries and loss of life, disruption of services and significant property damage.

METHOD OF COOPERATION
In order that the
_____ and
Jackson County Emergency Management will work in cooperation in performing services during disaster situations, the organizations have agreed as follows:

1. Liaison will be maintained between the organizations at a local/county level in planning and disaster situations.

2. The Red Cross will not undertake or provide any pet relief efforts.

3. Jackson County Emergency Management will provide_____ with available data regarding the effects of a disaster and progress of relief efforts.

4. Activities of the
   _____ in
   responding to pet disaster relief will be coordinated with the appropriate local government agencies. This could include:

   - the provision of shelter
   - the provision of food
   - the provision of medical treatment
   - tagging of pets for the return to their owners, etc., and
   - (other responsibilities, as necessary)

Exhibit 19f, Jackson Cty Evac, pg 6

5. The Jackson County Animal Shelter will serve as the coordinating agency for all pet relief efforts. Through Jackson County Animal Shelter, all efforts will be expended to reunite pets with owners subsequent to a disaster. Pets will be sheltered as long as possible or until reasonable possibilities of placement have been exhausted.

6. The cost of boarding and other pet disaster expenditures will be the responsibility of the pet's owner. The boarding facility will bill as they would under normal situations or at its discretion based on the disaster situation. The boarding facility may rely on its paid staff, volunteer network and/or local resources to offer pet housing and care.

7. No government agency will assume any financial responsibilities for pet disaster relief.

8. Jackson County Emergency Management will provide technical assistance, as appropriate, for disaster preparedness activities, such as the development of local response plans and training programs.

9. To keep the public fully informed, Jackson County Emergency Management, and the _____ will coordinate public information and education efforts.

10. This statement of understanding will end following one week notification by either _____ or Jackson County Emergency Management and will be subject to annual review, if requested by either party.

_____   _____
John Elliott, Director   Date
Jackson County Emergency Management

_____   _____
Agency Representative   Date

Exhibit 20a

Telcon; Subj: emergency preparedness for pet animals

7/25/06, Emily, Non-Preparedness – COSART

JS: Okay so you're Emily. So my understanding is a bill was passed in light of Katrina because of people who would stay with their pets. For example, so that there were emergency provisions so that people could be evacuated with their dogs or cats. That[1] was my understanding with the bill, was I wrong in that?

ED: Um I can't tell you what the purpose of the bill was because I didn't draft it or author it (she chuckles). But I think it came out of those circumstances and I think people had big hearts didn't necessarily bulk up the legislation in the way that it needed to be done.

JS: Okay so as it exists right now, for Joe Doe who has a dog or a cat, he cannot do pre-emergency planning, because a) there is no list that's required of designated places

ED: Well, I think we have two separate issues. You're asking about the act and it does not require a list.

JS: It does not require a list of pre-designated places which in an emergency and people have their adrenaline going, would have been helpful but it does not require that?

ED: It requires a plan it does not require a specific listing you're asking for.

---

[1] Transcribed by S. Chandler 2/12/06

JS: Okay, now,

ED: Now, the question as to whether or not such a list exists in the Seat of Colorado is a different question and it's a long and complicated answer and, um to say that we're not prepared, I don't think anyone in the state of Colorado or New York is totally prepared for anything at this point. We're not prepared for a Katrina-like situation. And I think we would all acknowledge that freely.

JS: Okay, let's segment or compartmentalize it. I just want to talk about the dogs or cats. I'm not interested in indicting anybody about an overall disaster for humans, I'm saying provisions

ED: Let me just ask a question first, are you a reporter?

JS; No, but I can get this to a reporter

ED: No, we don't need, I mean we can get our own press. I just heard you typing and wondered why.

Exhibit 20b

JS: I'm not typing.

ED: My, let's go back to segmenting. The list is a totally different issue than the legislation. Like I said, the legislation is more general in requiring, the City and County of Denver has a list, it's not that detailed.

JS: I live in Arapahoe County–I'm just inquiring about my own dogs. Right now there's no list that can be provided according to Heckendorf or anybody as to where I would go because a) there is no list, b) the list could change because circumstances could change.

ED: And that's what I was getting to, even in Denver which has a little bit more planning done than I would say other counties. I'm not speaking specifically to Arapahoe County but I'd say smaller counties than Denver are a little more behind. Jefferson County just by way of example is really kind of a model citizen in this regard because they have a full county animal response team that would respond to animal disasters and they have some of these things already created. I don't know because I don't run their program, if they have a predetermined list but I would imagine that they do. And—

JS: Is there someone in Arapahoe County that is that person's colleague, for example, that there would an Arapahoe County response team?

ED: Yes, I know they have a major effort now to ramp up animal issues. I don't know if they are created an animal response team at this time.

JS: And would be under the Animal Control Division?

ED: That's the first place I would start.

JS: Okay, they won't even respond.

ED: Um, the other complicating factor, I would say is that even though Dr. Jonathan does this everyday, and is prepared to help people respond in disaster coordinating as a resource or necessity, we don't ever know when a disaster is going to happen, so we don't have a list of shelters for every area. The way that we operate is that we are trying to co-locate shelters with the Red Cross. The Red Cross currently does not allow animals in their shelters except for service animals so what we have to do is use their—we have a model that basically has concentric circles coming out from a disaster and they don't ever know where they're going to have their disaster shelters either. They have a bunch of contacts, they have churches, and they have schools that they are potentially going to be able to locate their shelter at. But until the event happens, they don't know exactly where they're going to set it up.

JS: That's like saying; we shouldn't plan, because we won't be 100 percent sure. We shouldn't even have 30 or 40 percent planning to have a pre-designated possible area.

Exhibit 20c

ED: No, no, they have possible areas, as do we. We work with them so we can have co-locations.

JS: Okay, so why can't a list of possible locations be provided?

ED: Well, that's something we're working on. We don't have a complete list because we haven't been able to get a total list from Red Cross. This is a very new effort, all this recently happened. Again, we're privately funded, our budget every year is much smaller than most people and we're doing as much as we can. We're also helping to train County animal response teams; we're also trying to get together a veterinary response team program. We're doing a bunch of things with no money so to ask us to have all of this done and ready and prepared for you is a little bit difficult at this time because we're not being funded by the state.

JS: But isn't that always the point is people always—if it's education, if it's health, it's always money-money. The point of it is that there is no list at this time in time regardless of cause, regardless of what the legislation says or doesn't say.

ED: Would you agree with me that it actually takes staffing, money and time to prepare something like that?

JS: I'm not going to agree with you because why would you, they put out legislation. I don't know. All I'm saying is here I'm Joe Doe; I've had at least 16 calls.

ED: I agree–I share your frustration.

JS: What's gonna happen in a disaster when somebody has got the adrenaline running and they're getting tossed around if they can given even get through and the phones are going off the hook?

ED: I share your frustration. I mean, I'm not saying you're wrong, I'm not saying your frustration is unfounded, I don't—providing you with a list is not going to happen right now. What I can ask you to do is pursue contacts in the Arapahoe County system because they're the ones that are going to be filling up.

JS: Four times–Okay, let me tell you who I am; some of my background. If you go to www.next2kin.org, I'm the guy who did the work on over-vaccination and since my work now, all 49 states have gone to three-years. Still 79% of the vets still give the annual shot even though their own medical associations say and all the vets say three-years and they last ten. I know my way around this stuff and–this is remarkable to me. This is remarkable–and I've been in dealings with Tancredo's office over stuff like this; they're not going to be happy. And I understand what you're saying, if you don't have funding, what can you do—

ED: I'm not we're not working on it I'm just saying we don't have immediately what you're asking for right now. Again, I'm not disagreeing with you and you're angry at me. And you know what; we're the ones who are trying to work on a solution. I think the people to be angry with are the people in the State Legislature, and to some extent, the people in the Federal Legislature because they're passing a plan that is not going to help with these types of questions. And it's certainly not funded to help with this type of question. So you know,

Exhibit 20d

I'm not disagreeing and I'm not saying that you're wrong I just can't give you what you want and one of the reasons I can't give you what you want is because we're trying to do too many things with absolutely no funding even though the state and counties send you to us. I mean, they're not funding us in any way and you're talking to me. (Laughter). Don't you find that a little bit absurd?

JS: I find it absurd that it should have stopped at Animal Control in Arapahoe County with Thea Thompson who did not respond. That's what I find absurd because that's the place that should be the place for the first contact.

ED: Well–is that is something that we have done wrong?

JS: No, you're just catching 16 phone calls—16.

ED: I understand that, that's frustrating. But what can I do for you.

JS: You can't, you don't have a list.

ED: I don't have a list but I can take your name and get you in touch with someone who will speak to you.

JS: (Laughs) And what are they gonna tell me–we don't have the funding, we don't have the list, Red Cross isn't helping us right at this point in time and we have too many things to do.

ED: I'll say Red Cross isn't helping us right now and they're behind the eight-ball like everyone else. That's the bottom line.

JS: And people could complain about the Red Cross misallocating dollars during 9/11 funding, which they got caught on. So when people say we don't have enough money and point to this or that one, they (RC) had enough money. That's a fact what I'm telling you.

ED: I have no position on that. We deal with animals; we don't deal with people so how can I help you? Let me help you.

JS: You can't.

ED: No, that's not true; they may have a system in place.

JS: Where? Arapahoe County? They're not responding.

ED: But that doesn't mean that they don't have—

Exhibit 20e

JS: How can I know that if they don't return phone calls?

ED: You know I'm not going to argue on their behalf. I'm not the Arapahoe County Sheriff or Animal Control. I'm not so I'm not going to engage in this debate with you. So how may I, Emily, help you?

JS: You have nobody to give me to that can respond to me.

ED: That's not true. I will try to make some contacts for you.

JS: Okay, let me give you...its Jim Schwartz. Maybe the best way I can help everybody is for the Post and the News, which I've dealt with in great lengths before to get on top of this–that the act or the intent of the act, for whatever reason, is not being fulfilled whether it's funding or not but it's become—16...

ED: No, the act was never intended to deal with this particular question. It just wasn't. It was never intended to reach down to the local level, it just wasn't. It was intended to have states to say hey I have a plan and therefore I can get FEMA funding. It never said this is what you have to have in your plan and this is how it's done—(She's speaking a couple of words inaudibly) Federal Legislation is not going to do that.

JS: Also, you said to me that a plan could be one piece of paper with one line on it.

ED: Right, it could be because they have no—

JS: There is no mandate, there's no requirement is what you're saying.

ED: Practically, I don't think they can go down to that level and tell states what they need to have in their plan because every state differs. For example, when you're looking at Florida vs. Colorado, we talking about two totally different natural disasters that are going to affect and two totally different types of evacuation plans and two totally different types of situations with animals—

JS: But potential places to put the dog and people, that you know, sheltering is a factor in—-

ED: Right but its done on a totally local level and not everyone uses Red Cross sheltering. In Florida they have what are called colloquies; it's shelters and also animal friendly shelters where they put two types of systems where non Cross Red shelters where they are also co-located shelters. So animals are in shelters right next to humans. They also have shelters where people are able to bring their animals into a shelter but they have to sign off and say I'm willing to stay in a shelter with my animal and other people's animals. They take care of their own animals in both of those situations. So, as I'm saying, it's a totally local issue how people feel with sheltering, because the federal government doesn't know that there's a school on the 100th block of Vine St. They just don't know that and that's not the level to which they should rule them. So, they keep it at a local level and I don't think the Legislation was ever meant to deal with that local issue. What it is asking for, or saying is—what is happening at the sort of North Central region of Colorado which includes Denver, they're working on evacuation plans right now, they're working on sheltering plans right now and they're trying to come with answers to your questions and answers to a whole bunch of other questions: If we have to evacuate downtown Denver and people have Fluffy and Fido with them, are we going to let them on an RTD bus, are we going to do things like that? So people are trying to answer these questions, they just haven't gotten to where you would like them to be yet.

JS: I don't know if it's just me when you make that assertion. I think...

ED: No, it's me too but I'm just saying that people aren't just standing around and saying hey, we're going to wait and draft this plan that's not going to work. What they're trying to do is have a more comprehensive scheme than we've seen in other places where these huge disasters have hit. And they're trying to say, well hey, we're not only moving people on RTD buses, we have to think of special needs cases, we have to think about animals, we have to think about the moving and the hospitals so they're trying to do it all at once, which takes longer. And it means that if something happened today, we may not be prepared but it also means the system will be smarter when they eventually get it done.

JS: So the bottom line is that nothing is basically prepared at this point in time and that's why Ms. Thompson has not returned four phone calls?

ED: I can't answer for Arapahoe County. I think there are resources in place; they may not be ... it's not on an official list. But I certainly think they could give someone a call and help you direct yourself to a shelter when these things are happening. The other thing is I mean they're not going to know until, oftentimes, the governor makes the call if it's a large enough constituency. So they're not going to tell you where to go because that might change if a disaster—

JS: No, but they could say here's a list of potential places that could be called so you could plan accordingly and if and when it actually occurs, you would not be one of ten million calling at the same time getting a busy signal.

ED: No, that's true, that's true and I would say that generally, we're looking at the types of places you're looking at are going to be fairgrounds because those are large areas where they can put kennels and runs for animals and they also have parking lot facilities where they can house people in tents or put them inside. You're also looking at places near animal shelters that have large areas where they can shelter people. And those are sort of the general areas you're going to be sheltered in. But even if they have a list, I'm not sure it's something they're going to issue to the public, because they don't want this information going to the wrong places.

JS: Okay, thank you.

Exhibit 21 – Knowing When

Criteria	weight	1	2	3	4	5	6	7	8	9	10	11	12	13	14
Pain - Acute															
Cries/wimpering															
Can no longer walk															
Chronic Pain															
Can't get up without help															
Stiff - gets up slower & slower															
Doesn't want to be touched															
Mobility															
Can't jump up															
Doesn't want to walk															
Can't navigate steps															
Falls off bed etc.															
Dignity															
Accidents															
Painful urination/defecation															
Urinates/defecates on self															
Eating															
Not eating or drinking															
Loss of appetite															
Loss of weight															
Indifference															
Doesn't want affection															
Doesn't greet at door															
Does The Dog/Cat want to graduate/ready to go?															

Knowing when...

A large number of guardians have told me the same thing about asking their vets when it's time to say goodbye. In response to the question: "How do we know when it's time?," the response is something like: "Oh, you'll know when it's time."

That wasn't good enough for me – nor for a lot of people who dread making a decision if there's any chance it isn't necessary. But reducing the question – and answer – to some kind of mathematical equation is impossible, of course. Yet there must be some way to give us more assurance that we're doing the right thing.

The above matrix may be of some help. It came from an idea in *Animal Wellness* magazine. There are several ways to assess the importance of these morbidity indicators and I'll leave it up to you to decide how much weight each one gets. You can use the chart to indicate a change over a period of days or just to enumerate the weaknesses in a terminal friend.

I hope it will help you make a critical decision – the time when you must help your Ambassador from God to graduate.

Exhibit 22a

e-mails about microchipping

Date:	Sun, 16 Apr 2006 10:44:29 -0700 (PDT)
From:	"james schwartz"
Subject:	HomeAgain (The Microchip) or Home Affront? A Story for Pet Owner/Guardians? from Jim Schwartz
To:	swheeler@denverpost.com

Ms. Wheeler - fyi

Home Again or Home Affront?

The purpose of HomeAgain (1-800-738-4324) is to reunite lost companion animals with their guardians/owners through insertion of a microchip within the companion animal AND an identifying plastic tag on the companion animal's collar. The molded-in data on one side says 'HomeAgain Animal Retrieval System' and stamped on the other side, 'Call 1-800-252-7994'. On the same side as the call number is stamped – in ink – the ID number of the companion animal.

In gathering information to place into a Top Tag ID USB (for placement on my dog Elle's collar), I noticed her ID number on the Home Again collar tag was imperceptible.

Now granted, if she is lost and returned to a shelter or vet clinic, they will scan the chip (assuming it still works) for identification, but what about a neighbor three blocks away

– how would they be able to identify her to the 800 number with an imperceptible number?

There are 160 million dogs and cats in the US. Assume only 15% have been chipped or 24 million companion animals. Assume 1% of those that get chipped get lost per year or 240,000 companion animals. Assume a 1/3 of these dogs and cats are found by people who do not have scanners – 80,000. Assume if just 10% don't know to take the dog or cat to a shelter – that's 8000 dogs and cats unnecessarily not retrieved because of a faded or imperceptible tag. Of course, one can run these numbers on even 4 million having been chipped by all the companies chipping and it still would be too many dogs and cats unnecessarily unidentified

What was Nate at HomeAgain's response?

First, it was a cost issue. According to Nate, the service would cost more ($8 more onto the $12.5 for the service at the time 6 years ago) and less people would take the service. Upon pressing that I never was given the option of a more durable tag (i.e. stainless steel), **he indicated that these tags were just made available 'in the last couple of years."** Furthermore, he then blamed the veterinarians for not making this option available to owners as the optional tags are mentioned in the Home Again Kit.

Exhibit 22b

Upon chatting with Dr. Melanie Poundstone (303)-761-7063 – she indicated the kit comes as is with the plastic tag – and no mention to her recollection of any tag option. Dr. Poundstone also suggested at one's companion animals' yearly exam to scan the chip to see if it is still operable.

Nate's supervisor has yet to respond.

What good is a retrieval system that in part requires identification by tag number – if the tag number is inked-on rather than stamped – and subject to fading and imperceptibility?

Home Again or Home Affront?

To date, Ms. Wheeler who often covers companion animal related stories for the Denver Post – has yet to respond...

From:	"Karen Kennedy" <karenk@padcare.com>
To:	"james schwartz"
Subject:	Collar Tag Orders
Date:	Thu, 4 May 2006 13:20:58 -0400

Mr. Schwartz,

Please be advised that two complimentary stainless steel collar tags have been ordered for Max with microchip # 40304C305A and Moshe with microchip # 4041644658.

I have also sent you email confirmations of all three of your pets. If you have any corrections or updates, please respond to the email confirmation or this notice. I apologize for the inconvenience in the order of the collar tags.

Karen Kennedy

Operations Manager

HomeAgain Pet Recovery Service

From:	"Karen Kennedy" <karenk@padcare.com>
To:	"james schwartz"
Subject:	RE: Collar Tag Orders
Date:	Wed, 17 May 2006 15:47:51 -0400

Thank you for keeping me abreast of the status of your tags. We are doing a special re-order of these tags with shipment to your address on file. Our status does reflect an

Exhibit 22c

order for those tags but no delivery. We will reorder. I apologize for the inconvenience and thank you for your patience.

Karen Kennedy

From:	james schwartz
Sent:	Wednesday, May 17, 2006 1:10 PM
To:	karenk@padcare.com
Subject:	Re: Collar Tag Orders

Ms. Kennedy

Please be advised - today is May 17th and I have still not received these tags as promised

Jim Schwartz

Date:	Fri, 26 May 2006 08:10:24 -0700 (PDT)
From:	"james schwartz"
Subject:	Pet Chipping and Unintended Consequences
To:	fspielman@suntimes.com

Ms. Spielman

Relative to requiring the microchip in Chicago - good idea but a flawed system. Here is the flaw the councilman may not be aware of. Things not worth doing are not worth doing well. But there is a way to rectify the problem

As you are probably aware, 5-10 million or more people have their companion animal 'chipped' for identification in case of loss. (All shelters in the Denver area 'chip' dogs and cats for adoption.)

As part of the reunification system - a tag worn on the collar comes with the chip. (Why? Because estimates are that 40% of the companion animals found are by those who do not have the requisite scanner to identify the pet.) The tag has stamped in for example the Home Again number - but inked - not stamped in - is the id # for the pet.

(Home Again alone on its website brags of over 4 million dogs and cats chipped with their service.)

Exhibit 22d

Unfortunately, the tag is often inoperable over time - as the id # not stamped gets smudged or not legible. So the identification system is minimized in effect by those finding without a scanner.

My experience has not been exemplary with Home Alone. (Home Again (the largest purveyor) said there were stainless steel alternatives for the vet to offer at the time. Not so according to the vets I talked with - the plastic comes standard in the kit without info on alternatives.

So anyone with an older pet - may have a partially inoperable system if my experience is an indicator (and I've called others to see if the tag was smudged etc - illegible - and they had the same experience.)

Furthermore, it has come to my attention that _these chips can burn out_ - and so when a guardian owner sees their vet - at least annually they should be scanned to see if their chip is operable.

Finally the chip business has been trying to get Fed legislation for standardization - despite the flaws in the underlying system above. So this is another interesting hook to the story.

jim schwartz

PS Home Again didn't even have my right name etc in their data base to identify my dogs - and couldn't sort. I had to call the vet to get numbers. So much for the database as well. Home Again has their own website.

CODA

(Interesting material arriving at publishing deadline.)

January 10, 2008 –

This website below is not new, but for the pet guardian faced with giving informed consent for ANY kind of vaccination, before you do so, be sure to check in with:

www.critteradvocacy.com   (Essential read: "The Science Has Been Done")

You may feel that there is "too much information" on this site, but when you see that it is all carefully researched, referenced, and footnoted by Dr. Rogers – and speaks to your own dog or cat – you will have the satisfaction of being able to discuss your decision intelligently with your veterinarian. Better insist that your vet visit this website, too.

January 12, 2008–

The American International Group (AIG Insurance) commercial flatly states, "having a pet can increase your life by 7 years."

Check out the The Long Life Equation by Trisha Macnair, MD, MA (Adams Media, 2007 p. 29: "Studies have found that stroking or being near a familiar animal can lower heart rates and blood pressure levels. One New York study looked at male and female stockbrokers already taking medication to control high blood pressure. (I believe these were the Prof. Karen Allen studies - jds). Those with pets had significantly lower heart rate and blood pressure levels, which didn't increase when the subjects were asked to do mental arithmetic and other stressful tests. This was particularly marked when the pet was nearby during the stressful event, when there was just half the increase in blood pressure compared with participants who did not own a pet."

Another New York study, conducted by Allen, Blascovich and Mendes in 2002, reported that, "after suffering a heart attack, those people who owned a dog were 6 times more likely to be alive one year later than those who did not."

Can one's 42" plasma TV do this? A powerful legislative argument for "living property!"

January, 2008 –

It was time.
It was time to give legislation a third try.

The first attempt to reclassify our companion animals from 'personal property' (TV's) to 'beyond mere property' failed in 1999. The second attempt – with the addition of loss of companionship non-economic damages – in 2003 – not only failed but was hammered by the Colorado Veterinarians – at best 'stretching the truth,' in reality showing a great regard for the truth as they used it so sparingly.'

We thought it was time then. We were wrong. Several thousands of dollars wrong.

Last Summer (2007) Next To Kin Foundation sent a letter to every Colorado legislator in search of a sponsor for a bill that would:

(A) Reclassify licensable companion animals as 'living property' in the sense of duty of care; (B) Require informed consent (in plain language) relative to vaccination options (especially rabies) with an affirmative defense (a hold harmless clause) if informed consent as to the benefits and risks were given by companion animal owner/guardians; and (C) Create a non-economic loss of companionship damages recourse up to $100,000 with the above affirmative defense as well as the requirement of exhausting alternative dispute resolution to minimize frivolous lawsuits.

February 15, 2008 -

Colorado State Representative Debby Stafford (D-Aurora) was the only legislator answering our letter. Today she introduced into the General Assembly HB 08-1308, a bill which would (1) change the legal status of domestic dogs and cats from "mere property" to "living property," (2) recognize the value of companionship with these pets, and (3) make available civil remedies up to $100,000 for loss of that companionship due to negligence. The bill also (4) called for informed consent, protecting from legal action a vet who required the informed consent of his client prior to vaccinating. It would (5) prohibit any governmental requirement for vaccination more frequently than triennially, or according to the "Compendium;" and (6) required alternative dispute resolution prior to litigation.

Stafford, a former Republican who switched parties last year (2007) and is in her last year in the legislature due to term limits, had previously sponsored animal protection acts. In 2007, along with Rep. Morgan Carroll, she carried a bill that makes aggravated animal cruelty a class-6 felony with a fine up to $100,000. Furthermore, her sister is a holistic veterinarian. And finally, as Rep. Stafford told us, she is involved in the feasibility and creation of a human /companion animal cemetery/crematorium. Thus, despite a paucity of legislator interest, we felt we had a sponsor who has a real interest in companion animals.

The bill in its entirety is printed here for those readers who dare to enter the legislative swamp.

HB1308_L.006

HOUSE COMMITTEE OF REFERENCE REPORT

Chairman of Committee   Date

Committee on Judiciary.

After consideration on the merits, the Committee recommends the following:

HB08-1308 be amended as follows:

1 Amend printed bill, strike everything below the enacting clause and
2 substitute the following:

3 "**SECTION 1.** Article 21 of title 13, Colorado Revised Statutes,
4 is amended BY THE ADDITION OF A NEW PART to read:

5   PART 12

6   CIVIL LIABILITY FOR INJURY
7   TO COMPANION AND ASSISTANCE ANIMALS

8   **13-21-1201. Legislative declaration.** (1) THE GENERAL
9 ASSEMBLY HEREBY FINDS AND DETERMINES THAT:

10   (a) HARM TO COMPANION OR ASSISTANCE ANIMALS IS AN
11 INCREASING PROBLEM FOR COLORADO PET OWNERS;

12   (b) CURRENT LAWS DO NOT ADEQUATELY ADDRESS THE RECOVERY
13 OF DAMAGES FOR HARM CAUSED TO COMPANION AND ASSISTANCE
14 ANIMALS BY ANIMAL CRUELTY OR BY THE NEGLIGENT ACTS OF ANIMAL
15 HEALTH CARE PROFESSIONALS OR VETERINARIANS NOR DO CURRENT LAWS
16 DETER THAT HARM;

17   (c) CURRENT LAWS FAIL TO MAKE THE OWNER OF THE INJURED
18 COMPANION OR ASSISTANCE ANIMAL WHOLE, AND THEY DO NOT
19 ACCURATELY REFLECT SOCIETY'S FAVORABLE ATTITUDE TOWARD

COMPANION AND ASSISTANCE ANIMALS;

(d) CURRENT LAWS PRECLUDE COMPANION AND ASSISTANCE ANIMAL OWNERS FROM UTILIZING AN EFFECTIVE REMEDY TO COMPENSATE FOR THE INTENTIONAL OR NEGLIGENT HARM CAUSED TO THEIR COMPANION OR ASSISTANCE ANIMALS;

(e) COMPANION AND ASSISTANCE ANIMALS ARE OFTEN TREATED AS MEMBERS OF A FAMILY, AND AN INJURY TO OR THE DEATH OF A COMPANION OR ASSISTANCE ANIMAL IS PSYCHOLOGICALLY AND EMOTIONALLY SIGNIFICANT AND OFTEN DEVASTATING TO THE OWNER.

(2) THE GENERAL ASSEMBLY, THEREFORE, DECLARES THAT:

(a) CERTAIN ECONOMIC AND NONECONOMIC DAMAGES RESULTING FROM EITHER ANIMAL CRUELTY OR THE NEGLIGENT ACTS OF ANIMAL HEALTHCARE PROFESSIONALS THAT HARM COMPANION AND ASSISTANCE ANIMALS SHOULD BE RECOGNIZED UNDER THE LAW; AND

(b) COMPANION AND ASSISTANCE ANIMALS ARE NOT MERE PROPERTY BUT COMPRISE "LIVING PROPERTY" AND AS SUCH SHOULD BE GRANTED SPECIAL RECOGNITION UNDER COLORADO LAW.

13-21-1202. Definitions. AS USED IN THIS PART 12, UNLESS THE CONTEXT OTHERWISE REQUIRES:

(1) "ASSISTANCE ANIMAL" MEANS:

(a) AN ASSISTANCE DOG AS DEFINED IN SECTION 24-34-803 (7) (a), C.R.S.; OR

(b) AN ANIMAL THAT HAS BEEN OR IS BEING SPECIFICALLY TRAINED TO BE A THERAPY ANIMAL TO AID AN INDIVIDUAL WITH EPILEPSY OR ANY OTHER MEDICALLY DISABLED PERSON, OR TO AID A LAW ENFORCEMENT OFFICER IN CARRYING OUT HIS OR HER DUTIES.

(2) "COMPANION ANIMAL" MEANS A DOMESTICATED DOG OR CAT, OR OTHER DOMESTICATED NONFARM ANIMAL THAT MAY BE LICENSED OR REGISTERED BY A LOCAL GOVERNING BODY THAT IS OWNED OR KEPT BY A PERSON FOR COMPANIONSHIP, FOR PROTECTION, OR FOR SALE TO ANOTHER PERSON FOR SUCH PURPOSES.

(3) "ECONOMIC DAMAGES" MEANS MONEY DAMAGES, INCLUDING BUT NOT LIMITED TO THE REPLACEMENT COST OF THE COMPANION OR ASSISTANCE ANIMAL, REASONABLE VETERINARY EXPENSES, REASONABLE BURIAL EXPENSES FOR THE COMPANION OR ASSISTANCE ANIMAL, AND THE COST OF ANY TRAINING NECESSARY TO REPLACE THE SERVICES OF THE COMPANION OR ASSISTANCE ANIMAL.

(4) "NONECONOMIC DAMAGES" MEANS MONEY DAMAGES FOR LOSS OF SOCIETY, COMPANIONSHIP, COMFORT, PROTECTION, AND ASSISTANCE SERVICES.

(5) "OWNER" MEANS A PERSON OWNING, POSSESSING, HARBORING, KEEPING, HAVING A FINANCIAL INTEREST OR PROPERTY INTEREST IN, OR HAVING CONTROL OR CUSTODY OF, A COMPANION OR ASSISTANCE ANIMAL.

(6) "PERSON" MEANS AN INDIVIDUAL, CORPORATION, PARTNERSHIP, ASSOCIATION, OR OTHER LEGAL ENTITY.

(7) "VETERINARIAN" MEANS A PERSON WHO HAS RECEIVED A DOCTORAL DEGREE IN VETERINARY MEDICINE, OR ITS EQUIVALENT, FROM A SCHOOL OF VETERINARY MEDICINE AND WHO IS LICENSED TO PRACTICE VETERINARY MEDICINE PURSUANT TO ARTICLE 64 OF TITLE 12, C.R.S.

(8) "VETERINARY SERVICE" MEANS A SERVICE OR PROCEDURE INCLUDED WITHIN THE PRACTICE OF VETERINARY MEDICINE, AS DEFINED IN SECTION 12-64-103 (10), C.R.S.

13-21-1203. Damages - companion or assistance animals - cruelty - negligent health care practices. (1) AN OWNER MAY ASSERT A CLAIM THROUGH MEDIATION PURSUANT TO SUBSECTION (3) OF THIS SECTION TO RECOVER ECONOMIC DAMAGES AND NONECONOMIC DAMAGES FROM A PERSON WHO TORTURES, NEEDLESSLY TORMENTS, OR NEEDLESSLY KILLS A COMPANION OR ASSISTANCE ANIMAL. IF MEDIATION IS UNSUCCESSFUL, THE OWNER MAY BRING A CIVIL ACTION TO RECOVER THE DAMAGES DESCRIBED IN THIS SUBSECTION (1).

(2) AN OWNER MAY ASSERT A CLAIM THROUGH MEDIATION PURSUANT TO SUBSECTION (3) OF THIS SECTION TO RECOVER ECONOMIC DAMAGES AND NONECONOMIC DAMAGES FROM A VETERINARIAN WHO, IN THE COURSE OF NEGLIGENT VETERINARY PRACTICE, NEGLIGENT VETERINARY PERFORMANCE, OR THE NEGLIGENT PRESCRIBING OF

VETERINARY SERVICES, CAUSES SERIOUS PHYSICAL INJURY OR DEATH TO A COMPANION OR ASSISTANCE ANIMAL. IF MEDIATION IS UNSUCCESSFUL, THE OWNER MAY BRING A CIVIL ACTION TO RECOVER THE DAMAGES DESCRIBED IN THIS SUBSECTION (2).

(3) UPON AN OWNER'S REASONABLE BELIEF THAT A PERSON HAS TORTURED, NEEDLESSLY TORMENTED, OR NEEDLESSLY KILLED THE OWNER'S COMPANION OR ASSISTANCE ANIMAL, OR THAT A VETERINARIAN HAS NEGLIGENTLY CAUSED SERIOUS PHYSICAL INJURY TO OR THE DEATH OF THE OWNER'S COMPANION OR ASSISTANCE ANIMAL, THE ANIMAL'S OWNER SHALL REQUEST, IN WRITING, THAT THE PERSON PARTICIPATE IN MEDIATION WITH A MUTUALLY AGREED UPON MEDIATOR CONCERNING THE OWNER'S CLAIM. THE MEDIATION SHALL TAKE PLACE WITHIN FORTY-FIVE DAYS OF THE OWNER'S WRITTEN REQUEST. IF, THROUGH NO FAULT OF THE OWNER, THE MEDIATION DOES NOT TAKE PLACE, OR IF THE MEDIATION DOES NOT RESOLVE ALL OF THE OWNER'S CLAIMS, THE OWNER MAY BRING A CIVIL ACTION TO RECOVER DAMAGES PURSUANT TO SUBSECTIONS (1) AND (2) OF THIS SECTION. ADMISSIONS OF LIABILITY OR ANY STATEMENT OR OFFER IN SETTLEMENT MADE IN MEDIATION ARE INADMISSIBLE IN A SUBSEQUENT CIVIL ACTION PURSUANT TO RULE 408 OF THE COLORADO RULES OF EVIDENCE.

(4) A VETERINARIAN SHALL NOT BE LIABLE PURSUANT TO SUBSECTION (2) OF THIS SECTION FOR NEGLIGENCE RESULTING IN SERIOUS PHYSICAL INJURY OR DEATH TO A COMPANION OR ASSISTANCE ANIMAL DUE TO FAILURE TO INOCULATE IF THE VETERINARIAN CERTIFIES IN WRITING THAT, BASED UPON THE VETERINARIAN'S EDUCATION IN ANIMAL IMMUNOLOGY, DEMONSTRATED EXPERIENCE WITH ALTERNATIVE METHODS OF DETERMINING ANTIBODY STRENGTH SUCH AS BLOOD TITERING, AND IN THE BEST INTERESTS OF THE ANIMAL, THE VACCINATION OF THE COMPANION OR ASSISTANCE ANIMAL IS CONTRAINDICATED. ANY SUCH CERTIFICATION SHALL BE ACCEPTABLE TO ANY ANIMAL LICENSING AUTHORITY IN LIEU OF EVIDENCE OF VACCINATION FOR THE PURPOSE OF ISSUING AN ANIMAL LICENSE.

(5) THIS SECTION SHALL NOT APPLY TO ANY NOT-FOR-PROFIT ENTITY OR GOVERNMENTAL AGENCY, OR ITS EMPLOYEES, CAUSING SERIOUS PHYSICAL INJURY OR DEATH TO A COMPANION OR ASSISTANCE ANIMAL WHILE ACTING ON BEHALF OF THE PUBLIC HEALTH OR ANIMAL WELFARE.

(6) A VETERINARIAN SHALL NOT BE LIABLE FOR DAMAGES PURSUANT TO THIS SECTION IF HE OR SHE ACTED PURSUANT TO THE INFORMED CONSENT PROVISIONS CONTAINED IN SECTION 13-21-1204.

(7) AN AWARD FOR LOSS OF COMPANIONSHIP DAMAGES UNDER THIS SECTION MAY NOT EXCEED FIVE THOUSAND DOLLARS PER COMPANION OR ASSISTANCE ANIMAL.

(8) DAMAGES AWARDED UNDER THIS SECTION SHALL BE IN ADDITION TO, AND NOT IN LIEU OF, ANY FINE, SUSPENSION, REVOCATION, OR OTHER DISCIPLINARY ACTION IMPOSED BY THE STATE BOARD OF VETERINARY MEDICINE PURSUANT TO SECTION 12-64-111, C.R.S.

(9) THIS SECTION SHALL NOT BE CONSTRUED TO LIMIT OR ABROGATE ANY OF THE FOLLOWING:

(a) A CRIMINAL ACTION BROUGHT TO PROSECUTE AN ACT DESCRIBED IN THIS SECTION OR IN PART 2 OF ARTICLE 9 OF TITLE 18, C.R.S.; OR

(b) ANY RIGHT OR CAUSE OF ACTION THAT A CRIME VICTIM MAY ASSERT OR BRING.

13-21-1204. Informed consent - hold harmless. (1) PRIOR TO PERFORMING OR PRESCRIBING A VETERINARY SERVICE THAT INVOLVES A SUBSTANTIAL RISK TO THE LIFE OR HEALTH OF A COMPANION OR ASSISTANCE ANIMAL, A VETERINARIAN SHALL DISCUSS THE SERVICE WITH THE OWNER. THE DISCUSSION SHALL INCLUDE, BUT NEED NOT BE LIMITED TO, THE FOLLOWING:

(a) A DISCLOSURE BY THE VETERINARIAN OF ANY MATERIAL RISK ASSOCIATED WITH THE VETERINARY SERVICE THAT MAY AFFECT THE HEALTH OF THE COMPANION OR ASSISTANCE ANIMAL;

(b) THE OWNER'S DECISION TO CONSENT IN WRITING TO THE VETERINARY SERVICE;

(c) APPLICABLE STATE OR LOCAL LAWS AFFECTING THE VETERINARY SERVICE; AND

(d) ANY ALTERNATIVE APPROACHES TO THE VETERINARY SERVICE

TO BE PERFORMED.

(2) A VETERINARIAN SHALL NOT BE REQUIRED TO COMPLY WITH THE CONSENT REQUIREMENTS SET FORTH IN SUBSECTION (1) OF THIS SECTION IF HE OR SHE REASONABLY BELIEVES THAT A COMPANION OR ASSISTANCE ANIMAL REQUIRES IMMEDIATE VETERINARY CARE IN ORDER TO AVOID SUBSTANTIAL HARM OR DEATH TO THE ANIMAL.

13-21-1205. Attorney fees. THE PREVAILING PARTY IN AN ACTION BROUGHT UNDER THE PROVISIONS OF THIS PART 12 SHALL BE ENTITLED TO RECOVER REASONABLE ATTORNEY FEES AND THE COSTS OF SUIT.

SECTION 2. 12-64-111 (1), Colorado Revised Statutes, is amended BY THE ADDITION OF A NEW PARAGRAPH to read:

12-64-111. Discipline of licensees. (1) Upon signed complaint by any complainant or upon its own motion, the board may proceed to a hearing in conformity with section 12-64-112. After a hearing, and by a concurrence of a majority of members, the board may revoke or suspend the license of, place on probation, or otherwise discipline or fine, any licensed veterinarian for any of the following reasons:

(ee) FAILING TO COMPLY WITH THE INFORMED CONSENT REQUIREMENT DESCRIBED IN SECTION 13-21-1204, C.R.S.

SECTION 3. 25-4-607, Colorado Revised Statutes, is amended to read:

25-4-607. Order of board of health requiring inoculation of animals. (1) (a) When it is deemed advisable in the interest of public health and safety, the board of health of an organized health department or a county board of health may order that all dogs, cats, other pet animals, or other mammals in the county or district be vaccinated against rabies, such vaccination to be performed by a licensed veterinarian.

(b) Notwithstanding the provisions of this section, no PARAGRAPH (a) OF THIS SUBSECTION (1) A board of health of an organized health department or A county board of health shall NOT order the inoculation of animals against rabies:

(I) Any more frequently than is recommended in the

"Compendium of Animal Rabies Control" as promulgated by the national association of state public health veterinarians, OR TRIENNIALLY, WHICHEVER IS LESS FREQUENT; OR

(II) WHEN THE VETERINARIAN BELIEVES THAT, IN THE INTEREST OF THE HEALTH OF THE ANIMAL, INOCULATION IS INAPPROPRIATE DUE TO THE AGE OR POOR HEALTH OF THE ANIMAL.

(2) A VETERINARIAN MAY ISSUE A WRITTEN WAIVER EXEMPTING AN ANIMAL FROM LOCAL INOCULATION REQUIREMENTS WHEN THE VETERINARIAN, IN HIS OR HER PROFESSIONAL OPINION, DETERMINES THAT THE WAIVER WILL BENEFIT THE HEALTH OF THE ANIMAL WITHOUT COMPROMISING THE PUBLIC HEALTH. A WAIVER EXECUTED PURSUANT TO THIS SECTION SHALL BE ACCEPTED AND RECOGNIZED BY ANY LOCAL OR REGIONAL AUTHORITY ISSUING LICENSES FOR THE OWNERSHIP OF ANIMALS.

SECTION 4. 25-4-615 (2), Colorado Revised Statutes, is amended, and the said 25-4-615 is further amended BY THE ADDITION A NEW SUBSECTION, to read:

25-4-615. Further municipal restrictions not prohibited. (2) Notwithstanding subsection (1) of this section, ~~no~~ A municipality shall NOT require any animal to be inoculated against rabies:

(a) Any more frequently than is recommended in the "Compendium of Animal Rabies Control" as promulgated by the national association of state public health veterinarians, OR TRIENNIALLY, WHICHEVER IS LESS FREQUENT; OR

(b) WHEN THE VETERINARIAN BELIEVES THAT, IN THE INTEREST OF THE HEALTH OF THE ANIMAL, INOCULATION IS INAPPROPRIATE DUE TO THE AGE OR POOR HEALTH OF THE ANIMAL.

(3) A VETERINARIAN MAY ISSUE A WRITTEN WAIVER EXEMPTING AN ANIMAL FROM MUNICIPAL INOCULATION REQUIREMENTS WHEN THE VETERINARIAN, IN HIS OR HER PROFESSIONAL OPINION, DEEMS THAT THE WAIVER WILL BENEFIT THE HEALTH OF THE ANIMAL WITHOUT COMPROMISING THE PUBLIC HEALTH. A WAIVER EXECUTED PURSUANT TO THIS SECTION SHALL BE ACCEPTED AND RECOGNIZED BY ANY MUNICIPAL AUTHORITY ISSUING LICENSES FOR THE OWNERSHIP OF ANIMALS.

1 **SECTION 5. Effective date.** This act shall take effect upon
2 passage.

3 **SECTION 6. Safety clause.** The general assembly hereby finds,
4 determines, and declares that this act is necessary for the immediate
5 preservation of the public peace, health, and safety.".

6 Page 1, strike lines 102 and 103 and substitute the following:

7 "ANIMALS.".

** *** ** *** **

February 25, 2008 –

Representative Stafford counts votes and determines that the civil penalty for loss of companionship will not fly in the Judiciary Committee and calls for a stripped-down version (L010) which would permit a veterinarian to issue a waiver exempting a pet from a rabies vaccination order on account of the pet's age or medical condition IF THE PET HAD ALREADY HAD A SERIES OF VACCINATIONS!

February 28, 2008 -

We told Representative Stafford that this substitute bill would not accomplish our purpose – would not help pets – and suggested she simply pull the bill.

March 7, 2008-

Rep. Stafford said she wanted to get a bill passed, and invited us to a session at the Capitol with:

John Pape, Chief Epidemiologist, Colorado Department of Health

Dr. Jed Rogers, DVM, President since 2005 of Colorado Veterinary Medicine Assoc.

Ralph Johnson, Executive Director, CVMA and Foundation

Dr. Bill Fredregill, DVM, Sterling, CO

Lobbyists Leo Boyle and Peter Minahan (working for the vets)

Representative Stafford, obviously tired from a demanding legislative session, invited comments about the already amended bill (L010). We obliged, emphasizing that our objective was not to protect Vets from malfeasance claims, but to reduce pet mortality from over-vaccination. We specifically questioned Director Johnson about his now five-year old statement regarding the obligation of his association to deal with the matters at hand. Silence.

The staff member from the Health Dept. then circulated suggestions for a bill which would strike the L010 language and substitute a provision calling for the Health Department to make some rules about vaccination. Mrs. Stafford had obviously approved this action and wished to close the meeting.

We asked three questions of Dr. Rogers:

(1) Your organization opposes having the triennial vaccination frequency in the statute? Answer: "Yes."

(2) Your organization opposes a statutory requirement for informed consent to any risky veterinary procedure? Answer; "Yes."

(3) You are certain that your membership will be more comfortable with rules imposed by the Health Dept. bureaucracy than the simple requirements of our bill? Answer: "Yes."

"That which we intend becomes its exact opposite in time."

Guirjeff's Law of Seven

Sponsor Stafford directed the legislative drafting staff to turn the VCMA suggestion into a bill.

The bill in its new form was introduced into the Committee on March 12 and passed on an 7-4 vote.

> "A foolish faith in authority is the worst enemy of the truth'
> *Einstein*

Even Though – HB1308

In the end, HB1308, did not contain reclassification of licensable companion animals as living property *even though*:

- The American Animal Hospital Association's study showed 98% of companion animal owners viewed their dogs and cats as members of the family
- The veterinarians have promoted the concept of the 'animal/human bond' as well as pets as members of the family
- 67% of Americans in a Gallup Poll would not take $1,000,000 for their dog or cat
- AIG insurance company's currently running TV commercial claims that having a companion animal increases longevity an average of 7 years
- Thirty-nine states allow a companion animal, unlike other 'personal property' to be beneficiaries of a trust.

Nor did the final version of HB1308 include informed consent relative to over-vaccination of rabies companion animals, *even though:*

- The Colorado legislature passed a law in 1999 allowing the three year rabies shot but 79% of vets were still giving the one year shot and 62% of Colorado's pet owners didn't know about this option 6 years later (Hill Research Consulting study, 9/05)
- The veterinarian's own canon of ethics requires informed consent
- There have been only two cases of human/dog rabies from 1980-1996! That's three billionths of 1% incidence a year, compared to 21 deaths from *sky-diving* in 2004 alone!
- The AVMA's Protocol of Vaccination states 'the practice of annual rabies vaccination is based to historical precedent and government regulation NOT scientific data.'
- In Colorado, alone, over the next 10 years, the cost to guardians for the rabies shot alone, not including the cost of the vaccine, required office visit, or curing adverse reactions will be in excess of $ONE BILLION DOLLARS$!

Lastly, HB1308 did NOT incorporate an <u>enforceable deterrent</u> for loss of companionship damages, leaving our dogs and cats as the equivalent of TVs and couches in the eyes of the law, *even though:*

- The Veterinarian Board's revocation of license rate averages less than 20/100,000ths of 1% per year
- It costs $20,000 to $25,000 to sue for damages under the Colorado Consumer Protection Act for deceptive trade practices, with a probable return of only economic damages and no legal fees (for regulated professions). (Your plumber losing a suit would have to pay treble damages and legal fees [he's not a professional].)
- In the vast majority of court cases our companion animals are mere personal property – depreciable property at that – and damages are merely economic value.
- When the California veterinarians, suddenly enlightened, sought legislation to have non-economic damages pegged in law at $25,000, guess what? They were defeated by the vaccine manufacturers! (Fort Dodge, a vaccine manufacturer, is the #1 Platinum supporter of the Colorado Veterinary Medical Association!)
- The average veterinary wellness visit increased 2.5x inflation from 2003-2005, from $30 to $39 while my recent wellness visit for Max in 2008 cost $51. Thus, the price of an annual office visit is up as much as $21 in 5 years.
- The veterinarian's cost of malpractice insurance, stable or declining over the past 14+ years for $1,000,000 per incident/ $3,000,000 aggregate is $246 or about 8 cents a companion animal.
- The cost of $100,000 loss of companionship damages would be approximately 50 cents per companion animal adding $800 to $1000 in premium.

- The average owner veterinarian's salary (not including fringe benefits which are another 35%+ of salary) went from $94,000 to $124,000 – 2003-2005 or 500% of the inflation rate. Their revenues averaged $398,000 while pediatricians averaged $402,000 and they pay $5000-$11,000 in liability insurance.

- Colorado Veterinary Medical Association Executive Director Ralph Johnson stated in a speech to the American Veterinary Medical Legal Association in July, 2003, after defeating the first attempt for loss of companionship non-economic damages:

"(our Association needs) to lead the way in developing a resolution to the issues… A proactive approach has its risks, certainly, but so does an approach that is solely reactive…(we have) made no decision yet about formulating and advancing a specific bill (but) we're doing our homework."

Three attempts to legislatively recognize our companion animals as living property, beyond mere property, etc., have now been made since 1999. And the small-animal vets have been satisfied to employ an association which has stonewalled our every effort to get a legal handle on continuing physical harm to our companion animals and fiscal harm to owner/guardians – knowingly and willingly in my opinion.

HB1308 in its present form does nothing for companion animals nor their owner guardians that is not presently in law and practice. We hope it dies in the Senate. If not, many vets will probably be surprised when they receive new rules from the

Colorado Department of Public Health, as they are accustomed to "self regulation." HB1308 is immunity with impunity for the veterinarians and and also for the Colorado Public Health Department, a 'silver supporter' of the Colorado Veterinary Medical Association – probably with taxpayer cash.

HB1308 has been spayed/neutered – from the original bill we asked our sponsor to carry – even though...

Enough 'even thoughs.'

No dog before his time.

(To be continued....)

Next-to-Kin Foundation
www.trustmeimnotaveterinarian.com
www.next2kin.org

Made in the USA